CHAPTER 1: INTRODUCTION TO SALESFORCE ADMINISTRATION

In embarking on our journey through Salesforce Administration, it is crucial to lay a solid foundation by understanding the core principles and elements that define the Salesforce platform. This chapter will unravel the architecture of Salesforce, introduce its fundamental features, and clarify the pivotal role of an administrator. By establishing these fundamentals, we prepare ourselves for a deeper dive into more intricate aspects of Salesforce administration that will follow.

Salesforce is a cloud-based customer relationship management (CRM) platform that provides businesses with tools to manage their interactions with customers and streamline their operations. At its core, Salesforce is designed to be a highly customizable and scalable solution that can cater to various business needs. The platform operates on a multi-tenant architecture, meaning that multiple organizations share the same infrastructure while maintaining data privacy and security through logical separation.

Understanding Salesforce's architecture is essential for appreciating how its various components work together to deliver a seamless experience. The platform is built on a foundation of cloud computing, which allows it to offer on-demand access to applications and data from anywhere with an internet connection. This architecture supports a range of features that contribute to its flexibility and functionality, including its data model, user interface, and development tools.

The data model in Salesforce is structured around objects, which are analogous to tables in a traditional database. Standard objects, such as Accounts, Contacts, and Opportunities, are provided out-of-the-box and cover many of the core functions needed for CRM. Custom objects, on the other hand, can be created to address specific business requirements, allowing organizations to tailor the system to their unique needs. Each object consists of fields, which store individual pieces of data, and records, which are instances of those objects.

Salesforce's user interface is designed to be intuitive and user-friendly. The platform offers a range of tools for users to interact with their data, including customizable dashboards, reports, and lists. The Lightning Experience is the latest user interface, providing a modern and dynamic environment that enhances productivity and user satisfaction. It features a customizable homepage, a streamlined navigation menu, and enhanced tools for managing and analyzing data.

As an administrator, your role is central to the effective operation of Salesforce within an organization. Administrators are responsible for configuring and maintaining the platform to ensure it meets the organization's needs. This involves setting up and managing user accounts, defining security settings, and customizing the user interface. Administrators also play a key role in data management, including importing and exporting data, managing data quality, and ensuring data integrity.

One of the primary responsibilities of a Salesforce administrator is user management. This involves creating and managing user accounts, assigning roles and profiles, and setting up permission sets. By configuring these elements, administrators control who has access to different features and data within Salesforce. Proper user management ensures that users can perform their tasks efficiently while maintaining the security of the organization's data.

Another critical aspect of Salesforce administration is security. Salesforce provides a range of security features, including user authentication, data encryption, and access controls, to protect sensitive information. Administrators must configure these settings to safeguard data against unauthorized access and potential breaches. This includes setting up password policies, enabling multi-factor authentication, and defining sharing rules to control data visibility.

Customization is a hallmark of the Salesforce platform, and administrators are at the forefront of implementing these customizations. Customization allows organizations to tailor Salesforce to their specific processes and workflows. This may involve creating custom objects and fields, setting up validation rules, and designing page layouts to enhance user experience. Administrators use tools such as the Salesforce Schema Builder and the Lightning App Builder to make these customizations.

In addition to customization, administrators also manage automation within Salesforce. Automation tools, such as Workflow Rules, Process Builder, and Flow, help streamline business processes by automating repetitive tasks and ensuring that critical actions are taken based on predefined criteria. Administrators design and configure these automation processes to improve efficiency and reduce manual effort.

Understanding the role of an administrator and the capabilities of the Salesforce platform is essential for effectively managing and optimizing its use. As we progress through this book, we will explore these aspects in greater detail, diving into the technical configurations and strategies that will enable you to become proficient in Salesforce administration.

The significance of Salesforce for businesses cannot be overstated. The platform enhances operational efficiency by centralizing customer information, automating processes, and providing actionable insights through advanced analytics. By integrating Salesforce into their operations, organizations can achieve greater visibility into their customer interactions, improve decision-making, and drive overall business growth.

In summary, this introductory chapter has provided an overview of Salesforce's architecture, core features, and the role of an administrator. With a solid understanding of these foundational elements, we are well-prepared to delve into more specialized topics and techniques that will be covered in subsequent sections. As we continue, we will build on this knowledge to explore the more advanced aspects of Salesforce administration, equipping you with the skills and insights needed to excel in this dynamic field.

As we progress in our exploration of Salesforce, it's important to understand the key features that contribute to its functionality and adaptability. One of the standout features of Salesforce is its robust customization capability. This flexibility allows organizations to mold the platform to fit their specific business processes and needs, thereby maximizing its effectiveness. Customization within Salesforce is not just about altering the appearance of the interface but also about modifying the underlying data structures and business logic to align with organizational goals.

Customization begins with objects and fields. Standard objects, which come pre-configured with the platform, cover a wide array of business scenarios. However, to address unique business requirements, administrators can create custom objects. These custom objects enable the capture of data that is specific to an organization's needs. For example, a company might require an object to track proprietary information about product warranties or customer service tickets. Custom fields can be added to both standard and custom objects, providing additional dimensions to data records and enhancing the granularity of data capture.

Beyond objects and fields, Salesforce also offers a powerful tool for building and managing relationships between different data sets: relationships. These are established through lookups, master-detail relationships, and junction objects. Lookups create a loose connection between objects, while master-detail relationships establish a more dependent link, with child records inheriting ownership and sharing settings from the parent. Junction objects are used to create many-to-many relationships, which are essential for complex data structures where a single record needs to relate to multiple other records.

Another critical area of customization involves the user interface. The Salesforce Lightning Experience provides a modern and flexible interface that allows for extensive personalization. Administrators can configure page layouts, which define how information is presented to users. Page layouts can be customized to include or exclude specific fields, sections, and related lists, tailored to different user profiles or roles. This personalization ensures that users have access to the information and tools they need most, enhancing productivity and user satisfaction.

Customizing Salesforce also involves the creation of custom

applications. Salesforce's AppExchange offers a wealth of pre-built applications, but organizations can also develop their own. Custom apps can be built using the Lightning App Builder, which allows administrators to design applications by dragging and dropping components onto a canvas. This process does not require extensive programming knowledge, making it accessible for administrators to create tailored solutions that fit their business requirements.

Workflow automation is another pivotal aspect of Salesforce that significantly enhances its utility. Automation helps in streamlining repetitive tasks and ensuring consistency in processes. Workflow Rules are one of the foundational tools for automation, allowing administrators to define criteria and specify actions that should be triggered when these criteria are met. For example, a workflow rule might automatically assign a task to a sales representative when a new lead is created or send a notification to a customer when a case is closed.

For more complex automation needs, Process Builder offers a more advanced set of capabilities. Process Builder allows for the creation of intricate workflows with multiple steps and conditional logic. Administrators can design processes that involve updating records, creating new records, and executing actions based on a series of conditions. This tool provides greater flexibility and control compared to Workflow Rules, enabling more sophisticated automation scenarios.

Another powerful tool within Salesforce is Flow, which facilitates the creation of user-driven processes. Flows can be used to build guided workflows that interact with users through screens and input forms. This capability is especially useful for processes that require user input or decision-making, such as onboarding new employees or handling complex customer service scenarios. Flows can be integrated with other automation tools and can be customized to fit specific business needs.

Data management is an integral part of Salesforce administration. Ensuring data accuracy and consistency is critical for maintaining the reliability of the system. Salesforce provides various tools for managing data, including data import and export utilities, as well as tools for deduplication and data cleansing. The Data Import Wizard allows for the bulk import of data from external sources, while the Data Loader tool provides more advanced options for managing large datasets. Regular data maintenance tasks, such as deduplication and validation, are essential for preserving data integrity and ensuring that users can rely on the information within the system.

The security features of Salesforce are designed to protect sensitive data and maintain compliance with various regulations. Security settings include user authentication, data encryption, and access controls. Administrators are responsible for configuring these settings to safeguard data from unauthorized access. Salesforce provides robust mechanisms for defining user roles, profiles, and permission sets, which control access to different features and data within the platform. By carefully managing these settings, administrators can ensure that users have the appropriate level of access while maintaining the security and confidentiality of the organization's information.

In summary, understanding and leveraging the core features of Salesforce is essential for effective administration. Customization, automation, and data management are fundamental to optimizing the platform's functionality and aligning it with business objectives. As we continue to explore these concepts, we will delve into more advanced topics and practical applications, equipping you with the knowledge and skills to master Salesforce administration.

As we delve deeper into the Salesforce platform, it is essential to grasp the role and responsibilities of a

Salesforce administrator. Administrators are the custodians of the Salesforce environment, tasked with ensuring that the platform operates smoothly and aligns with the organization's needs. Their responsibilities are multifaceted, encompassing system maintenance, user management, and ongoing support.

One of the primary roles of an administrator is to maintain and configure the Salesforce environment. This involves ensuring that the system remains up-to-date with the latest releases and features provided by Salesforce. Regular updates are crucial, as they often include security patches, performance improvements, and new functionalities that can enhance the user experience and system capabilities. Administrators need to be proactive in applying these updates and testing them to ensure that they do not disrupt existing processes or integrations.

User management is another critical responsibility. Administrators are tasked with creating and managing user accounts, assigning roles and profiles, and setting up permissions. Roles and profiles define what users can see and do within Salesforce, determining their access to various objects, fields, and functionalities. Setting up appropriate access controls is vital for maintaining data security and ensuring that users can only access the information and features relevant to their roles. This process involves configuring user access rights, defining hierarchies, and setting up sharing rules to manage data visibility and collaboration.

In addition to user management, administrators are responsible for supporting users and addressing any issues they encounter. This support role includes troubleshooting problems, providing training, and creating documentation to assist users in navigating the Salesforce platform. Effective communication and problem-solving skills are essential in this aspect of the role, as administrators need to understand user concerns and provide timely solutions to enhance their experience.

Data quality and integrity are paramount in Salesforce administration. Administrators must implement processes and tools to ensure that data entered into the system is accurate, consistent, and up-to-date. This involves establishing data validation rules to prevent incorrect or incomplete data from being saved, as well as implementing deduplication strategies to avoid duplicate records. Regular data audits and cleansing activities are also part of maintaining data quality, ensuring that the information within Salesforce remains reliable and useful for decision-making.

Another significant aspect of the administrator's role is managing and optimizing Salesforce integrations. Salesforce is often used in conjunction with other systems and applications, such as marketing automation tools, financial software, or customer support platforms. Administrators are responsible for configuring and maintaining these integrations to ensure seamless data flow between systems. This includes setting up APIs, managing integration connections, and troubleshooting any issues that arise during data synchronization.

Custom reports and dashboards are vital tools for organizations to gain insights from their Salesforce data. Administrators play a crucial role in designing and implementing these analytical tools. Reports allow users to extract and analyze data from Salesforce, while dashboards provide visual representations of key metrics and performance indicators. Administrators must understand the reporting needs of various stakeholders and create customized reports and dashboards that provide actionable insights. This involves using Salesforce's reporting tools to define report types, filters, and aggregations, as well as designing dashboards that present data in an easily digestible format.

Security management is an ongoing responsibility for Salesforce administrators. Ensuring that sensitive information is protected and that the system complies with relevant data protection regulations requires vigilance and expertise. Administrators must configure security settings, including field-level security, object-level permissions, and login policies. They also need to stay informed about best practices and regulatory requirements related to data security and privacy, implementing measures to safeguard information and address any security concerns promptly.

In conclusion, the role of a Salesforce administrator is both dynamic and multifaceted. It requires a comprehensive understanding of the Salesforce platform, from its core features and customization options to its integration capabilities and security settings. Administrators are essential in maintaining the health of the Salesforce environment, supporting users, and ensuring data quality. As we progress further, we will delve into more specialized topics and advanced techniques, building upon this foundational understanding to equip you with the skills necessary for mastering Salesforce administration.

CHAPTER 2: NAVIGATING THE SALESFORCE INTERFACE

To effectively manage the Salesforce platform, understanding its user interface is essential. The Salesforce interface is designed to facilitate ease of use while providing robust functionality. By becoming acquainted with its various components, you can navigate the system more efficiently and tailor it to meet your organization's needs.

Our exploration begins with the Home page, which serves as the central hub for Salesforce users. When you first log into Salesforce, the Home page provides a snapshot of your tasks, notifications, and important updates. This page is customizable, allowing users to add components that are relevant to their roles. For instance, a sales manager might include a component displaying current sales figures, while a customer service representative might add a list of open support cases. Customizing the Home page to display pertinent information not only enhances efficiency but also ensures that users have immediate access to the tools and data they need.

The App Launcher is another crucial element of the Salesforce interface. It provides a menu of available applications and tabs, making it easy to switch between different Salesforce modules. Whether you need to access Sales Cloud, Service Cloud, or any custom applications, the App Launcher streamlines this process. The applications listed here can be organized according to user preferences or departmental needs. For administrators, understanding how to configure and manage the App Launcher is key to ensuring that users have access to the appropriate tools and can quickly find what they need.

Tabs and menus within Salesforce further organize the interface and enhance navigation. The primary tabs, such as Home, Accounts, Contacts, Opportunities, and Cases, serve as gateways to various functions and data. Each tab is associated with a specific object or feature within Salesforce. For example, the Accounts tab allows you to view and manage information related to customer accounts, while the Opportunities tab focuses on sales opportunities and pipeline management. Understanding the purpose and function of each tab helps in effectively utilizing Salesforce's capabilities and streamlining workflows.

Navigating through the different sections of Salesforce involves interacting with these tabs and using the navigation bar. The navigation bar is designed to provide quick access to frequently used functions and recent records. It allows users to search for specific records, access recently viewed items, and utilize various tools without having to navigate through multiple screens. For administrators, configuring the navigation bar to align with user needs and preferences can significantly enhance productivity and user satisfaction.

Customizing the Salesforce interface is an integral aspect of managing the platform. Salesforce offers a range of customization options to tailor the interface to better fit organizational needs. This customization can be as simple as changing the layout of the Home page or as complex as creating custom tabs and apps. Administrators have the ability to modify page layouts, add custom fields, and configure record types to ensure that the interface aligns with the specific requirements of different user roles.

For instance, the Page Layout Editor allows administrators to customize the layout of detail pages for different objects. This editor provides a drag-and-drop interface for arranging fields, sections, and related lists. Customizing page layouts ensures that users see the most relevant information and can efficiently perform their tasks. Additionally, administrators can create different page layouts for different profiles, providing a tailored experience for various user roles.

Another important aspect of interface customization is the use of Lightning App Builder. This tool allows for the creation of custom Lightning pages, which can be used to design personalized user experiences. With the Lightning App Builder, administrators can drag and drop components onto a page, configure their settings, and define the layout. This level of customization enables the creation of dynamic and responsive interfaces that cater to specific business needs.

In addition to customizing individual pages, administrators can also configure Salesforce's global search functionality. The global search bar at the top of the interface provides users with the ability to search across all objects and records within Salesforce. Configuring search settings, including search filters and search layouts, ensures that users can quickly find the information they need without sifting through irrelevant results. Effective search configuration enhances user efficiency and reduces the time spent locating records.

Understanding the nuances of the Salesforce interface is crucial for optimizing its use and ensuring that users can perform their tasks efficiently. By customizing the Home page, App Launcher, tabs, menus, and search functionalities, administrators can tailor the platform to meet organizational needs and enhance user satisfaction. As we continue our exploration of Salesforce, these foundational elements of navigation and customization will support more advanced configurations and management strategies, enabling you to leverage Salesforce's full potential.

As we delve deeper into the Salesforce interface, it's crucial to examine the detailed aspects of each component and how they interplay to create an efficient user experience. Each part of the interface is designed to streamline processes and improve accessibility, but understanding their configuration and functionality will truly optimize your administrative efficiency.

Let's start with the Home page, which is often the first point of interaction for Salesforce users. The Home page is not just a static dashboard; it is a dynamic workspace that can be tailored to reflect the needs and preferences of its users. For administrators, the ability to customize the Home page means that you can create a personalized experience that enhances productivity. This includes adding or removing components based on the role and responsibilities of different users.

For example, a sales representative might benefit from a Home page featuring recent leads, a list of high-priority opportunities, and a visual representation of sales performance. Conversely, a customer support agent might need quick access to open cases, a summary of recent customer interactions, and a dashboard showing case resolution metrics. By understanding the types of information and tools that different roles require, you can configure the Home page to provide relevant insights at a glance.

Transitioning to the App Launcher, it's important to recognize its role as a navigation tool within Salesforce. The App Launcher is designed to give users quick access to the various apps and features available within the platform. This includes both standard Salesforce applications and any custom apps that may have been developed for specific business needs. Administrators should be adept at managing the App Launcher to ensure that users have access to the applications they need while avoiding clutter from unused or irrelevant apps.

The configuration of the App Launcher involves organizing apps into a logical order and setting permissions to control access. For instance, if your organization has different departments using Salesforce for distinct purposes, you can create custom app pages that group relevant apps together. This ensures that users can quickly find the tools they need without navigating through a long list of unrelated options.

Navigating through Salesforce involves more than just understanding the Home page and App Launcher; it also requires familiarity with the various tabs and menus that provide access to core features. The primary tabs, which include Home, Accounts, Contacts, Opportunities, and Cases, represent the main objects within Salesforce. Each tab serves as a gateway to detailed information and functions related to its respective object.

For example, the Accounts tab provides access to customer account records, where you can view detailed information about each account, including related contacts, opportunities, and activities. Similarly, the Contacts tab allows you to manage individual contact records, track interactions, and maintain a comprehensive view of your network. Understanding how to effectively use these tabs is essential for managing data and facilitating user workflows.

Menus within Salesforce are another key component of the user interface. The main menu bar provides access to a range of functions, including settings, reports, and dashboards. This menu can be customized to include frequently used features or tools, allowing users to streamline their navigation and access critical functions with ease. For administrators, configuring the menu to align with user roles and responsibilities ensures that the most relevant tools are readily accessible.

One of the powerful features of Salesforce is its ability to create and manage custom tabs and objects. Custom tabs allow you to extend Salesforce's functionality by adding new objects and related pages tailored to your organization's needs. This might involve creating custom fields, objects, and layouts that support unique business processes. By leveraging custom tabs, administrators can build a Salesforce environment that aligns closely with organizational requirements and enhances overall efficiency.

Another aspect of interface customization is the use of Lightning pages. Lightning Experience provides a modern user interface that is designed to be more intuitive and responsive compared to the classic interface. With Lightning pages, you can create custom layouts that cater to specific user needs, incorporating components such as charts, lists, and visual elements. This customization helps ensure that users can quickly access and interact with the most relevant data.

The Lightning App Builder is a tool that facilitates the creation and customization of these Lightning pages. Through a drag-and-drop interface, administrators can arrange components, configure their settings, and design pages that meet the specific needs of different user roles. This tool provides the flexibility to create tailored experiences that enhance productivity and user satisfaction.

Additionally, understanding the global search functionality is crucial for effective navigation within Salesforce. The global search bar allows users to search across all objects and records, providing a comprehensive view of relevant information. Administrators should be familiar with how to configure search settings, including search filters and layouts, to ensure that users can find the information they need quickly and efficiently.

In summary, mastering the Salesforce interface involves more than just knowing where to find tools and features. It requires a deep understanding of how to customize and configure the Home page, App Launcher, tabs, menus, and search functionalities to align with organizational needs and user preferences. By leveraging these capabilities, administrators can create an efficient and user-friendly environment that enhances productivity and supports effective data management.

The integration of various Salesforce features into the user interface is essential for maximizing administrative efficiency and user satisfaction. As we continue exploring the interface, it becomes evident that Salesforce's flexibility and customization capabilities are pivotal for tailoring the platform to meet specific organizational needs.

A key aspect to address is the use of dashboards and reports. Dashboards provide a visual representation of data and are instrumental in monitoring key performance indicators and metrics. They can be customized to display charts, graphs, and tables that aggregate information from multiple sources within Salesforce. Understanding how to create and manage dashboards involves configuring data sources, selecting appropriate visualization types, and setting up filters to ensure that the displayed information is relevant and actionable.

Reports, on the other hand, offer a more detailed view of data and are crucial for in-depth analysis. Salesforce's reporting tools allow for the creation of custom reports that can be tailored to focus on specific data sets or criteria. Administrators must be adept at using the report builder to design reports that meet organizational needs, including defining report types, setting up filters, and customizing layouts. The ability to schedule and automate report generation further enhances the efficiency of data management by ensuring that stakeholders receive timely updates.

Another critical feature to explore is the Salesforce mobile interface. With the increasing use of mobile devices for business operations, Salesforce's mobile capabilities are essential for providing users with access to the platform on the go. The mobile interface offers a streamlined version of the desktop experience, optimized for smaller screens and touch interactions. Administrators should ensure that mobile configurations are aligned with desktop settings, but also optimized for mobile-specific use cases. This includes setting up mobile layouts, managing mobile-specific features, and ensuring data synchronization between mobile and desktop environments.

Customization of page layouts is another area where administrators can significantly impact user experience. Page layouts determine the arrangement of fields, sections, and related lists on a record page. Customizing these layouts allows for a more intuitive user experience by presenting relevant information in a structured manner. This customization involves configuring field placements, adjusting section visibility, and adding or removing related lists based on user roles and needs. The goal is to ensure that users can quickly access and interact with the information they need without unnecessary distractions.

Additionally, the use of record types and page layouts can help streamline data entry and management by providing tailored forms for different business processes. Record types allow for the creation of different forms and layouts based on the type of record being created, such as opportunities or cases. This customization ensures that users are presented with the fields and options that are most relevant to their specific tasks, reducing errors and improving data accuracy.

Permissions and access controls are crucial components of the Salesforce interface that impact how users interact with the platform. Administrators must configure profiles and permission sets to control access to various features, objects, and records. This involves defining user roles, setting up field-level security, and managing sharing rules to ensure that users have appropriate access based on their responsibilities. Proper configuration of these permissions helps maintain data security and integrity while enabling users to perform their tasks efficiently.

The process of managing user interfaces also involves understanding and utilizing Salesforce's automation tools. Workflow rules, process builders, and flows are integral for automating repetitive tasks and streamlining business processes. These tools enable administrators to set up automated actions, such as sending notifications, updating records, or creating tasks, based on predefined criteria. By automating routine tasks, administrators can reduce manual effort and ensure that processes are executed consistently and accurately.

In addition to these automation tools, Salesforce's integration capabilities with other systems and applications play a vital role in enhancing the user experience. Integration with external systems allows for the seamless exchange of data and functionality between Salesforce and other platforms. This integration can be achieved through various methods, including APIs, middleware, and pre-built connectors. Administrators must be proficient in configuring and managing these integrations to ensure that data flows smoothly and that users have access to the information and tools they need.

Finally, it is essential to consider the ongoing maintenance and support of the Salesforce interface. Regular updates and enhancements to the platform may introduce new features or changes to existing functionality. Administrators must stay informed about these updates and assess their impact on the user interface. This involves testing new features, updating customizations, and providing training and support to users to ensure a smooth transition and continued efficiency.

In conclusion, mastering the Salesforce interface requires a comprehensive understanding of its various components, customization options, and integration capabilities. By effectively managing the Home page, App Launcher, tabs, menus, dashboards, reports, mobile interface, page layouts, permissions, automation tools, and integrations, administrators can create a tailored and efficient user experience that supports organizational goals and enhances productivity.

CHAPTER 3: USER MANAGEMENT AND SECURITY

Understanding user management and security is paramount to maintaining a robust and secure Salesforce environment. This segment will guide you through the essential components of user management, including the creation and administration of user accounts, the assignment of roles and profiles, and the configuration of security settings. Effective management in these areas ensures that users have the appropriate access to perform their duties while maintaining the security and integrity of the data within Salesforce.

To start with, the process of creating and managing user accounts in Salesforce is foundational to user management. When setting up a new user, it is crucial to provide accurate and comprehensive details to ensure that the user can effectively access and utilize the system. This involves entering information such as the user's name, email address, and user license type. Each user license type corresponds to a specific level of access and functionality, so selecting the appropriate license is essential for aligning user needs with the capabilities provided by Salesforce.

Once a user account is created, assigning roles is the next step in configuring user access. Roles in Salesforce define the hierarchy and data access levels within the organization.

A user's role determines what data they can view and interact with based on their position within the organizational structure. By establishing roles, you can control data visibility and ensure that users only have access to the information relevant to their responsibilities. It is important to design a role hierarchy that reflects the actual organizational structure, allowing for efficient data sharing and reporting while maintaining appropriate access controls.

Profiles are another critical aspect of user management. A profile in Salesforce defines a user's access to various objects, fields, and features within the platform. Each profile specifies the permissions and settings that govern what actions a user can perform and what data they can access. When configuring profiles, it is necessary to consider both standard and custom profiles to ensure that they align with the specific needs of different user groups. For instance, a sales profile might include permissions to manage opportunities and leads, while a support profile would focus on cases and service-related objects.

In addition to roles and profiles, permission sets provide a flexible way to grant additional permissions to users without changing their profile. Permission sets allow administrators to extend access to specific objects or features on an as-needed basis. This is particularly useful when users require temporary access or when there are exceptions to the standard permissions defined by their profile. Managing permission sets involves creating and assigning these sets based on user requirements and ensuring that they are updated as needs change.

Security settings are integral to protecting data and maintaining the integrity of the Salesforce environment. One of the fundamental aspects of security in Salesforce is the use of field-level security and object-level security. Field-level security controls access to specific fields within an object, ensuring that sensitive information is protected from unauthorized viewing or editing. Object-level security, on the other hand, governs access to entire objects and their records, allowing administrators to define which users can view, create, edit, or delete records within each object.

Another essential component of Salesforce security is the use of sharing rules and organization-wide defaults. Sharing rules are used to grant access to records based on specific criteria, such as role hierarchy or user groups. These rules help in managing record visibility and collaboration by allowing users to access records that they would not otherwise be able to see. Organization-wide defaults set the baseline level of access for all records in the organization, which can then be modified through sharing rules and manual sharing to tailor access as needed.

Auditing and monitoring are crucial for maintaining a secure Salesforce environment. Salesforce provides various tools and features to track changes and monitor user activity. The Setup Audit Trail is a valuable tool for reviewing recent changes made to the configuration of the Salesforce instance. It logs administrative changes, including modifications to settings, profiles, and permissions, providing insight into who made the changes and when. Similarly, login history and event monitoring features allow administrators to track user login activities and detect any unusual or unauthorized access patterns.

Regularly reviewing and updating user access and security settings is an essential practice for maintaining a secure Salesforce environment. This includes periodically auditing user roles, profiles, and permissions to ensure they are aligned with current organizational needs and security policies. Implementing best practices for user management, such as conducting periodic access reviews, enforcing strong password policies, and providing user training on security practices, further enhances the overall security posture of the Salesforce platform.

In conclusion, mastering user management and security in Salesforce requires a thorough understanding of user roles, profiles, permission sets, and security settings. By effectively creating and managing user accounts, assigning appropriate roles and profiles, and configuring robust security measures, you can ensure that users have the access they need while safeguarding the integrity of the data. Implementing best practices for security and regularly monitoring and updating settings will contribute to a secure and efficient Salesforce environment.

As we delve deeper into user management and security within Salesforce, understanding the role of access control mechanisms becomes crucial. Access control mechanisms are pivotal in ensuring that users can only interact with data and functionalities relevant to their roles. These mechanisms include profiles, permission sets, and field-level security, each of which plays a distinct role in managing user access and maintaining security.

Profiles are fundamental in defining what a user can see and do within Salesforce. Each profile consists of a collection of permissions and settings that apply to a group of users. These permissions encompass object access, field-level permissions, and various system permissions. When configuring profiles, it is essential to carefully select permissions that match the user's role and responsibilities. For instance, a user profile for a sales representative might include permissions to create and modify opportunities and leads, while a support profile would be tailored to managing cases and service-related records.

Field-level security is a critical component that determines whether users can view or edit specific fields within an object. This feature is particularly important for safeguarding sensitive data, such as financial information or personal details. By setting field-level security, administrators can ensure that only authorized users have access to particular fields, thus minimizing the risk of data exposure. It's a practice that should be implemented thoughtfully, aligning with organizational policies and compliance requirements.

Permission sets offer a flexible approach to granting additional permissions to users beyond what their profile provides. They allow administrators to assign specific permissions to individual users or groups without altering the base profile. For example, if a user needs temporary access to a new feature or object, a permission set can be applied to grant this access without modifying the user's existing profile. Managing permission sets effectively involves creating and assigning them based on evolving user needs and ensuring that they are regularly reviewed and updated.

To complement profiles and permission sets, sharing rules and organization-wide defaults help manage data visibility across the Salesforce platform. Sharing rules enable administrators to extend access to records based on criteria such as role hierarchy, public groups, or territory management. This functionality ensures that users can collaborate effectively by accessing records that are relevant to their role while still adhering to the principle of least privilege. Organization-wide defaults establish the baseline level of access for records, which can be adjusted through sharing rules and manual sharing to grant additional access as needed.

Security settings in Salesforce also involve configuring password policies and session settings to protect user accounts from unauthorized access. Password policies define the rules for password complexity, expiration, and history, which are critical for maintaining secure user authentication. By enforcing strong password policies, organizations can reduce the risk of unauthorized access due to compromised credentials. Additionally, session settings govern aspects such as session timeout and concurrent login limits, further enhancing security by controlling how long users remain logged in and how many sessions they can have open simultaneously.

Auditing and monitoring tools play a vital role in maintaining a secure Salesforce environment. The Setup Audit Trail provides a detailed log of changes made to the configuration of the Salesforce instance, including modifications to user permissions, profiles, and settings. This log is invaluable for tracking administrative activities and identifying any unauthorized or unintended changes. Similarly, login history and event monitoring features allow administrators to review user login patterns and detect any anomalies or suspicious behavior. Regularly reviewing these logs can help in identifying potential security issues and ensuring compliance with security policies.

Best practices for user management and security involve not only implementing robust controls but also maintaining a proactive approach to security management. This includes conducting regular access reviews to ensure that user roles and permissions remain aligned with their current responsibilities. Implementing strong password policies, providing user training on security awareness, and staying informed about security updates and best practices are all essential for safeguarding the Salesforce environment.

As organizations continue to rely on Salesforce for their business operations, effective user management and security practices are crucial for protecting data and ensuring operational efficiency. By understanding and applying the principles of user roles, profiles, permission sets, and security settings, administrators can create a secure and well-managed Salesforce environment that supports both organizational needs and user productivity.

As we continue to explore the facets of user management and

security in Salesforce, it's crucial to understand the intricacies of managing user access through various administrative tools and strategies. One significant aspect is managing public groups and queues, which play a role in organizing and distributing records and tasks among users. Public groups allow administrators to create collections of users, roles, and other groups to facilitate record sharing and collaboration. For example, you might establish a public group for a sales team, which can be used to grant access to opportunities and leads specific to that team. Additionally, queues enable the efficient distribution of records like cases or leads by placing them into a centralized pool that can be accessed and claimed by users based on predefined criteria.

Managing record access through role hierarchies is another essential element of user security. Salesforce uses a role hierarchy to ensure that users higher in the hierarchy can access the data owned by users lower in the hierarchy. This hierarchical structure reflects the organization's reporting structure and supports data visibility and management. For instance, a sales manager would naturally have access to all opportunities created by their team members, facilitating oversight and ensuring they can support their team effectively. It's important to configure role hierarchies carefully to balance visibility and data security, ensuring that users have access appropriate to their position within the organization.

Effective management of data visibility extends beyond role hierarchies to include sharing rules and manual sharing. Sharing rules are an automated way to extend access to records beyond the role hierarchy. They can be configured to provide access based on record attributes or user groups. For example, you might create a sharing rule that grants access to all high-value opportunities to a specific team of executives, regardless of their role hierarchy. Manual sharing provides a more granular approach, allowing users or administrators to individually share records with specific users or groups. This flexibility ensures that sensitive data can be protected while still enabling necessary collaboration.

Furthermore, it's vital to consider the implications of login access and session management on security. Login access policies can be configured to control where and how users can log into Salesforce. For instance, administrators might restrict login access to specific IP ranges or set up two-factor authentication to add an additional layer of security. These settings help mitigate the risk of unauthorized access and ensure that user accounts are protected from potential threats. Similarly, managing session settings such as session timeout and login history provides additional security measures by reducing the risk of session hijacking and tracking login patterns for suspicious activity.

Regular audits and reviews are integral to maintaining robust security and effective user management. Periodic audits of user accounts and permissions ensure that access levels remain appropriate as roles and responsibilities evolve. These audits help identify any discrepancies or excessive permissions that could pose security risks. Reviewing login history and user activity logs also provides insights into potential security breaches or misuse of the system. By conducting these reviews regularly, administrators can proactively address any security concerns and ensure compliance with organizational policies.

In conclusion, navigating the complexities of user management and security within Salesforce requires a thorough understanding of the platform's various tools and configurations. By effectively managing profiles, permission sets, sharing rules, and role hierarchies, administrators can ensure that users have the appropriate level of access while maintaining data security. Implementing strong security practices, such as configuring login access policies and conducting regular audits, further enhances the platform's overall security posture. As Salesforce continues to be a critical tool for managing business operations, mastering these aspects of user management and security is essential for creating a secure and efficient environment that supports organizational success and user productivity.

CHAPTER 4: CUSTOMIZING SALESFORCE: FIELDS AND OBJECTS

Customizing Salesforce to fit unique business requirements is a critical aspect of effective administration. This process begins with understanding how to create and manage custom fields and objects, which are fundamental to tailoring the Salesforce platform to your organization's specific needs. In this section, we will delve into the methods for defining custom fields, creating new objects, and adjusting page layouts to enhance both functionality and user experience.

To start, it is essential to grasp the concept of custom fields within Salesforce. Custom fields allow you to extend the standard data model by adding specific attributes that are unique to your business processes. When defining custom fields, you will begin by selecting the appropriate field type based on the kind of data you need to capture. Salesforce offers a range of field types, including text, number, date, and picklist, each serving a different purpose. For instance, if your business requires tracking a custom product code, you might use a text field, while a numerical value like discount percentages would be best suited to a number field.

Once you have determined the field type, you will proceed to configure the field's properties. This includes setting field-level security, which dictates which profiles or permission sets can view or edit the field. It's also crucial to consider the field's placement on page layouts to ensure it aligns with the user's workflow. Custom fields can be used in various ways across Salesforce, such as in reports, formula fields, and validation rules, providing a high degree of flexibility in how data is captured and utilized.

Creating new objects is another significant aspect of customization. Objects in Salesforce are essentially tables in the database that store data records. While Salesforce comes with standard objects like Accounts, Contacts, and Opportunities, you can create custom objects to handle data that falls outside the scope of these standard objects. Custom objects are useful for managing unique business entities, such as a "Projects" object for tracking project details or a "Cases" object for handling customer service requests.

To create a new object, you will navigate to the Object Manager in Salesforce Setup and choose the option to create a new custom object. During this process, you will define key attributes such as the object's name, record name, and whether it will be available in the Salesforce mobile app. Custom objects also support custom fields, allowing you to extend their functionality in a way that is specific to your organization's needs. Once created, these objects can be linked to standard and other custom objects through relationships, such as lookups or master-detail relationships, which enable complex data modeling.

Customizing page layouts is equally important as creating fields and objects. Page layouts determine how information is presented to users and how they interact with records. By customizing page layouts, you can control the arrangement of fields, sections, and related lists on a record page, ensuring that users have quick access to the most relevant information.

Page layouts can be tailored to different user profiles or record types, providing a personalized experience that enhances productivity.

To customize a page layout, you will use the Page Layout Editor, which offers a drag-and-drop interface for adding, removing, and rearranging components. For instance, you might add a new section to a page layout to display custom fields related to a specific business process, or you might rearrange existing sections to prioritize the most frequently used information. Additionally, you can create multiple page layouts for different record types, ensuring that each layout is optimized for the unique needs of different departments or user roles.

In addition to standard page layouts, Salesforce also supports Lightning App Builder, a tool for creating custom Lightning pages. Lightning pages offer enhanced functionality and user experience by providing components like tabs, charts, and custom links that can be arranged to suit specific business needs. With Lightning App Builder, you can create home pages, record pages, and app pages that align with your organization's workflow and provide a cohesive user experience across the platform.

Through careful customization of fields, objects, and page layouts, Salesforce administrators can create a tailored solution that meets the specific needs of their organization. By leveraging these customization capabilities, you not only enhance the functionality of the Salesforce platform but also improve the overall user experience, ensuring that the system supports your business processes effectively and efficiently.

To further enhance the customization of Salesforce, it's crucial to understand how to utilize relationships between objects. Salesforce's data model allows for the creation of complex structures through relationships such as lookups and master-detail. These relationships help establish connections between different types of data, providing a more organized and interconnected data model.

Lookup relationships create a link between two objects, allowing one object to reference another. For example, if you have a custom object for "Projects" and another for "Clients," you might establish a lookup relationship where each project record can reference a specific client. This relationship is more flexible and does not enforce strict dependencies between the objects, making it suitable for scenarios where records are loosely related.

Master-detail relationships, on the other hand, are more rigid and enforce a parent-child relationship between objects. In this setup, the detail (or child) record is tightly bound to the master (or parent) record. For example, if you have a "Projects" object and a "Tasks" object, you could create a master-detail relationship where each task is directly tied to a specific project. This relationship ensures that when the master record is deleted, all associated detail records are also deleted, thereby maintaining data integrity and consistency.

Another critical aspect of customization involves creating and managing custom record types. Record types allow for different business processes and page layouts for the same object. By defining multiple record types for an object, you can tailor the data entry and user experience to match various business requirements. For example, if your organization uses a "Cases" object to handle customer service requests, you might create different record types for "Technical Support" and "Billing Issues," each with its own page layout and set of fields.

To implement record types, you first define the record types for the object and then configure the picklist values available for each type. This customization ensures that users see only the relevant options based on the type of record they are working with, streamlining data entry and improving accuracy.

Beyond fields, objects, and relationships, Salesforce also offers powerful tools for customizing user interfaces through the use of Lightning Components. Lightning Components are reusable building blocks that can be combined to create dynamic user experiences. With Lightning App Builder, you can design custom pages and applications using these components, enhancing the user interface to better meet your organization's needs.

Lightning Components come in various types, including standard components, custom components, and third-party components from the Salesforce AppExchange. Standard components are pre-built elements provided by Salesforce, such as charts and related lists. Custom components, on the other hand, are developed using the Lightning Component framework, allowing you to build tailored functionality that aligns with specific business processes. Third-party components can be installed from the AppExchange and integrated into your Salesforce environment, providing additional features and enhancements.

Customizing Salesforce also involves the use of validation rules and workflow automation. Validation rules are essential for ensuring data quality by enforcing specific criteria when records are created or edited. For instance, you might create a validation rule to ensure that a "Due Date" field on a "Tasks" object cannot be set in the past. By defining these rules, you help prevent incorrect or incomplete data from entering the system, maintaining the integrity of your records.

Workflow automation, including process builder and flows, allows you to automate repetitive tasks and business processes. Process Builder enables the creation of automated workflows based on certain criteria, such as sending email notifications or updating field values when a record meets specific conditions. Flows offer a more advanced level of automation, allowing you to create complex, multi-step processes that can involve user interactions and integration with external systems.

Effective customization requires not only the technical skills to implement these features but also an understanding of how these customizations impact users and processes. By taking a user-centric approach, you can ensure that the customizations you implement align with the needs and workflows of your organization, ultimately enhancing both efficiency and user satisfaction. As you continue to customize Salesforce, always consider the broader implications of your changes and how they fit into the overall structure and objectives of your Salesforce environment.

As we delve deeper into the realm of Salesforce customization, it becomes evident that the process extends beyond mere field creation and object modification. A significant aspect of tailoring Salesforce to fit your business needs is the customization of page layouts. Page layouts define the arrangement and visibility of fields, related lists, and other components on the user interface. The customization of these layouts plays a crucial role in optimizing user experience and ensuring that relevant information is readily accessible.

Page layouts can be customized to display different sets of fields and related lists based on user profiles, record types, or specific business requirements. For instance, within the "Opportunity" object, you may want to display different fields and related lists for different sales stages or teams. By creating distinct page layouts for various scenarios, you can ensure that users interact with the most pertinent information and tools relevant to their role. This customization not only enhances the efficiency of data entry but also improves the overall usability of the Salesforce platform.

Another powerful feature in Salesforce customization is the

ability to use custom formulas and validation rules to further refine data handling and user interaction. Custom formulas allow you to calculate values based on other fields within the same record or related records. For example, you might create a formula field on the "Opportunity" object to automatically calculate the "Expected Revenue" based on the "Amount" and "Probability" fields. These formulas can greatly reduce manual data entry and ensure consistency across records.

Validation rules are essential for maintaining data integrity by enforcing specific criteria during record creation or modification. They help ensure that data adheres to business rules and standards. For example, you might use a validation rule to prevent users from saving a "Lead" record unless a valid email address is provided. These rules can be customized to address a wide range of scenarios, providing real-time feedback to users and preventing erroneous data from entering the system.

In addition to custom fields, objects, and page layouts, Salesforce also provides the ability to create and utilize custom objects, which are integral to expanding the platform's functionality. Custom objects are user-defined entities that can hold data unique to your organization. For instance, if your organization needs to track "Assets" or "Projects" beyond the standard Salesforce objects, you can create custom objects to manage this data. Each custom object can have its own set of fields, relationships, and page layouts, offering flexibility in how data is organized and presented.

Managing relationships between custom objects and standard objects or other custom objects is crucial for maintaining a cohesive data model. Custom relationships, such as lookup or master-detail, allow you to establish connections and dependencies between different data entities. This relational data model ensures that users can navigate between related records seamlessly and that data integrity is preserved across the platform.

Furthermore, it is important to consider the implications of customizations on data security and user permissions. As you customize Salesforce, you must ensure that field-level security and object-level permissions are appropriately configured to protect sensitive information and control access based on user roles. For example, you might restrict access to certain fields or objects for specific user profiles, ensuring that only authorized personnel can view or edit sensitive data.

Salesforce's customization capabilities also extend to user interface enhancements through the use of Lightning App Builder and Lightning Components. The Lightning App Builder allows you to create custom applications and pages using drag-and-drop components, enabling you to design tailored user experiences that align with your organization's needs. You can include custom Lightning Components, standard components, and third-party components to build comprehensive solutions that enhance functionality and user interaction.

By leveraging these customization features, you can create a Salesforce environment that is not only tailored to your business processes but also optimized for usability and efficiency. It is essential to approach customization with a strategic mindset, considering both immediate requirements and long-term scalability. The goal is to build a flexible and robust Salesforce environment that supports your organization's evolving needs while maintaining a high standard of data integrity and user satisfaction.

CHAPTER 5: AUTOMATING PROCESSES WITH WORKFLOW RULES AND PROCESS BUILDER

In the realm of Salesforce administration, automation serves as a pivotal mechanism for enhancing operational efficiency and reducing manual effort. This section will explore how to harness the power of workflow rules and Process Builder to automate processes effectively. By setting up and managing these automation tools, you can streamline business processes, minimize manual intervention, and ensure that critical tasks are executed consistently and accurately.

Workflow rules are one of the foundational tools for automation within Salesforce. They allow you to define specific criteria that, when met, trigger automated actions. This can include tasks such as sending email notifications, updating fields, creating tasks, or even sending outbound messages. The design of a workflow rule involves setting up rule criteria, defining the rule's evaluation criteria, and specifying the actions to be executed when the criteria are met. For example, you might create a workflow rule that automatically sends a reminder email to the account owner if a contract is nearing its renewal date. This ensures that important deadlines are not overlooked and that follow-up actions are taken in a timely manner.

In addition to creating workflow rules, it's important to understand the distinction between "Rule Criteria" and "Evaluation Criteria." Rule Criteria specify the conditions that must be met for the workflow to be triggered. These conditions can be based on field values, record types, or other factors relevant to your business needs. Evaluation Criteria determine when the workflow rule should be evaluated, such as when a record is created or edited. By carefully configuring these criteria, you can ensure that the automation aligns with your specific business processes and triggers the desired actions effectively.

Process Builder, on the other hand, offers a more advanced and flexible approach to automation compared to workflow rules. With Process Builder, you can create complex automation processes that involve multiple steps and criteria. The tool provides a visual interface that allows you to design and manage processes with ease. Unlike workflow rules, Process Builder enables you to create automated processes that can involve multiple related records, invoke Apex code, and handle more complex logic.

Creating a process in Process Builder begins with defining the criteria that initiate the process. This can be based on changes to a record or other events within Salesforce. After defining the criteria, you can specify a series of actions to be executed as part of the process. These actions can include updating records, creating new records, sending email alerts, or invoking other processes or flows. For example, you might use Process Builder to automate the creation of a follow-up task whenever a lead is assigned to a sales representative. The process can be designed to handle various conditions, such as different lead sources or stages, ensuring that each scenario is addressed appropriately.

Another key advantage of Process Builder is its ability to create "Immediate" and "Scheduled" actions. Immediate actions are executed as soon as the process is triggered, whereas scheduled actions occur at a later time. This feature allows you to design processes that not only handle immediate tasks but also schedule actions for future dates or times. For instance, you could design a process that updates a customer record and sends a thank-you email immediately after a purchase is made, and then schedules a follow-up call for a week later.

When designing automation strategies, it's crucial to consider best practices to ensure that your automation is effective and maintainable. One best practice is to avoid creating overly complex processes that can be difficult to manage and troubleshoot. Instead, focus on creating clear and concise automation rules that address specific business needs. Additionally, regularly review and update your automation processes to adapt to changing business requirements and ensure ongoing effectiveness.

In summary, both workflow rules and Process Builder play integral roles in automating processes within Salesforce. Workflow rules provide a straightforward approach to automating simple tasks based on predefined criteria, while Process Builder offers a more advanced and flexible solution for handling complex automation scenarios. By understanding the capabilities and appropriate use cases for each tool, you can design effective automation strategies that streamline business processes, improve efficiency, and reduce manual effort.

Building upon the foundation of workflow rules and Process Builder, it is crucial to understand how to leverage these tools to address specific business needs and improve overall efficiency. To do this, we must dive deeper into the practical applications and strategic considerations for designing effective automation processes.

One of the key aspects of successful automation is ensuring that the processes align with the goals and workflows of the organization. For instance, when setting up a workflow rule, it is essential to clearly define the trigger conditions. These conditions determine when the workflow will be activated. A common scenario might involve automating customer support processes. Suppose a company wants to ensure that every time a new case is created in Salesforce, an automatic notification is sent to the support team. To achieve this, you would configure a workflow rule that triggers when a case is created. The rule's criteria could specify that the case status is "New," and the associated action could be an email alert to the support team. This setup ensures that the team is promptly informed of new cases and can address them in a timely manner.

In contrast, Process Builder offers a more sophisticated approach to automation, allowing for multi-step processes and complex logic. A notable advantage of Process Builder is its ability to manage related records and perform actions across multiple objects. For example, consider a scenario where a company wants to automate the lead-to-opportunity conversion process. Using Process Builder, you can create a process that triggers when a lead is converted. This process might involve updating the lead record, creating a new opportunity, and assigning tasks to the sales team. By defining criteria and actions for each step, you can ensure that the conversion process is handled seamlessly and consistently.

When designing automation in Process Builder, it is helpful to visualize the entire process flow. The visual interface provided by Process Builder allows you to map out each step and its associated actions. This visualization not only aids in the design but also helps in identifying potential issues or inefficiencies. For example, if a process involves creating related records and updating fields across multiple objects, the visual flow can reveal if any steps are missing or if the logic needs refinement.

Another important consideration when working with automation tools is managing exceptions and ensuring data integrity. While automation can greatly reduce manual effort, it is essential to account for scenarios where the automation might not work as expected. For instance, you might set up a workflow rule to update a field based on specific criteria, but if the rule inadvertently updates records incorrectly, it could lead to data inconsistencies. To mitigate such risks, it is crucial to thoroughly test your automation rules and processes in a sandbox environment before deploying them to production. Testing allows you to verify that the automation behaves as intended and that any potential issues are addressed.

Additionally, regularly monitoring and auditing your automation processes can help maintain their effectiveness over time. Salesforce provides tools and reports that allow you to track the performance of your workflow rules and processes. By reviewing these reports, you can identify any anomalies or areas where the automation might need adjustments. For example, if a workflow rule is not triggering as expected, examining the execution logs can provide insights into the cause and help you refine the rule's criteria or actions.

As organizations grow and evolve, their automation needs may change. Therefore, it is important to periodically review and update your automation processes to ensure they continue to meet the organization's objectives. For instance, if a business introduces new products or services, you might need to adjust your automation rules to accommodate these changes. Staying proactive in managing and optimizing your automation processes ensures that they remain aligned with the organization's evolving requirements.

In summary, automation through workflow rules and Process Builder is a powerful means of enhancing efficiency and streamlining business processes within Salesforce. By carefully designing and managing these automation tools, you can achieve significant improvements in operational effectiveness. Leveraging the capabilities of both workflow rules and Process Builder allows you to address a wide range of automation needs, from simple task automation to complex multi-step processes. Through thoughtful configuration, testing, and ongoing management, you can ensure that your automation strategies deliver tangible benefits and support the overall success of your organization.

In the realm of Salesforce automation, the successful implementation of workflow rules and Process Builder not only streamlines operations but also drives consistency and accuracy in data handling. As we explore these tools further, it becomes clear that each serves distinct but complementary roles in the automation landscape.

Workflow rules are ideal for straightforward, single-action automations. They excel in scenarios where a simple trigger, such as a record update or creation, necessitates a specific follow-up action. For instance, consider a business process where every time a contract is marked as "Approved," an automatic task should be assigned to the legal team for final review. In this case, the workflow rule is configured with a trigger based on the contract's status field. The action, in this case, would be the creation of a task with pre-defined details. This simple but effective use of workflow rules ensures that essential follow-up actions are systematically executed, minimizing the risk of overlooked tasks.

However, for more complex scenarios that require multi-step actions or involve multiple objects, Process Builder provides a robust solution. Its ability to handle intricate logic and interact with related records makes it a powerful tool for advanced automation needs. Take, for example, an automated process for handling customer feedback. When a feedback record is created, Process Builder can initiate a series of actions, such as updating related customer records, creating follow-up tasks for support staff, and sending a thank-you email to the customer. This multi-step process demonstrates the flexibility of Process Builder in managing more elaborate workflows that go beyond the capabilities of basic workflow rules.

An important aspect of using Process Builder effectively is understanding the concept of process criteria and actions. Criteria define the conditions under which the process is triggered, while actions specify what should happen when those conditions are met. For example, if we consider an automation process that triggers when a sales opportunity reaches a certain stage, the criteria might include conditions like opportunity amount or close date. The actions could involve updating fields on the opportunity record, creating related tasks, and notifying the sales team. Crafting these criteria and actions thoughtfully ensures that the process aligns with business goals and operational requirements.

Furthermore, while setting up automation processes, it is essential to consider how they will interact with existing workflows and other automation tools. Overlapping or conflicting automation rules can lead to unexpected outcomes or inefficiencies. For instance, if a workflow rule and a Process Builder process both attempt to update the same field on a record, it could result in data inconsistencies or conflicting updates. To avoid such issues, thorough planning and testing are necessary. It is advisable to document all automation processes and their interactions, ensuring that they complement rather than interfere with each other.

Another critical consideration in automation is handling

exceptions and ensuring that processes do not inadvertently cause disruptions. For example, if a workflow rule triggers an email notification but the email template contains outdated information, it could lead to miscommunication. To address this, it is important to establish a review and approval process for automation rules and their associated actions. Regular audits and updates help maintain the accuracy and relevance of automation processes, ensuring that they continue to meet organizational needs.

In addition to setting up and managing automation, monitoring and analyzing its performance are key to optimizing its effectiveness. Salesforce provides various tools and reports to track automation activity and performance. By analyzing these reports, administrators can gain insights into how automation processes are functioning and identify areas for improvement. For example, if a particular workflow rule is not triggering as expected, examining the execution logs can help diagnose the issue and make necessary adjustments.

Ultimately, the goal of leveraging workflow rules and Process Builder is to enhance efficiency, reduce manual effort, and improve data accuracy. By understanding the strengths and limitations of each tool, administrators can design and implement automation strategies that effectively address business needs. Through thoughtful configuration, testing, and ongoing management, automation becomes a powerful asset in achieving operational excellence and driving business success.

In conclusion, Salesforce's automation tools offer substantial benefits for streamlining processes and improving efficiency. Workflow rules provide a straightforward solution for single-action tasks, while Process Builder supports more complex, multi-step processes. By mastering these tools and applying best practices in their implementation, you can significantly enhance your Salesforce environment and support the achievement of your organizational objectives.

CHAPTER 6: MANAGING DATA: IMPORTING, EXPORTING, AND DATA QUALITY

Effectively managing data is a cornerstone of Salesforce administration, and mastering the intricacies of data import, export, and quality management is essential for maintaining the integrity and functionality of the Salesforce environment. This discussion begins with a comprehensive look at the tools and methodologies for importing and exporting data, focusing on the Data Loader and other integral tools designed to handle large volumes of information. Subsequently, we will delve into the crucial aspects of data quality management, including validation rules, deduplication techniques, and best practices for data stewardship.

Data import and export are fundamental processes in Salesforce that allow administrators to move information into and out of the system. The Data Loader is one of the primary tools used for these tasks. It is a powerful, client-based application that enables bulk data operations, including inserting, updating, upserting, and deleting records. When preparing for a data import, it is essential to understand the structure of the data being imported and how it aligns with Salesforce objects and fields. Proper mapping of fields is crucial to ensure that the data is accurately populated into the correct Salesforce records.

The Data Loader supports CSV files for data import, which necessitates that the data be organized in a format compatible with Salesforce's data model. For example, when importing account data, the CSV file should include columns for all relevant fields such as Account Name, Account Number, and any custom fields that have been defined. Before performing an import, it is advisable to conduct a data quality check on the CSV file to identify and rectify any inconsistencies or errors that might cause issues during the import process.

In addition to the Data Loader, Salesforce provides other tools for data management, such as the Import Wizard. This tool offers a more user-friendly interface and is suitable for smaller data volumes. It guides users through a step-by-step process to import data into standard and custom objects, making it accessible for those who may not require the advanced capabilities of the Data Loader. The Import Wizard also provides options for data mapping and error handling, which can be useful for ensuring data integrity during the import process.

Exporting data from Salesforce is equally important for data analysis, reporting, and backup purposes. The Data Loader can be used to export data in CSV format, which is suitable for offline analysis or integration with other systems. Additionally, Salesforce offers report-based exports, allowing administrators to generate reports and export data directly from the reporting interface. This method provides flexibility in selecting the specific data subsets and formats needed for various business needs.

As we transition from data import and export to data quality management, it becomes evident that maintaining accurate and reliable data is crucial for the effective use of Salesforce. Data quality management involves implementing strategies to ensure that data is accurate, consistent, and up-to-date. One of the primary tools for maintaining data quality is the use of validation rules. These rules define criteria that data must meet before it can be saved in Salesforce, helping to prevent the entry of invalid or incomplete information.

For example, a validation rule might be configured to require that all opportunity records have a close date in the future, ensuring that only realistic and actionable opportunities are recorded. Validation rules can be tailored to enforce specific business rules and data standards, thereby supporting the overall data governance strategy and improving the reliability of the data stored in Salesforce.

Another critical aspect of data quality management is deduplication. Duplicate records can lead to inefficiencies and inaccuracies, making it imperative to have processes in place to identify and eliminate duplicates. Salesforce provides built-in tools for deduplication, such as matching rules and duplicate rules. These tools help identify potential duplicate records based on predefined criteria and provide options for merging or handling duplicates as needed.

Deduplication is not a one-time activity but rather an ongoing process that should be integrated into regular data maintenance routines. By routinely checking for and resolving duplicates, administrators can ensure that the data remains clean and reliable. Implementing deduplication practices also supports the accuracy of reporting and analytics, as it prevents the distortion of results caused by duplicate entries.

Effective data stewardship is the practice of overseeing and managing data throughout its lifecycle, ensuring that it remains accurate, secure, and compliant with organizational standards. This involves not only implementing validation and deduplication strategies but also establishing data governance policies and procedures. Data stewardship includes regular audits of data quality, user training on data entry best practices, and continuous monitoring of data-related processes.

In conclusion, managing data effectively in Salesforce requires a thorough understanding of both the tools available for importing and exporting data and the strategies needed to maintain data quality. By leveraging tools such as the Data Loader and Import Wizard, and implementing robust data quality practices like validation rules and deduplication, administrators can ensure that Salesforce remains a reliable and valuable asset for their organization. The focus on data stewardship and ongoing maintenance supports the integrity and utility of the data, ultimately driving better decision-making and operational efficiency.

When managing data within Salesforce, it is critical to maintain an ongoing focus on data quality to ensure the reliability and effectiveness of the platform. Data quality management involves a range of practices and tools designed to address issues such as inaccuracies, inconsistencies, and redundancies that can impact the integrity of the data. One of the primary strategies for managing data quality is the implementation of validation rules.

Validation rules are custom conditions that must be met before data can be saved in Salesforce. They act as gatekeepers, ensuring that only data which meets predefined criteria is entered into the system. By configuring these rules, administrators can enforce data standards and reduce the likelihood of errors or incomplete entries. For example, a validation rule might be set to require that all new contacts have an email address, ensuring that no contact records are created without essential contact information. Validation rules can be as simple or as complex as needed, and they can be tailored to suit various business requirements.

Creating effective validation rules involves defining the criteria that will be used to assess data entries. This is achieved through a combination of logical expressions and field references. For instance, if a business requires that the "Close Date" of opportunities must always be in the future, a validation rule can be set up to compare the Close Date field with the current date. If the rule conditions are not met, Salesforce will prevent the record from being saved and provide an error message to the user, guiding them to correct the issue.

In addition to validation rules, deduplication is another essential aspect of data quality management. Duplicate records can clutter the system, lead to inaccurate reporting, and create inefficiencies. To address this issue, Salesforce provides several tools to identify and merge duplicate records. Matching rules and duplicate rules are two key components in this process.

Matching rules determine the criteria for identifying potential duplicates. They can be based on various fields, such as email addresses, phone numbers, or names. For example, a matching rule might be configured to flag any contact records with the same email address as potential duplicates. Duplicate rules then use these matching rules to define how duplicate records should be handled. Administrators can choose to allow or block duplicate records, or to alert users when duplicates are detected, providing options to merge or discard the entries.

Effective deduplication requires ongoing vigilance and periodic review of the data. Implementing a regular schedule for deduplication processes can help maintain data cleanliness and prevent the accumulation of duplicate records. Additionally, educating users on best practices for data entry and encouraging adherence to standardized formats can help minimize the creation of duplicates in the first place.

Another crucial element of data quality management is data stewardship. Data stewardship encompasses the policies, procedures, and responsibilities associated with maintaining high-quality data. This involves establishing data governance practices, including roles and responsibilities for data management, data entry standards, and procedures for monitoring and improving data quality.

Data stewardship also includes performing regular data audits to identify and address any issues with data accuracy and consistency. These audits may involve analyzing data trends, reviewing records for accuracy, and conducting data quality assessments. By implementing a comprehensive data stewardship program, organizations can ensure that data remains accurate, secure, and aligned with business goals.

To support data stewardship efforts, Salesforce offers various features and tools that assist in maintaining data quality. Data quality dashboards, for example, provide visual representations of data quality metrics, allowing administrators to quickly identify areas that require attention. Additionally, reports and analytics can be used to track data quality trends and measure the effectiveness of data management strategies.

Ultimately, effective data management in Salesforce requires a combination of robust tools and strategic practices. By mastering the use of data import and export tools such as the Data Loader and Import Wizard, and implementing comprehensive data quality management strategies including validation rules, deduplication, and data stewardship, administrators can ensure that their Salesforce environment remains a valuable and reliable asset. The focus on maintaining high-quality data not only enhances operational efficiency but also supports informed decision-making and drives overall business success.

To ensure the effective management of data within Salesforce, it is essential to understand the tools available for importing and exporting data, as well as to apply best practices for maintaining data quality. The ability to efficiently handle data operations is crucial for any Salesforce administrator, and mastering these processes can significantly enhance the performance and reliability of the platform.

Data import processes involve transferring data from external sources into Salesforce. One of the primary tools for this task is the Data Import Wizard, which is a user-friendly tool that provides a guided interface for importing data. It supports a variety of standard and custom objects and allows for the bulk import of records. When using the Data Import Wizard, it is important to follow a systematic approach. This involves selecting the appropriate object to import data into, mapping the fields from the source data to Salesforce fields, and configuring any necessary settings, such as data transformations or error handling options. For smaller data volumes or one-time imports, the Data Import Wizard can be a straightforward and effective solution.

For more complex or large-scale data imports, the Data Loader is the preferred tool. The Data Loader is a client application that allows for more advanced data manipulation and supports a wider range of operations, including insertions, updates, deletions, and upserts. It can handle large volumes of data and offers greater flexibility in terms of data processing. To use the Data Loader effectively, you need to understand the structure of your Salesforce objects and the relationships between them. This knowledge will help you prepare your data files correctly and ensure that data is imported accurately and efficiently.

Data export processes are equally important, as they allow for the extraction of data from Salesforce for analysis, reporting, or backup purposes. The Data Export Wizard, available within Salesforce, provides an intuitive interface for exporting data. It allows you to select specific objects or all data and choose the desired export format, such as CSV files. For regular data backups or large-scale exports, using the Data Export Wizard can simplify the process and ensure that you have access to up-to-date data.

Additionally, the Data Loader can also be used for exporting data. This tool offers greater control over the export process, including the ability to filter records based on specific criteria and export data in various formats. By leveraging the Data Loader for exports, administrators can generate detailed reports and backups, ensuring that important data is preserved and accessible when needed.

In parallel with the import and export processes, maintaining data quality is a critical aspect of data management. As previously mentioned, validation rules play a significant role in ensuring data integrity by enforcing data standards and preventing incorrect data entries. By configuring validation rules that align with business requirements, administrators can help ensure that data entered into Salesforce is accurate and consistent.

Another important aspect of data quality management is data deduplication. Duplicate records can create confusion, lead to erroneous reporting, and affect overall system performance. Implementing deduplication processes involves using tools such as matching rules and duplicate rules to identify and address duplicate records. Regular deduplication activities, including automated processes and manual reviews, are essential for maintaining a clean and efficient database.

Effective data stewardship also plays a pivotal role in data quality management. Data stewardship encompasses the ongoing management of data quality, including establishing data governance practices, defining data entry standards, and monitoring data integrity. A well-defined data stewardship program ensures that data management responsibilities are clearly assigned, data entry practices are standardized, and data quality issues are promptly addressed.

To support data stewardship efforts, Salesforce provides various features and tools, such as data quality dashboards and reporting capabilities. These tools offer insights into data quality metrics and trends, allowing administrators to identify areas for improvement and measure the effectiveness of data management strategies. By leveraging these features, administrators can proactively manage data quality and ensure that the Salesforce environment remains a reliable and valuable resource.

In summary, the effective management of data within Salesforce involves a comprehensive approach to data import, export, and quality management. By mastering the use of tools such as the Data Import Wizard, Data Loader, and Data Export Wizard, and applying best practices for validation, deduplication, and data stewardship, administrators can enhance the performance and reliability of the Salesforce platform. Ensuring data accuracy and consistency is essential for maximizing the value of Salesforce and supporting the overall success of the organization.

CHAPTER 7: REPORTS AND DASHBOARDS: CREATING AND CUSTOMIZING

In this section, we will immerse ourselves in the world of Salesforce reports and dashboards, fundamental tools that empower users to analyze and visualize data effectively. As an administrator, mastering these tools is crucial for creating meaningful insights and supporting data-driven decision-making within your organization.

Understanding the core components of Salesforce reporting starts with familiarizing yourself with different report types. Salesforce offers several report formats, each suited to various data analysis needs. The primary report types include Tabular Reports, Summary Reports, Matrix Reports, and Joined Reports. Each format serves a distinct purpose and provides different ways to organize and view data.

Tabular Reports are the most basic type and display data in a simple table format. They are useful for straightforward lists where no grouping or summarization is required. For example, a tabular report could list all contacts in a specific region. While straightforward, this type of report lacks depth and is best used for simple, quick lists.

Summary Reports, on the other hand, allow for data grouping and summarization. This type of report is ideal when you need to organize data by certain criteria and perform aggregate calculations. For instance, a summary report could group opportunities by stage and calculate the total revenue for each stage. This format is useful for understanding data trends and patterns at a higher level than tabular reports.

Matrix Reports offer a more complex view by allowing data to be grouped both horizontally and vertically. This type of report is beneficial for cross-referencing multiple data points and providing a more comprehensive analysis. For example, a matrix report could compare sales performance across different regions and time periods, giving a multidimensional view of the data.

Joined Reports provide the capability to combine data from multiple report types into a single view. This format is particularly useful for comparing and analyzing different data sets side by side. For example, a joined report could show sales data alongside customer support case data, allowing for a comparison of sales performance and customer satisfaction.

Creating effective reports requires an understanding of how to apply filters and customize report settings. Filters enable you to refine your data to focus on specific criteria, such as a particular date range or record type. By applying filters, you can narrow down the data displayed in your reports and ensure that the information is relevant and actionable.

Customizing report settings involves selecting the appropriate fields, grouping options, and summarization methods to align with your analysis needs. You can adjust report columns, add or remove fields, and set up summaries and calculations based on your requirements. This customization ensures that your reports present the data in a meaningful way that supports your objectives.

Once reports are created, the next step is to design and customize dashboards. Dashboards provide a visual representation of data and offer an intuitive way to monitor key metrics and performance indicators. Salesforce dashboards are composed of various components, including charts, graphs, tables, and gauges, each designed to convey different types of information.

When creating dashboards, it is essential to consider the audience and purpose of the dashboard. For example, a sales manager may require a dashboard that displays real-time sales performance metrics, while a customer service manager might need a dashboard focused on case resolution times and customer satisfaction scores. Tailoring the dashboard components to meet these needs ensures that the information presented is relevant and useful.

Customization options for dashboards include selecting the appropriate report sources, configuring chart types, and arranging components to create a cohesive view. You can choose from a range of chart types, such as bar charts, line charts, and pie charts, to represent data visually. Additionally, dashboards can be set up to display dynamic data by incorporating filters and interactive elements, allowing users to drill down into specific details as needed.

One of the key features of Salesforce dashboards is the ability to create multiple dashboard views. This functionality enables users to switch between different perspectives of the data, such as viewing performance by region or by sales team. By offering multiple views, dashboards provide flexibility and allow users to analyze data from different angles.

In summary, mastering reports and dashboards in Salesforce is crucial for leveraging the full potential of the platform's data analysis and visualization capabilities. By understanding the various report types and customization options, you can create insightful reports that address specific business needs. Designing effective dashboards requires careful consideration of the intended audience and purpose, ensuring that the visual representations of data are both meaningful and actionable. As you progress through this material, you will develop the skills necessary to harness the power of Salesforce reporting and dashboards to drive informed decision-making and support your organization's strategic goals.

Creating insightful and functional dashboards requires a clear understanding of the data you wish to present and the most effective ways to visualize it. Dashboards are composed of various components that allow for a comprehensive view of key metrics and performance indicators. To design dashboards that provide meaningful insights, one must carefully select and configure these components to reflect the needs of the end users.

When designing a dashboard, the first consideration is the choice of components. Salesforce dashboards include charts, graphs, tables, and gauges, each serving different purposes. For instance, bar charts are ideal for comparing quantities across categories, while line charts are suited for showing trends over time. Pie charts can effectively display proportions and percentages, and tables are useful for detailed, tabular data presentations. Gauges provide a quick visual indication of performance against a target, making them valuable for monitoring goals.

Selecting the right component involves understanding the type of data you have and what you want to communicate. For example, if you need to show sales performance over different quarters, a line chart would effectively highlight trends and fluctuations. If your goal is to illustrate the market share distribution among competitors, a pie chart might be more appropriate. Each component has its strengths, and using them effectively requires thoughtful consideration of what each visualization can best convey.

Customizing these components is the next step in creating impactful dashboards. This process involves configuring the data sources for each component, setting up filters, and adjusting the visual presentation to ensure clarity and usability. For instance, you might need to pull data from specific reports or objects, apply filters to focus on relevant subsets, and adjust the display settings to enhance readability. Effective customization ensures that the dashboard accurately represents the data and aligns with the specific needs of the users.

Filters play a crucial role in dashboard customization. They allow users to interact with the dashboard by drilling down into specific data sets or time periods. For example, a sales dashboard might include filters for regions, product lines, or time frames, enabling users to view performance metrics tailored to their particular interests. By implementing filters, you enhance the dashboard's interactivity and make it a more powerful tool for data analysis.

The layout of a dashboard also significantly impacts its effectiveness. A well-organized dashboard should present information in a logical and intuitive manner. Grouping related components together and ensuring that the most critical metrics are prominently displayed can improve user experience and make the data easier to interpret. For instance, placing key performance indicators (KPIs) at the top of the dashboard ensures that users can quickly assess the most important information without scrolling through less relevant details.

Beyond the basic layout and component customization, dashboards in Salesforce can be made even more dynamic with the use of interactive features. Adding dynamic filters, drill-down capabilities, and interactive charts allows users to engage with the data more deeply. For example, interactive charts can enable users to click on specific data points to see more detailed information or to filter the entire dashboard based on a selected category. These features enhance the functionality of the dashboard and allow users to explore the data in a more nuanced way.

Creating dashboards also involves setting up proper sharing and security settings to ensure that the right users have access to the appropriate data. Salesforce allows for granular control over dashboard sharing, enabling administrators to set permissions based on user roles or groups. By configuring these settings, you can ensure that sensitive data is only accessible to authorized individuals while still providing relevant insights to those who need them.

In conclusion, mastering the creation and customization of reports and dashboards in Salesforce is essential for harnessing the platform's full potential in data analysis and visualization. By understanding the various report types and their applications, customizing report settings, and designing effective dashboards with appropriate components and interactive features, you can provide valuable insights that support informed decision-making. The ability to create tailored, dynamic dashboards not only enhances data visibility but also empowers users to engage with and analyze data more effectively, driving better business outcomes.

The effective utilization of Salesforce reports and dashboards hinges on their ability to convey actionable insights clearly and efficiently. As we navigate through the nuances of creating and customizing these tools, it becomes clear that their power lies not just in their design, but in their alignment with business objectives and user needs.

When it comes to reports, understanding the various types available in Salesforce is fundamental. Each report type serves a specific purpose and is suited for different kinds of data analysis. Tabular reports, for example, present data in a straightforward table format and are useful for generating lists, such as a list of contacts or leads. Summary reports, on the other hand, allow users to group data and summarize it with subtotals, which is invaluable for analyzing sales figures or tracking progress against goals. Matrix reports offer a more complex structure, enabling users to cross-tabulate data across rows and columns, ideal for comparing performance metrics across different dimensions. Finally, joined reports provide a flexible way to combine multiple report types into a single view, offering a comprehensive perspective on related data sets.

Customization of reports involves tailoring them to meet specific analytical needs and ensuring they deliver the most relevant insights. This process begins with selecting the appropriate report type and then configuring filters to narrow down the data. Filters are crucial for honing in on the specific data points that matter to the user, whether it's sales data from a particular region or customer interactions within a given timeframe. By applying filters, you can refine the report to present only the most pertinent information, which enhances its usefulness and clarity.

Another essential aspect of report customization is the layout and formatting. Salesforce offers various options to modify the appearance of reports, such as adjusting column widths, changing text alignment, and applying conditional formatting. These adjustments help make the report more readable and visually appealing. Conditional formatting, for instance, allows you to highlight key figures or trends, such as flagging sales figures that exceed targets or displaying negative performance indicators in red. These visual cues facilitate quicker interpretation of the data and aid in identifying important trends at a glance.

Moving on to dashboards, the key to creating effective

dashboards lies in their ability to provide a snapshot of performance metrics and key indicators in a cohesive manner. Dashboards aggregate data from multiple reports, offering a consolidated view that can highlight overall trends and performance. Each component of a dashboard—whether it's a chart, graph, or table—should be carefully selected to represent the most critical data effectively. When designing dashboards, it's important to prioritize clarity and focus. Place the most important metrics at the top or in prominent positions to ensure that users can quickly access and interpret key information.

In addition to static reports and dashboards, Salesforce offers dynamic features that can further enhance data interaction. Interactive dashboards, for example, enable users to drill down into specific data points to uncover more detailed insights. This interactivity allows users to explore different aspects of the data, such as filtering by a particular time period or region, and provides a more granular view of performance. Incorporating such features into your dashboards can significantly improve their usability and effectiveness, as it empowers users to engage with the data on a deeper level.

Another crucial consideration when working with dashboards is ensuring they are aligned with user roles and responsibilities. Different users may require access to different sets of data based on their roles within the organization. Salesforce allows for customization of dashboard visibility, enabling you to configure settings so that users only see the dashboards relevant to their function. This ensures that sensitive or irrelevant data is not exposed and that users have access to the information they need to perform their roles effectively.

Finally, maintaining and updating reports and dashboards is an ongoing process. As business needs evolve and new data becomes available, it's important to periodically review and adjust your reports and dashboards to ensure they continue to provide valuable insights. This might involve updating report filters, modifying dashboard components, or adding new visualizations to reflect changes in business strategy or objectives.

In summary, creating and customizing reports and dashboards in Salesforce requires a thoughtful approach to data presentation and user needs. By understanding the different report types, utilizing effective filters, and designing dashboards that align with business goals, you can leverage Salesforce's powerful tools to drive data-driven decision-making and enhance organizational performance. The ability to tailor these tools to specific analytical needs and user requirements not only improves data visibility but also supports more informed and strategic business decisions.

CHAPTER 8: MANAGING AND CONFIGURING APPLICATIONS

Salesforce provides a robust platform with a plethora of applications and features that can be tailored to fit the specific needs of an organization. Navigating and managing these applications effectively is crucial for maximizing the platform's potential and ensuring it aligns with business objectives. This section delves into the processes involved in managing and configuring applications within Salesforce, including both installed packages and custom applications.

When beginning to manage applications in Salesforce, it is essential to first understand the distinctions between installed packages and custom applications. Installed packages refer to third-party solutions that have been added to your Salesforce environment through the AppExchange, Salesforce's marketplace for apps and components. These packages can range from simple add-ons to comprehensive systems that extend Salesforce's native capabilities. Custom applications, on the other hand, are designed and built specifically for your organization within the Salesforce platform. They leverage Salesforce's native tools and functionalities to address unique business processes and requirements.

The initial step in managing applications is app setup. This involves configuring both installed packages and custom applications to ensure they are properly integrated and optimized for use. For installed packages, this typically includes reviewing the documentation provided by the vendor to understand the necessary setup procedures. This might involve configuring package-specific settings, mapping data fields to Salesforce objects, and integrating with other systems or processes within Salesforce. It is also important to review the security settings associated with the package to ensure that access is appropriately controlled and that sensitive data is protected.

Custom applications require a different approach. The setup process begins with defining the application's purpose and requirements. This involves identifying the business processes that the application will support and determining the necessary Salesforce components and features. Once the application's scope is defined, the next step is to configure its components, such as custom objects, fields, and page layouts. Custom objects are critical for storing data that does not fit within Salesforce's standard objects, while custom fields allow you to capture additional information pertinent to your business processes. Page layouts are designed to enhance user experience by organizing how data is displayed and interacted with on record pages.

A crucial part of managing and configuring applications is understanding and utilizing Salesforce's configuration options. These options provide flexibility in how applications are tailored to meet specific needs. For example, Salesforce allows for the customization of object relationships, which can define how different objects interact with each other. This includes setting up master-detail relationships, which enforce data integrity by creating a parent-child relationship between objects, and lookup relationships, which provide a more flexible association between objects.

Additionally, configuring application settings involves adjusting user interface elements to enhance usability. This includes setting up custom tabs to provide easy access to various parts of the application, configuring list views to display relevant records, and customizing compact layouts to ensure key information is visible at a glance. Each of these configuration options plays a role in creating a streamlined and efficient user experience.

Another important aspect of application management is optimizing performance. As applications are used and data accumulates, it is essential to regularly review and optimize their performance to ensure they continue to operate efficiently. This might involve analyzing data usage patterns, identifying and addressing performance bottlenecks, and implementing best practices for data management. For instance, regularly archiving old or unnecessary data can help maintain optimal performance and reduce system clutter.

User adoption and training are also critical components of successful application management. Even the most well-configured application will only be effective if users understand how to use it and are comfortable with its features. Providing thorough training and support ensures that users can leverage the application's capabilities to their fullest extent. This might include creating user guides, conducting training sessions, and providing ongoing support to address any issues or questions that arise.

Finally, it is essential to monitor and evaluate the application's performance continuously. This involves gathering feedback from users, tracking key performance indicators, and assessing whether the application continues to meet the organization's evolving needs. Regular evaluations help identify areas for improvement and ensure that the application remains aligned with business objectives.

In summary, managing and configuring applications within Salesforce involves a comprehensive approach that includes understanding the differences between installed packages and custom applications, setting up and configuring components, optimizing performance, and ensuring user adoption. By focusing on these areas, Salesforce administrators can effectively tailor the platform to meet their organization's unique requirements, enhance operational efficiency, and support business success.

Continuing with the exploration of managing and configuring applications within Salesforce, it is crucial to delve deeper into the practical aspects of application setup and optimization. As previously established, the effective management of Salesforce applications involves a detailed approach to both installed packages and custom applications. This section will provide a more granular look at the processes involved, including app-specific configurations, performance considerations, and ongoing management practices.

When configuring installed packages, one of the initial tasks is to review and understand the package's configuration settings. Installed packages often come with a set of predefined configurations and default settings, which might need adjustment based on the specific needs of your organization. This could involve modifying field mappings, adjusting workflows that the package integrates with, and setting up custom permissions to ensure that users have appropriate access levels. It is also essential to test the package thoroughly to ensure that it integrates seamlessly with existing Salesforce processes and does not disrupt other functionalities.

Custom applications require a more hands-on approach to configuration. After setting up the basic components of a custom application, such as custom objects and fields, the next step is to focus on the configuration of user interfaces and user experiences. This includes designing intuitive page layouts that facilitate easy data entry and retrieval, configuring related lists to provide relevant information, and setting up custom tabs for quick access to application components. Effective configuration of user interfaces is crucial for enhancing productivity and ensuring that users can efficiently navigate and utilize the application.

An important aspect of configuring custom applications is defining and implementing business processes through automation. Salesforce provides various tools, such as workflow rules, Process Builder, and Flow, to automate routine tasks and streamline business processes. For instance, you might configure a workflow rule to send an email alert when a record meets certain criteria or use Process Builder to update related records automatically. By leveraging these tools, you can ensure that the application not only meets business requirements but also operates efficiently and with minimal manual intervention.

Optimizing applications for performance is another critical aspect of management. As the volume of data and the complexity of processes increase, it is essential to monitor application performance and make adjustments as needed. Salesforce offers various tools and features to help with performance optimization, such as the Salesforce Optimizer, which provides insights into potential areas for improvement and recommendations for optimizing your Salesforce instance. Regularly reviewing performance metrics, such as page load times and system usage patterns, helps identify potential bottlenecks and ensures that the application remains responsive and efficient.

Data management plays a significant role in application optimization. Properly managing data within the application involves implementing data governance practices, such as defining data ownership, establishing data quality standards, and ensuring compliance with data privacy regulations. This includes setting up validation rules to enforce data accuracy and consistency, using deduplication tools to remove duplicate records, and implementing data archiving strategies to manage historical data effectively. By maintaining high data quality, you can ensure that the application delivers accurate and reliable insights, which is essential for informed decision-making.

User training and support are integral to the successful deployment and management of Salesforce applications. Even with the most well-configured application, user adoption can be a challenge if users are not adequately trained or supported. Providing comprehensive training sessions, creating user documentation, and offering ongoing support are essential for helping users become proficient with the application. Additionally, gathering feedback from users can provide valuable insights into potential areas for improvement and help identify any issues that may need to be addressed.

Finally, ongoing management of Salesforce applications involves regular reviews and updates to ensure that they continue to meet the evolving needs of the organization. This includes staying informed about new Salesforce features and updates, reviewing application performance periodically, and making adjustments based on user feedback and changing business requirements. By maintaining a proactive approach to application management, you can ensure that your Salesforce instance remains aligned with organizational goals and continues to deliver value.

In summary, managing and configuring Salesforce applications involves a multifaceted approach that includes detailed setup and configuration, performance optimization, effective data management, and comprehensive user support. By focusing on these areas, you can tailor the Salesforce platform to meet your organization's unique needs, enhance operational efficiency, and support business success.

In managing and configuring Salesforce applications, understanding the nuances of app deployment and maintenance is crucial for ensuring ongoing effectiveness and alignment with business needs. This part will explore advanced aspects of application management, including how to handle upgrades, manage user access, and maintain application health over time.

Once an application is set up and optimized, it is vital to consider the implications of updates and upgrades. Salesforce regularly releases new versions of its platform, which can introduce new features, enhancements, and bug fixes. When an application is updated, whether it's an installed package from the AppExchange or a custom-built solution, it is essential to evaluate the changes thoroughly. This involves reviewing release notes, testing the updates in a sandbox environment, and assessing the impact on existing configurations and customizations.

For instance, when an installed package is upgraded, the new version might include changes that affect the application's functionality or compatibility with other Salesforce components. It is prudent to perform regression testing to ensure that existing workflows, reports, and integrations continue to function as expected. In cases where the upgrade introduces significant changes, additional training may be necessary to help users adapt to the new features or interfaces.

Managing user access to applications is another critical aspect of configuration. Salesforce provides granular control over user permissions through profiles and permission sets, allowing administrators to define what users can see and do within an application. Profiles serve as the baseline for user permissions, defining access to objects, fields, and record types. Permission sets, on the other hand, provide additional permissions that can be assigned to users on top of their profile settings.

When configuring user access, it is essential to balance security with usability. For example, while restricting access to sensitive data is necessary to maintain security, overly restrictive permissions can hinder user productivity. Regularly reviewing and updating user permissions ensures that access levels remain appropriate as roles and responsibilities within the organization evolve. Additionally, implementing role hierarchies can simplify the management of data visibility by automatically granting access based on the user's position in the hierarchy.

Maintaining the health of an application involves ongoing monitoring and management to address issues as they arise and to ensure continued performance. Salesforce provides several tools to aid in this process, such as the Salesforce Optimizer, which offers recommendations for improving the performance and efficiency of your Salesforce instance. Regular use of these tools can help identify areas for improvement and prevent potential issues before they impact users.

Monitoring application performance is also crucial for maintaining health. Performance metrics such as page load times, error rates, and user feedback can provide insights into how well an application is functioning. Salesforce's built-in reports and dashboards can be customized to track these metrics and provide alerts when performance thresholds are exceeded. Addressing performance issues promptly helps ensure that users have a positive experience and that the application continues to meet business needs.

Data management remains a critical component of application health. As applications grow and evolve, ensuring that data remains accurate, consistent, and up-to-date is essential. Regular data quality checks, such as deduplication and validation, help maintain data integrity and prevent issues related to data inaccuracies. Implementing data archiving strategies can also help manage the volume of data and improve application performance by keeping the database lean and efficient.

User training and support are key to successful application management. Even the best-configured application can face challenges if users are not adequately trained or supported. Providing ongoing training sessions, creating user guides, and establishing a support system for addressing user questions and issues can enhance user adoption and satisfaction. Additionally, soliciting feedback from users can provide valuable insights into how the application can be improved or adjusted to better meet their needs.

In summary, effective management and configuration of Salesforce applications require a comprehensive approach that includes handling updates, managing user access, maintaining application health, and ensuring data quality. By focusing on these areas, Salesforce administrators can optimize the functionality of their applications, enhance user experience, and support organizational goals. As the Salesforce platform continues to evolve, staying informed about new features and best practices will be key to maintaining a successful and efficient application environment.

CHAPTER 9: IMPLEMENTING AND MANAGING SALESFORCE COMMUNITIES

Salesforce Communities, now known as Salesforce Experience Cloud, serve as a powerful tool for creating online spaces where organizations can interact with their customers, partners, and employees. The ability to implement and manage these communities effectively can transform how businesses engage with various stakeholders and streamline communication and collaboration. This section will guide you through the critical aspects of setting up and managing Salesforce Communities, focusing on the essential steps to ensure that these platforms are tailored to meet organizational needs and enhance user experience.

The first step in implementing a Salesforce Community is to understand the types of communities available and select the one that aligns with your organizational goals. Salesforce Communities can be broadly categorized into customer communities, partner communities, and employee communities. Customer communities are designed to facilitate customer support and engagement, offering a space for customers to access knowledge bases, participate in forums, and interact with support teams. Partner communities focus on providing a platform for business partners to collaborate, share leads, and track joint sales activities. Employee communities aim to enhance internal collaboration, knowledge sharing, and employee engagement.

Once the type of community is determined, the next phase involves setting up the community. This begins with enabling the Communities feature in Salesforce. To do this, navigate to the Salesforce Setup menu, search for "Communities," and enable the feature. After activation, you will need to create a new community. This process involves defining basic community details, such as its name, URL, and type. You will also select a community template that aligns with the intended use of the community. Salesforce offers various templates, including Customer Service, Partner Central, and Build Your Own, each tailored to different use cases.

The selection of a template is critical as it influences the initial layout and functionality of the community. For instance, the Customer Service template is optimized for support interactions and includes features such as a case management console and knowledge base. On the other hand, the Partner Central template is designed for collaboration with business partners and includes tools for managing leads, opportunities, and partner-specific reports. Custom templates can also be created if the available options do not fully meet your needs.

After setting up the basic structure of the community, the next step is configuration and customization. Salesforce provides a range of tools to customize the appearance and functionality of the community. The Community Builder, a drag-and-drop interface, allows administrators to design and personalize community pages. This tool enables the addition of components such as banners, links, and custom widgets, which can be configured to match the organization's branding and user requirements.

Page layouts within the community can be customized to enhance user experience. This involves arranging components in a manner that aligns with user workflows and ensures that critical information and tools are easily accessible. For instance, in a customer community, it might be beneficial to place the knowledge base and support request forms prominently on the homepage to facilitate easy access to support resources. Similarly, in a partner community, dashboards and lead management tools might be prioritized to streamline partner interactions.

User management is another essential aspect of community administration. Salesforce Communities require careful configuration of user access and permissions to ensure that the right individuals have appropriate levels of access. This involves creating and assigning community-specific profiles and permission sets that define what users can view and do within the community. For instance, customers might need access to knowledge articles and support cases but should not have the ability to edit community settings. Partners might require access to leads, opportunities, and collaboration tools but should be restricted from internal company resources.

Effective user management also involves setting up community roles and hierarchies. Salesforce allows for the definition of roles that can be used to control data visibility and access within the community. By establishing a role hierarchy, you can ensure that users at higher levels have access to data and features relevant to their roles while restricting access for lower-level users.

Ongoing management of Salesforce Communities involves monitoring user engagement, managing content, and addressing any issues that arise. Salesforce provides analytics tools to track community activity, user interactions, and content performance. These insights can help you identify areas for improvement and make data-driven decisions to enhance community engagement and effectiveness.

In conclusion, implementing and managing Salesforce Communities involves a structured approach to setup, configuration, and ongoing administration. By selecting the appropriate community type, customizing the platform to meet organizational needs, and managing user access effectively, you can leverage Salesforce Communities to foster collaboration, improve customer and partner interactions, and streamline communication within your organization.

When delving deeper into the management and customization of Salesforce Communities, it's crucial to address several additional aspects to ensure that your community not only meets initial setup requirements but also evolves effectively to meet changing business needs and user expectations.

One of the critical components of a successful community is content management. Content within a Salesforce Community can significantly impact user engagement and satisfaction. To manage content effectively, you must first understand the types of content that can be included in a community. This includes knowledge base articles, discussion forums, FAQ sections, and custom pages.

Knowledge base articles, for example, are vital for providing self-service support to community members. These articles should be well-organized and easy to search. To achieve this, ensure that articles are categorized properly and use tags to facilitate searchability. It is also beneficial to use a combination of rich text formatting, images, and links to enhance the clarity and usefulness of the articles.

Discussion forums and FAQ sections serve as interactive elements where community members can ask questions and share information. Proper configuration of these features is essential for fostering engagement and providing timely responses. For discussion forums, setting up categories and sub-categories will help in organizing discussions and making it easier for users to find relevant topics. In the FAQ section, ensure that common questions are addressed comprehensively and that answers are updated regularly based on new inquiries or changes in procedures.

Custom pages can be used to highlight important announcements, upcoming events, or featured content. These pages can be designed using the Community Builder, allowing you to place various components such as text blocks, images, and embedded links. Custom pages should be updated periodically to reflect current information and maintain user interest.

User engagement is another critical aspect of managing a Salesforce Community. To maximize engagement, it's important to create a welcoming environment where users feel valued and encouraged to participate. Implementing features such as gamification, which includes badges and leaderboards, can motivate users to contribute more actively.

Monitoring user activity through Salesforce's reporting and analytics tools provides insights into how users interact with the community. Analyzing this data can reveal trends, such as which areas of the community are most popular or where users are experiencing difficulties. This information can be used to make informed decisions about content updates, feature enhancements, or additional training for community managers.

Another vital component of community management is the handling of community security and data privacy. Ensuring that sensitive information is protected and that users only have access to the data relevant to their roles is paramount.

Salesforce Communities allow for granular control over data access through the use of sharing rules and permission sets.

It is essential to regularly review and update these permissions to accommodate changes in user roles or business requirements. Additionally, monitoring user activity for unusual or unauthorized access can help prevent potential security breaches. Implementing best practices for data protection, such as encryption and secure login methods, further enhances the security of the community.

Customization of community branding is also a key factor in creating a professional and cohesive user experience. Salesforce allows for extensive customization of community appearance, including the use of custom logos, color schemes, and page layouts. Ensuring that the community branding aligns with your organization's overall branding strategy helps in creating a seamless experience for users and reinforces brand identity.

Beyond the visual and functional aspects, it's important to continuously gather feedback from community users. User feedback can be collected through surveys, feedback forms, or direct interactions. Understanding user needs and concerns helps in making targeted improvements and addressing any issues promptly.

Implementing a feedback mechanism within the community itself can also facilitate ongoing improvements. For instance, enabling users to rate articles or post suggestions can provide valuable insights into the effectiveness of content and community features.

In summary, effective management and customization of Salesforce Communities involve a multifaceted approach. From content management and user engagement to security and branding, each aspect plays a crucial role in creating a successful community platform. By focusing on these areas and leveraging Salesforce's tools and features, you can build and maintain a dynamic community that meets organizational objectives and provides value to its users.

To ensure a robust and successful Salesforce Community implementation, ongoing management and fine-tuning are essential. This involves not only maintaining the community's functionality and appearance but also adapting to evolving user needs and business requirements.

One key area of focus is the continuous evaluation and optimization of community performance. Salesforce provides a suite of analytics and reporting tools designed to help administrators track and assess community activity. By regularly reviewing these reports, administrators can gain insights into user behavior, content engagement, and overall community health. Metrics such as page views, post interactions, and user logins can highlight areas where the community is thriving and identify opportunities for improvement.

For instance, if certain content or discussion threads are receiving significantly higher engagement, it might be worth exploring why they are popular and how similar content can be developed to maintain user interest. Conversely, if certain areas of the community are underutilized, it could indicate a need for better promotion or content updates to make them more relevant and appealing.

Another critical aspect of managing Salesforce Communities is ensuring that the community evolves in alignment with organizational changes. As businesses grow and change, so too should the community. This may involve updating community content, adjusting user permissions, or integrating new features to support emerging business needs. Regularly revisiting the community's objectives and aligning them with the broader organizational strategy helps in maintaining its relevance and effectiveness.

Engagement strategies must also adapt to keep pace with user expectations. Regularly introducing new features, content, or engagement activities can help sustain user interest and encourage ongoing participation. For example, incorporating new tools for user collaboration, such as enhanced discussion forums or interactive content, can revitalize a community and attract more active involvement.

Additionally, integrating feedback loops into the community experience is crucial. Providing mechanisms for users to easily submit feedback, report issues, or suggest improvements helps in creating a responsive and user-centered environment. Salesforce offers built-in tools for collecting feedback, such as surveys and suggestion forms, which can be embedded directly into the community. Analyzing this feedback enables administrators to make data-driven decisions about future enhancements and ensure that the community continues to meet user needs.

Managing user roles and permissions effectively is another important aspect of community administration. As your community grows, the complexity of user roles and permissions can increase. Regularly reviewing and updating these settings ensures that users have appropriate access levels and that sensitive information remains protected. Salesforce's flexible permission settings allow administrators to tailor access controls precisely, but it requires ongoing vigilance to balance user access with data security.

Furthermore, ensuring that community members are engaged and motivated to contribute requires implementing and managing community incentives. Salesforce Communities can benefit from gamification elements such as badges, leaderboards, and recognition programs. These features not only reward active participants but also encourage others to engage more deeply with the community. Setting up these incentives involves configuring gamification settings and defining criteria for earning rewards, which can be aligned with community goals and user behavior.

It is also important to stay informed about new Salesforce features and updates that could impact the community. Salesforce regularly releases updates and new functionalities that can enhance community management. Keeping abreast of these changes ensures that you can leverage new tools and features to improve community performance and user experience. Salesforce's release notes, webinars, and community forums are valuable resources for staying updated on these developments.

Finally, integrating the Salesforce Community with other business systems and applications can enhance its utility and effectiveness. For example, linking community data with CRM systems or marketing automation tools can provide a more comprehensive view of user interactions and facilitate targeted outreach. Ensuring smooth integration involves configuring APIs, data synchronization, and ensuring that all systems work cohesively to support community objectives.

In summary, managing and configuring Salesforce Communities requires a proactive and strategic approach. Regular performance evaluations, adapting to organizational changes, integrating user feedback, and leveraging new features are all crucial for maintaining an effective and engaging community. By focusing on these aspects and continually optimizing the community experience, administrators can create a vibrant platform that supports meaningful interactions and drives business success.

CHAPTER 10: INTEGRATING SALESFORCE WITH OTHER SYSTEMS

Integration plays a pivotal role in creating a cohesive and efficient business ecosystem. It involves connecting Salesforce with other systems and applications to ensure that data flows seamlessly between different platforms and that various business functions work together harmoniously. The integration process can vary in complexity, depending on the systems involved and the specific needs of the organization. This discussion will provide an in-depth look at the methods and best practices for achieving effective Salesforce integration.

To start, it's important to understand the various integration options available for Salesforce. The most commonly used methods include APIs, middleware solutions, and third-party tools. Each of these options has its own set of advantages and use cases, and the choice of which to use depends on factors such as the complexity of the integration, the volume of data being transferred, and the specific requirements of the business processes.

Salesforce provides a robust set of APIs that can be used to integrate with other systems. The Salesforce API ecosystem includes several types of APIs, each designed for different purposes. The REST API, for instance, is commonly used for simpler integrations and is well-suited for web and mobile applications. It uses standard HTTP methods and returns data in JSON format, making it accessible and easy to use for developers familiar with web technologies.

The SOAP API, on the other hand, is designed for more complex integrations that require a higher level of security and more robust data handling capabilities. It is often used in enterprise-level applications and supports both synchronous and asynchronous operations. SOAP API interactions are based on XML, which can be beneficial for systems that already use XML for data exchange.

Another important API is the Bulk API, which is specifically designed for handling large volumes of data. This API is ideal for operations such as data migration or batch processing, where large amounts of data need to be inserted, updated, or deleted efficiently. The Bulk API supports both REST and SOAP protocols, allowing for flexibility in integration approaches.

When it comes to integrating Salesforce with other systems, middleware solutions can play a crucial role. Middleware acts as an intermediary layer between Salesforce and other applications, facilitating data exchange and ensuring that different systems can communicate effectively. Middleware platforms often provide additional features such as data transformation, error handling, and monitoring, which can simplify the integration process and enhance overall system reliability.

Popular middleware solutions for Salesforce integration include tools like MuleSoft, Jitterbit, and Dell Boomi. These platforms offer pre-built connectors and integration templates that can accelerate the implementation process. They also provide user-friendly interfaces for configuring and managing integrations, which can be particularly valuable for organizations with limited in-house development resources.

Third-party integration tools also offer valuable capabilities for connecting Salesforce with other systems. These tools are designed to address specific integration needs and often provide out-of-the-box solutions for common scenarios. For example, integration platforms like Zapier or Workato offer pre-configured workflows that can connect Salesforce with various other applications, including email platforms, CRM systems, and productivity tools.

When planning and executing an integration project, several best practices should be considered to ensure seamless data flow and maintain integration integrity. First and foremost, it's essential to define clear integration objectives and requirements. This involves understanding the specific data that needs to be exchanged, the frequency of data updates, and any transformation or validation rules that must be applied. A well-defined integration scope helps in selecting the right tools and designing an integration architecture that meets the organization's needs.

Data mapping and transformation are critical components of successful integration. Data mapping involves aligning fields and data structures between Salesforce and the other systems being integrated. This ensures that data is correctly interpreted and processed by both systems. Transformation rules may be needed to convert data formats or values to match the requirements of the target system. Proper data mapping and transformation are essential for maintaining data consistency and avoiding errors during data exchange.

Testing is another crucial aspect of integration. Comprehensive testing ensures that the integration works as expected and that data flows correctly between systems. It's important to conduct both functional testing, which verifies that the integration performs the required tasks, and end-to-end testing, which ensures that the entire data flow and process work smoothly. Testing should be conducted in a controlled environment before deploying the integration to production to minimize the risk of disruptions.

Monitoring and maintaining integrations is also important for ongoing success. Integrations should be monitored for performance and reliability to detect and address any issues that may arise. Regular maintenance, such as updating integration components or adjusting configurations, helps in adapting to changes in business processes or system updates. Implementing logging and alerting mechanisms can provide early warnings of potential problems and facilitate prompt resolution.

In conclusion, integrating Salesforce with other systems involves leveraging APIs, middleware solutions, and third-party tools to create a cohesive business ecosystem. By understanding the available integration options and adhering to best practices for data mapping, testing, and monitoring, organizations can ensure that their integrations are effective and reliable. This enables seamless data flow and enhances the overall efficiency of business processes, contributing to a more unified and responsive organization.

When integrating Salesforce with other systems, it is crucial to delve into the specific methodologies and considerations that ensure data integrity and system coherence. The integration process not only involves choosing the appropriate tools and technologies but also requires a detailed understanding of how data interacts between systems and how business processes are affected.

One significant aspect of integration is the use of Salesforce's outbound messaging. This feature allows Salesforce to send messages to external systems via HTTP or HTTPS requests. Outbound messages are particularly useful for scenarios where immediate updates to external systems are needed, such as triggering notifications or updating records in another application. This approach is often used in conjunction with workflow rules or process automation tools, which define when and how messages should be sent.

For more complex integration needs, Salesforce's Apex code can be utilized. Apex is a proprietary programming language developed by Salesforce that enables developers to execute flow and transaction control statements on the Salesforce platform's server side. With Apex, developers can write custom logic to interact with external systems through HTTP callouts. This flexibility allows for the development of tailored solutions that can handle intricate integration requirements, such as custom authentication or sophisticated data processing.

Another important consideration is the use of Salesforce Connect. This feature allows Salesforce to access data from external systems in real time without physically importing it into Salesforce. Salesforce Connect uses OData (Open Data Protocol) to connect to external data sources, providing a way to view and interact with external data directly within Salesforce. This is particularly valuable for organizations that need to integrate with systems that hold large volumes of data or where data is frequently updated.

When setting up integrations, it is crucial to consider the security implications. Ensuring that data is transmitted securely and that integrations adhere to organizational security policies is paramount. Salesforce provides a range of security features, such as OAuth for authentication, which ensures that only authorized users and systems can access data. Additionally, Salesforce supports encryption both in transit and at rest, providing protection for sensitive information during and after transmission.

Monitoring and managing the performance of integrations is another critical factor. Integrations should be designed to handle various loads and respond to changes in data volume or system demand. Tools such as Salesforce's built-in monitoring dashboards and external application performance management tools can help track the health of integrations and identify any issues that may arise. Regular reviews and updates to integration configurations can help address performance bottlenecks and ensure that integrations continue to meet organizational needs.

Data consistency and quality are fundamental to the success of any integration. To maintain data integrity, it is important to implement thorough data validation and error-handling mechanisms. This involves checking for data anomalies or discrepancies during the data transfer process and ensuring that any issues are promptly addressed. Error logs and notifications can provide valuable insights into integration performance and help diagnose and resolve issues.

Furthermore, change management is a vital aspect of maintaining integrations. As systems evolve and business requirements change, it is essential to manage updates and modifications to integrations carefully. This includes keeping track of changes in external systems, updating integration configurations accordingly, and testing changes in a staging environment before deploying them to production. Effective change management practices help minimize disruptions and ensure that integrations remain functional and effective over time.

In addition to these technical considerations, effective communication and collaboration with stakeholders are essential for successful integrations. Engaging with business users, IT teams, and external partners ensures that integration requirements are well understood and that the solutions developed align with business objectives. Clear documentation of integration processes, configurations, and dependencies is also important for facilitating ongoing support and future enhancements.

In summary, integrating Salesforce with other systems requires a comprehensive approach that includes leveraging Salesforce's APIs, utilizing middleware solutions, and employing third-party tools. Security, performance monitoring, data consistency, and change management are critical components of a successful integration strategy. By addressing these considerations and following best practices, organizations can achieve seamless data flow and maintain the integrity of their integrations, ultimately enhancing their business operations and supporting their strategic goals.

In the realm of Salesforce integration, it is essential to thoroughly understand the different methodologies available and their impact on business operations. As we further explore integration strategies, let us examine specific considerations for choosing the right approach and maintaining a robust integration framework.

One critical consideration is the selection of integration tools and methods based on the complexity and scale of the integration needs. For instance, when dealing with simple, one-way data transfers or updates, Salesforce's native integration tools such as the Data Import Wizard or the Data Loader may suffice. These tools are designed to handle bulk data operations efficiently, making them ideal for straightforward scenarios where large volumes of data need to be imported into or exported from Salesforce.

However, for more complex integrations involving real-time data exchange or sophisticated business logic, leveraging Salesforce's API capabilities is often necessary. The Salesforce API provides a comprehensive set of endpoints that support various types of data operations, including querying, creating, updating, and deleting records. The choice of API—whether REST, SOAP, Bulk, or Metadata—depends on the specific requirements of the integration. REST APIs, for instance, are well-suited for mobile and web applications due to their lightweight and easy-to-use nature, while SOAP APIs offer robust support for enterprise-level integrations requiring strong data integrity and security.

Middleware solutions also play a significant role in integrating Salesforce with other systems. Middleware acts as an intermediary layer that facilitates communication between Salesforce and external applications. This approach is particularly beneficial when integrating with legacy systems or when complex data transformations are needed. Middleware platforms such as MuleSoft, which is now part of Salesforce, provide extensive tools for building, deploying, and managing integrations. These platforms offer pre-built connectors and templates that simplify the integration process, reduce development time, and enhance scalability.

When implementing integrations, it is crucial to adhere to best practices for ensuring data integrity and system performance. One such practice is the use of error-handling and logging mechanisms. Effective error-handling strategies involve setting up processes to catch and manage exceptions that may occur during data exchange. This ensures that any issues are identified and addressed promptly, preventing data loss or corruption. Comprehensive logging of integration activities also provides valuable insights into the operational status of integrations and aids in troubleshooting and performance monitoring.

Another important best practice is to establish clear data mapping and transformation rules. When integrating systems with different data structures, it is essential to define how data fields and values are mapped between Salesforce and the external system. This involves creating transformation rules that convert data formats and ensure consistency across systems. By meticulously planning and documenting these rules, you can avoid data mismatches and ensure accurate data exchange.

Security is an integral aspect of any integration strategy. It is vital to implement robust authentication and authorization mechanisms to protect sensitive data and ensure that only authorized users and systems have access. Salesforce supports various authentication methods, including OAuth, which allows for secure token-based access. Additionally, encrypting data both in transit and at rest helps safeguard it from unauthorized access or breaches.

Performance optimization is another key consideration. Integrations should be designed to handle varying loads and adapt to changes in data volume. This involves optimizing API calls, reducing the frequency of data updates, and employing efficient data processing techniques. Regular performance assessments and scalability testing help identify potential bottlenecks and ensure that the integration can support growing business needs.

Finally, continuous monitoring and maintenance are essential for ensuring the long-term success of integrations. This includes regularly reviewing integration logs, assessing performance metrics, and staying updated with changes in both Salesforce and external systems. Proactive maintenance involves updating integration configurations as needed, addressing any issues that arise, and adapting to evolving business requirements.

In summary, integrating Salesforce with other systems involves a multifaceted approach that requires careful consideration of tools, methodologies, and best practices. By leveraging Salesforce's APIs, middleware solutions, and adhering to best practices for data integrity, security, and performance, organizations can achieve seamless and effective integrations. This ultimately enables a cohesive business ecosystem, supports data-driven decision-making, and enhances overall operational efficiency.

CHAPTER 11: ADVANCED CUSTOMIZATION: APEX AND VISUALFORCE

As we delve into advanced customization within Salesforce, Apex and Visualforce emerge as essential tools for extending the platform's capabilities beyond its out-of-the-box functionality. This exploration into Apex programming and Visualforce pages provides a deeper understanding of how to create tailored solutions that address unique business requirements and enhance user experiences.

Apex is a strongly typed, object-oriented programming language specifically designed for the Salesforce platform. It is executed on Salesforce's servers and enables developers to write custom business logic that can be executed on-demand or in response to database events. Apex code is crucial for implementing complex logic that cannot be achieved through declarative tools alone. To start using Apex effectively, it is essential to understand its syntax and execution context.

Apex code is executed in a multitenant environment, meaning that code written by different organizations runs on the same infrastructure. Salesforce imposes governor limits to ensure fair use of resources among all tenants. These limits include constraints on the number of database operations, CPU time, and memory usage. Therefore, optimizing Apex code to operate within these limits is vital for ensuring performance and reliability. Efficient code practices involve minimizing SOQL queries within loops, using bulk processing techniques, and leveraging asynchronous operations when necessary.

Writing Apex code typically involves creating Apex classes and triggers. Apex classes are used to define custom objects and methods that encapsulate specific business logic. For instance, you might write a class to handle custom calculations or integrate with external systems. Triggers, on the other hand, are pieces of Apex code that run before or after a record is inserted, updated, deleted, or undeleted. They are used to enforce business rules or automate processes based on changes to Salesforce data. Understanding the lifecycle of triggers and the context in which they execute is crucial for developing effective triggers that do not disrupt the standard data operations.

Visualforce is Salesforce's framework for building custom user interfaces. It allows developers to create pages that interact with Salesforce data and integrate with Apex controllers. Visualforce pages are built using a markup language that resembles HTML, supplemented with Salesforce-specific tags and components. These pages can be used to design custom layouts, create complex user interactions, and display data in ways that are not possible with standard Salesforce page layouts.

To create a Visualforce page, you start by defining the page's structure using Visualforce markup. This markup includes standard HTML elements and Visualforce components, which are rendered dynamically based on the data from Salesforce. Components such as `<apex:form>`, `<apex:inputText>`, and `<apex:dataTable>` are used to build interactive forms, display data in tables, and capture user input. Each Visualforce page is associated with an Apex controller, which manages the logic and data interactions for that page.

Apex controllers are written in Apex and are responsible for handling user actions and managing data within a Visualforce page. There are two types of controllers: standard controllers and custom controllers. Standard controllers provide built-in functionality for standard Salesforce objects and are automatically provided for Visualforce pages that work with these objects. Custom controllers are written by developers to handle complex logic or interactions not covered by standard controllers. Additionally, you can use controller extensions to augment the functionality of standard or custom controllers.

When integrating Apex and Visualforce, it is important to consider how these components work together to deliver a seamless user experience. For example, you might create a Visualforce page with custom forms and interactive elements, while using an Apex controller to process user inputs, perform calculations, and update Salesforce records. This integration allows for the creation of sophisticated applications that leverage the full power of Salesforce's platform.

The development process for Apex and Visualforce includes several stages, from writing and testing code to deploying and maintaining it. Salesforce provides tools such as the Developer Console, which offers an integrated development environment for writing, testing, and debugging Apex code. Additionally, you can use Salesforce's deployment tools like Change Sets or Salesforce DX to manage the deployment of customizations between different Salesforce environments.

Testing is a critical aspect of working with Apex and Visualforce. Salesforce requires that all Apex code is covered by unit tests before it can be deployed to production. These tests ensure that the code performs as expected and helps identify potential issues before they impact users. Writing effective unit tests involves creating test methods that simulate various scenarios and validate the behavior of the code under different conditions.

In summary, Apex and Visualforce provide powerful capabilities for advanced customization within Salesforce. Apex allows for the implementation of custom business logic through its object-oriented programming language, while Visualforce enables the creation of tailored user interfaces. Mastering these tools involves understanding their syntax, execution contexts, and integration points, as well as adhering to best practices for code efficiency, testing, and deployment. With these skills, you can build robust solutions that meet specific business needs and enhance the functionality of the Salesforce platform.

Apex and Visualforce, while powerful tools for advanced Salesforce customization, require careful integration and thoughtful design to fully realize their potential. Delving deeper into the practical applications of these tools, it becomes clear how they can be employed to address specific business needs and enhance Salesforce functionalities.

One common use case for Apex involves creating custom business logic that cannot be achieved with Salesforce's declarative tools alone. For instance, imagine a scenario where a business needs to automate the process of calculating commissions based on complex rules that involve multiple objects and dynamic criteria. While Salesforce's standard formula fields and workflow rules offer some automation capabilities, they might fall short when it comes to handling intricate logic. Apex comes into play here by allowing developers to write custom code that performs these calculations and updates records accordingly.

Apex triggers, for example, can be employed to execute code before or after specific events such as the insertion, update, or deletion of records. Consider a trigger that calculates and updates a custom commission field on a related object whenever an opportunity record is modified. This trigger would listen for changes to the opportunity object, perform the necessary calculations using Apex code, and then update the related commission record. Implementing such a trigger involves understanding the trigger context, managing bulk operations, and ensuring that the code adheres to Salesforce's governor limits.

Another powerful aspect of Apex is its ability to integrate with external systems. For instance, a business might need to fetch data from an external database or web service to enrich Salesforce records. Apex provides the `Http` and `HttpRequest` classes, which can be used to make HTTP requests to external APIs. By writing Apex code that handles these requests and processes the responses, developers can seamlessly integrate external data into Salesforce. This integration might involve handling authentication, parsing JSON or XML responses, and updating Salesforce records based on the retrieved data.

Visualforce pages complement Apex by offering a means to create custom user interfaces tailored to specific requirements. Building on the previous example of calculating commissions, a Visualforce page could be designed to provide a custom interface for users to view and interact with commission data. This page could include custom forms, charts, and tables that display the calculated commissions and allow users to enter or modify relevant information. Integrating this Visualforce page with an Apex controller would enable dynamic interactions and ensure that user inputs are processed and stored correctly.

To effectively utilize Visualforce, it is important to grasp the different types of components available. Visualforce components are categorized into standard components, which are provided by Salesforce, and custom components, which are created by developers. Standard components include elements like `<apex:page>`, `<apex:form>`, and `<apex:inputText>`, while custom components can be defined to encapsulate reusable pieces of functionality. For instance, a custom component might be created to display a reusable chart or data table that can be included on multiple Visualforce pages.

Another key consideration when working with Visualforce is understanding the relationship between Visualforce pages and Apex controllers. The controller is the heart of a Visualforce page, managing the data and logic behind the user interface. The controller interacts with Salesforce data, processes user inputs, and dictates the page's behavior. When designing a Visualforce page, it is crucial to ensure that the associated controller is well-structured and capable of handling all required operations efficiently. This might involve writing methods to query and update data, managing user interactions, and implementing error handling.

Testing and debugging are integral parts of working with Apex and Visualforce. Apex code must be thoroughly tested to ensure that it functions as expected and adheres to Salesforce's governor limits. Salesforce provides a testing framework that allows developers to write and run unit tests for Apex code. These tests help identify issues, validate code behavior, and ensure that changes do not introduce new bugs. For Visualforce pages, testing involves verifying that the user interface works correctly across different devices and browsers and that it integrates seamlessly with the associated Apex controllers.

Deployment of custom Apex and Visualforce components requires careful planning. Salesforce offers several tools for deploying changes between environments, including Change Sets and Salesforce DX. Change Sets are used to package and deploy customizations between Salesforce orgs, while Salesforce DX provides a more advanced development lifecycle management approach. Regardless of the tool used, it is essential to test changes in a sandbox environment before deploying them to production to avoid disrupting live operations.

In conclusion, Apex and Visualforce offer extensive capabilities for advanced customization within Salesforce. Apex provides a robust programming environment for implementing complex business logic and integrating with external systems, while Visualforce enables the creation of custom user interfaces tailored to specific needs. Mastering these tools requires an understanding of their syntax, execution contexts, and best practices for development, testing, and deployment. By leveraging Apex and Visualforce effectively, you can build sophisticated solutions that enhance Salesforce's functionality and meet unique business requirements.

When diving into the intricacies of Apex and Visualforce, it is essential to recognize how these tools can be leveraged to create a seamless and efficient user experience while addressing complex business requirements. Apex, as Salesforce's proprietary programming language, empowers developers to execute sophisticated operations on the Salesforce platform. Visualforce, on the other hand, allows for the creation of custom user interfaces that integrate closely with the Salesforce data model.

Apex code is executed in the Salesforce cloud, providing an environment where developers can write and deploy business logic and automation that goes beyond the capabilities of the point-and-click tools available in Salesforce. A critical aspect of working with Apex is understanding the asynchronous execution of code. Salesforce provides several mechanisms for executing code asynchronously, such as Queueable Apex,

Batch Apex, and Future methods. These mechanisms allow for processing large data volumes or performing operations that would otherwise exceed the governor limits if executed synchronously.

Queueable Apex is particularly useful for handling complex, long-running processes. It provides a more flexible and scalable approach compared to future methods or batch classes. With Queueable Apex, developers can chain multiple jobs together, manage job execution, and handle errors more effectively. This capability is crucial for scenarios where large volumes of data need to be processed or when complex logic must be executed in stages.

Batch Apex is another important feature for handling large datasets. It allows for the processing of records in manageable chunks, minimizing the risk of hitting governor limits. A batch class is composed of three main methods: `start`, `execute`, and `finish`. The `start` method initializes the batch job, the `execute` method processes each batch of records, and the `finish` method performs post-processing tasks. This approach is ideal for scenarios such as data migration, report generation, or any operation that requires the processing of many records.

Future methods provide a simpler way to perform asynchronous operations by executing code in the background. While less flexible than Queueable Apex or Batch Apex, future methods are useful for tasks that can be performed independently of the main execution flow, such as making HTTP callouts or performing operations that do not require immediate feedback.

Visualforce, as a framework for building custom user interfaces, integrates tightly with Apex to deliver tailored solutions. When designing Visualforce pages, developers use a markup language that closely resembles HTML but includes Salesforce-specific tags and components. For instance, `<apex:page>` defines a Visualforce page, while `<apex:form>` and `<apex:commandButton>` are used to create interactive forms and buttons.

One of the key features of Visualforce is its ability to create custom user interfaces that interact with Apex controllers. Controllers are Apex classes that manage the logic behind a Visualforce page. There are two types of controllers: standard and custom. Standard controllers are automatically provided by Salesforce for standard objects like Accounts or Contacts, while custom controllers are Apex classes that provide specific functionality for custom Visualforce pages.

A custom controller allows for full control over the data and interactions on a Visualforce page. By implementing a custom controller, developers can define methods that handle user input, query Salesforce data, and perform business logic. For example, a custom controller might handle the submission of a form that collects user feedback, processes the data, and updates records accordingly. The Visualforce page would use this controller to bind data, manage user interactions, and ensure that the UI responds to user actions appropriately.

Additionally, Visualforce supports the use of custom components, which can be reused across multiple pages to ensure consistency and reduce duplication. Custom components are defined using the `<apex:component>` tag and can include both standard and custom Visualforce components. By creating reusable components, developers can build modular and maintainable pages that adhere to design standards and best practices.

Testing is a crucial aspect of both Apex and Visualforce development. For Apex code, Salesforce provides a robust testing framework that allows developers to write unit tests to verify code functionality. These tests should cover various scenarios, including positive, negative, and boundary cases. Proper testing ensures that code changes do not introduce new issues and that the functionality behaves as expected in different conditions.

For Visualforce pages, testing involves validating the user interface across different devices and browsers to ensure that it functions correctly and provides a consistent experience. Additionally, integration tests should be performed to verify that Visualforce pages interact correctly with Apex controllers and that data is processed and displayed as intended.

Finally, deploying Apex code and Visualforce pages requires careful management to ensure a smooth transition from development to production environments. Salesforce provides tools like Change Sets and Salesforce DX for deploying customizations. Change Sets allow for the transfer of metadata between Salesforce orgs, while Salesforce DX offers a more advanced approach with version control and continuous integration capabilities.

In summary, Apex and Visualforce are powerful tools for advanced Salesforce customization. Apex allows for the implementation of complex business logic and asynchronous processing, while Visualforce provides the flexibility to create custom user interfaces tailored to specific needs. Mastering these tools requires a deep understanding of their features, limitations, and best practices, as well as a focus on thorough testing and careful deployment. By leveraging Apex and Visualforce effectively, developers can build sophisticated solutions that enhance Salesforce's capabilities and deliver tailored experiences to users.

CHAPTER 12: MANAGING SALESFORCE RELEASES AND UPDATES

In managing Salesforce releases and updates, it is crucial to maintain a well-organized and systematic approach to ensure that your Salesforce environment remains both current and functional. As Salesforce frequently releases updates, including new features, enhancements, and bug fixes, a robust release management process is essential to take full advantage of these changes while minimizing disruption to your operations.

The release management process begins with reviewing the Salesforce release notes. These notes provide detailed information about new features, improvements, and fixes included in each release. Salesforce typically publishes release notes for each seasonal update—Spring, Summer, and Winter. The release notes are comprehensive documents that outline changes across various aspects of the platform, including core functionality, user interface updates, and new tools. By thoroughly reviewing these notes, administrators can identify which updates are relevant to their organization and plan accordingly.

Planning for new features is a vital step in the release management process. After understanding the potential impact of new features from the release notes, it is important to assess how these features align with your organization's needs and objectives. This involves evaluating whether the new functionalities will enhance existing processes, address any pain points, or require adjustments to current configurations. Effective planning also includes setting priorities for the implementation of new features based on their potential benefits and the organization's readiness to adopt them.

A key aspect of handling updates effectively is the use of sandbox environments. Sandboxes are copies of your Salesforce environment that can be used for testing purposes without affecting your live data. Salesforce provides different types of sandboxes, including Developer, Developer Pro, Partial Copy, and Full sandboxes. Each type serves a different purpose and offers varying levels of data and metadata. For most update testing, a Partial Copy or Full sandbox is ideal, as it includes a representative set of data that allows for more realistic testing scenarios.

Testing updates in a sandbox environment involves several steps. First, administrators should deploy the new release or feature to the sandbox and verify that the installation process completes without errors. Next, they should conduct thorough testing to ensure that new features function as expected and that no existing functionality is adversely affected. This includes performing regression testing to check that previously working features remain operational and user acceptance testing to gather feedback from end users about the changes.

Addressing potential issues that arise during testing is

an important part of managing Salesforce updates. If any problems are identified, administrators should document them and work to resolve them before deploying the updates to the production environment. This may involve collaborating with Salesforce support, adjusting configurations, or implementing workarounds. In cases where issues cannot be resolved within the sandbox, it may be necessary to defer the update or request an extension from Salesforce to allow additional time for resolution.

Ensuring a smooth transition for users involves effective communication and change management strategies. Before rolling out updates to the production environment, it is essential to prepare users for the changes. This can be achieved through training sessions, informational materials, and user guides that explain the new features and any changes to existing processes. Additionally, providing support resources and a feedback mechanism can help users adapt to the updates and report any issues they encounter.

Another crucial consideration in managing Salesforce releases is the use of release management tools and best practices. Salesforce offers tools like Change Sets and Salesforce DX to facilitate the deployment of updates and customizations. Change Sets are used to move configurations and customizations between Salesforce environments, while Salesforce DX provides a more advanced approach with version control and continuous integration capabilities. By leveraging these tools, administrators can streamline the deployment process, track changes, and maintain consistency across environments.

Finally, maintaining a proactive approach to release management involves staying informed about upcoming releases and planning for future updates. Salesforce provides advance notice of upcoming releases through its Trust site, which includes information about scheduled maintenance and planned release dates. By keeping abreast of these updates and incorporating them into your release management strategy, you can better anticipate changes, allocate resources, and ensure that your Salesforce environment remains aligned with your organizational goals.

In summary, managing Salesforce releases and updates requires a comprehensive approach that includes reviewing release notes, planning for new features, testing updates in a sandbox environment, addressing potential issues, and ensuring a smooth transition for users. By adopting best practices, leveraging release management tools, and maintaining proactive communication, administrators can effectively navigate the release cycle and enhance the functionality of their Salesforce environment.

As you delve into managing Salesforce releases and updates, understanding the impact of these updates on your Salesforce environment is critical. Salesforce's continuous release cycle introduces new features, enhancements, and fixes that can influence various aspects of your organization's CRM system. This underscores the importance of a meticulous approach to managing these updates to ensure they align with your business processes and maintain system stability.

One of the initial steps in managing releases is to thoroughly analyze the release notes provided by Salesforce. These documents are comprehensive and detail all the new features, enhancements, and bug fixes introduced in each release. They are organized to highlight key changes and their potential impact on your Salesforce instance. By examining these notes, administrators can identify which updates are pertinent to their organization's needs. This involves understanding both the new capabilities offered and any deprecated features or changes to existing functionality that might affect current processes or integrations.

After reviewing the release notes, the next step is to

plan for the new features and changes. Effective planning involves assessing the relevance of new functionalities to your organization. For instance, if a release includes enhancements to the Sales Cloud that could streamline your sales processes, it may be beneficial to prioritize these updates. Planning also requires evaluating how these new features will integrate with existing configurations and customizations. This step may include updating your Salesforce strategy documents, revising process flows, and preparing a detailed rollout plan.

Testing updates in a sandbox environment is a crucial practice in managing Salesforce releases. Sandboxes are designed to mirror your production environment, allowing for safe testing and experimentation without impacting live data. To effectively test updates, deploy the new release or feature into the sandbox and verify its functionality. This includes not only confirming that the new features work as intended but also ensuring that they do not interfere with existing customizations and integrations. It is vital to conduct thorough regression testing to ensure that previously working functionalities remain unaffected. Engaging end-users in User Acceptance Testing (UAT) can also provide valuable feedback on how well the new features meet their needs and how intuitive they are to use.

Addressing potential issues that arise during testing is a fundamental aspect of managing Salesforce updates. If problems are identified, administrators need to troubleshoot and resolve them before proceeding to production. This might involve debugging Apex code, adjusting Visualforce pages, or reconfiguring settings. Collaboration with Salesforce support can be crucial for resolving complex issues. Documentation of issues and their resolutions can provide insights for future updates and help in managing similar challenges.

A smooth transition for users involves clear communication and change management. Before rolling out updates to the production environment, it is essential to inform users about the upcoming changes. This can be achieved through various channels such as emails, training sessions, and internal documentation. Providing users with guides and resources on how to navigate new features and changes can facilitate a smoother adoption process. Additionally, setting up support channels to address user queries and issues post-update can help in quickly resolving any challenges that arise.

In managing Salesforce releases, leveraging tools and best practices is essential for efficiency. Salesforce offers several tools to assist with deployment and version control. Change Sets, for example, allow administrators to transfer configurations between Salesforce environments, while Salesforce DX provides a more sophisticated approach for managing and deploying changes through version control and continuous integration. Utilizing these tools can streamline the update process, reduce the risk of errors, and ensure consistency across different environments.

Another important aspect of release management is staying informed about upcoming releases and their potential impact. Salesforce provides advance notices of release schedules and planned maintenance through its Trust site and other communication channels. By monitoring these updates, administrators can better prepare for changes and align their update strategies with Salesforce's release timeline. This proactive approach helps in mitigating potential disruptions and ensures that your Salesforce environment remains synchronized with Salesforce's evolution.

In summary, managing Salesforce releases and updates involves a comprehensive approach that includes reviewing release notes, planning for new features, testing updates in a sandbox environment, addressing potential issues, and ensuring smooth user transitions. By adopting effective testing strategies, leveraging Salesforce tools, and maintaining proactive communication, administrators can navigate the release cycle efficiently and enhance their Salesforce environment's functionality.

Maintaining an effective release management strategy requires careful coordination and adherence to best practices to ensure that updates are smoothly integrated into the Salesforce environment. One critical aspect of this process is managing data migration and integration during updates. As Salesforce evolves, new features and changes may necessitate adjustments in data structures or integrations with other systems. Therefore, it is imperative to review any data schema changes or integration modifications detailed in the release notes. This review helps identify potential impacts on existing integrations or custom data models.

During the testing phase, data migration is an essential component. It is crucial to test how updates affect data flow between Salesforce and external systems. For example, if an update introduces new fields or changes to existing objects, it's important to validate that these changes do not disrupt the data mapping or transformation processes in integrations. Testing should include running data migration scenarios to ensure that data remains accurate and that integrations continue to function as expected.

Another important consideration is managing custom code and configurations. Salesforce updates can sometimes affect custom Apex code or Visualforce pages. This is particularly relevant if the update includes changes to Salesforce's APIs or introduces new system limits. During testing, I would review all custom code and configurations to ensure compatibility with the new release. It is essential to check for any deprecated methods or changes in system behavior that could affect custom functionality. Engaging developers to conduct thorough code reviews and adjustments is a prudent approach to prevent disruptions in your Salesforce environment.

Moreover, as updates are applied, it's important to manage user expectations and provide adequate support. A structured rollout plan should include clear communication to users about what to expect with the new release. This plan should outline any changes in user interfaces, new features, or modifications to existing functionality. Providing training sessions or informational materials can help users adapt to the updates and leverage new features effectively. Additionally, setting up a feedback mechanism allows users to report issues or provide suggestions, which can be valuable for addressing any unforeseen problems that may arise post-update.

Monitoring and performance evaluation are also integral to managing Salesforce updates. After implementing a release in the production environment, continuous monitoring is necessary to ensure that the system performs as expected. This involves tracking system performance metrics and user activity to identify any issues promptly. Salesforce provides various tools and dashboards that can be used to monitor system health and performance. Regularly reviewing these metrics helps ensure that the updates do not negatively impact system performance or user experience.

Addressing any post-release issues quickly is essential for maintaining system stability. If users encounter problems or if performance issues are detected, it is crucial to have a process in place for rapid resolution. This includes having access to Salesforce support resources and maintaining a log of issues and their resolutions. Timely intervention helps minimize the impact on users and ensures that the system remains reliable and functional.

In addition to managing updates, administrators should also consider long-term strategies for release management. This includes developing a comprehensive release management plan that outlines procedures for testing, deployment, and support. Establishing best practices and standard operating procedures for handling updates can streamline the process and ensure consistency. Regular training for administrators and users on release management practices can also contribute to a more efficient update process.

Finally, embracing a culture of continuous improvement is vital for effective release management. This involves regularly reviewing and refining release management processes based on lessons learned from past updates. By staying informed about Salesforce's evolving features and best practices, administrators can adapt their strategies to better align with organizational needs and technological advancements.

In summary, managing Salesforce releases and updates is a multifaceted process that requires careful planning, testing, communication, and monitoring. By addressing data migration, custom code compatibility, user support, and performance evaluation, administrators can ensure a smooth transition and maintain a high-functioning Salesforce environment. Establishing long-term strategies and embracing continuous improvement further enhance the effectiveness of release management, ensuring that your Salesforce instance remains up-to-date and aligned with your organization's goals.

CHAPTER 13: DATA SECURITY AND COMPLIANCE

Ensuring robust data security and adhering to compliance standards are paramount in managing a Salesforce environment. As a Salesforce administrator, it is critical to understand and implement various security measures to protect sensitive information and ensure that the system remains compliant with applicable regulations.

To begin with, encryption is a fundamental component of data security. Salesforce provides several encryption options to safeguard data both at rest and in transit. The platform supports encryption through the use of Secure Socket Layer (SSL) for data transmitted between users and Salesforce, ensuring that data exchanged is encrypted during transit. Additionally, Salesforce Shield provides advanced encryption features, such as Platform Encryption, which allows for the encryption of data stored within Salesforce. Platform Encryption can be applied to standard and custom fields, files, and attachments, providing an added layer of security for sensitive information.

Implementing encryption requires a careful approach to ensure that it does not interfere with business processes. For example, while encryption protects data from unauthorized access, it is essential to consider the performance implications and potential impact on data visibility and searchability. Administrators must balance security with functionality to ensure that encryption enhances protection without disrupting users' ability to work effectively.

Another crucial aspect of data security is establishing and managing audit trails. Salesforce offers detailed auditing capabilities through features like Field History Tracking and Audit Trail. Field History Tracking allows administrators to monitor changes to specific fields in objects, capturing a history of modifications that can be reviewed for auditing purposes. This feature is particularly useful for tracking changes to sensitive data and ensuring accountability.

Audit Trail, on the other hand, provides a comprehensive log of administrative changes made within the Salesforce environment. It tracks modifications to setup and configuration, including changes to permissions, customizations, and integration settings. By regularly reviewing audit trails, administrators can identify and address any unauthorized or unexpected changes, thus maintaining the integrity of the Salesforce instance.

Compliance with regulations such as the General Data Protection Regulation (GDPR) is another critical consideration. GDPR, which applies to organizations handling personal data of individuals in the European Union, imposes stringent requirements on data protection and privacy. Salesforce offers various features to support GDPR compliance, including Data Protection and Privacy features such as data export and deletion capabilities.

To comply with GDPR, administrators need to implement mechanisms for handling data subject requests, such as the right to access and the right to be forgotten. Salesforce provides tools for exporting data, allowing users to retrieve their personal information upon request.

Additionally, Salesforce supports data deletion processes, enabling organizations to erase data in accordance with GDPR requirements.

Security controls within Salesforce are also essential for protecting data and ensuring compliance. These controls include user authentication, access controls, and permission settings. Multi-Factor Authentication (MFA) is a critical security measure that adds an extra layer of protection by requiring users to provide additional verification, such as a code sent to their mobile device, in addition to their password. MFA enhances security by reducing the risk of unauthorized access, even if user credentials are compromised.

Access controls are another key element of security. Salesforce allows administrators to define user profiles and permission sets to control access to various objects, fields, and records. By configuring these permissions appropriately, administrators can ensure that users only have access to the data necessary for their roles, minimizing the risk of data breaches and unauthorized access.

It is also important to monitor the Salesforce environment for potential security threats. Salesforce provides tools for monitoring and managing security, such as Security Health Check, which evaluates the security settings and practices against industry standards and best practices. Regular security assessments using these tools help identify vulnerabilities and ensure that the environment remains secure.

Additionally, integrating Salesforce with external security solutions, such as Security Information and Event Management (SIEM) systems, can enhance threat detection and response capabilities. SIEM systems aggregate and analyze security-related data from various sources, including Salesforce, to identify and respond to potential threats more effectively.

In summary, managing data security and compliance within Salesforce involves a comprehensive approach that includes implementing encryption, managing audit trails, and ensuring compliance with regulations like GDPR. By establishing robust security controls, monitoring for threats, and leveraging Salesforce's built-in features, administrators can protect sensitive information and maintain a secure and compliant Salesforce environment. Addressing these aspects proactively helps safeguard data, mitigate risks, and ensure that the Salesforce instance aligns with organizational and regulatory requirements.

When managing Salesforce environments, it's vital to understand and implement various security measures to ensure that data is both secure and compliant with relevant regulations. One of the fundamental security practices is the use of encryption to protect sensitive data. Salesforce provides multiple encryption options designed to safeguard data at rest and in transit. For instance, Salesforce Shield's Platform Encryption allows administrators to encrypt data stored within Salesforce, which includes standard and custom fields, files, and attachments. This level of encryption ensures that even if unauthorized access occurs, the data remains protected by robust encryption algorithms.

However, implementing encryption involves more than just enabling features. It requires a strategic approach to balancing security with functionality. Administrators need to ensure that encryption does not hinder user operations or disrupt workflows. For instance, encrypted data may affect reporting and searching capabilities, and administrators must consider these aspects when configuring encryption settings. Additionally, Salesforce's native encryption capabilities are complemented by SSL encryption for data transmitted between Salesforce and users, ensuring data remains secure during transit.

Alongside encryption, audit trails play a critical role in maintaining security and compliance. Salesforce offers tools like Field History Tracking and Audit Trail, which are essential for monitoring changes and maintaining oversight of the Salesforce environment. Field History Tracking enables the monitoring of modifications to specific fields in objects, capturing a history of changes that can be audited for accuracy and compliance. This is particularly important for tracking sensitive data changes and ensuring data integrity.

Audit Trail, on the other hand, provides a log of administrative changes made within Salesforce, including alterations to setup and configuration, such as permission changes and customizations. Regularly reviewing these logs helps administrators detect any unauthorized or unexpected changes, which could indicate potential security issues. This oversight ensures that the Salesforce environment remains stable and secure, and that any deviations from standard configurations are promptly addressed.

Compliance with regulations such as the General Data Protection Regulation (GDPR) is another significant aspect of managing Salesforce data security. GDPR sets stringent standards for data protection and privacy, particularly concerning the handling of personal data for individuals within the European Union. Salesforce provides several features to assist with GDPR compliance, such as Data Protection and Privacy tools. These tools facilitate data subject requests, including the right to access personal information and the right to request data deletion.

To comply with GDPR, administrators must implement processes for responding to data subject requests efficiently. Salesforce offers functionality for exporting data, enabling users to retrieve their personal data upon request. This capability supports transparency and user rights as mandated by GDPR. Additionally, Salesforce's data deletion features help administrators erase data in compliance with GDPR requirements, ensuring that personal information is not retained longer than necessary.

Implementing security controls is another crucial aspect of safeguarding data and ensuring compliance. Salesforce provides various security features, including Multi-Factor Authentication (MFA), which enhances user account protection. MFA requires users to provide an additional verification factor, such as a code sent to their mobile device, in addition to their password. This additional layer of security reduces the risk of unauthorized access, even if user credentials are compromised.

Access controls within Salesforce are also essential for protecting sensitive data. By defining user profiles and permission sets, administrators can manage access to objects, fields, and records, ensuring that users have access only to the information necessary for their roles. Proper configuration of these permissions is vital for minimizing the risk of data breaches and unauthorized access. Regular reviews and updates to these permissions help maintain a secure environment as roles and responsibilities evolve.

Monitoring for potential threats is a proactive approach to maintaining security. Salesforce offers tools such as Security Health Check, which evaluates the security settings and practices against industry standards and best practices. Conducting regular security assessments with these tools helps identify vulnerabilities and ensures that the Salesforce environment adheres to security best practices.

Integrating Salesforce with external security solutions can further enhance threat detection and response capabilities. Security Information and Event Management (SIEM) systems, for example, aggregate and analyze security-related data from various sources, including Salesforce. This integration allows for a more comprehensive view of security events and facilitates quicker responses to potential threats.

In summary, managing data security and compliance within Salesforce involves a multifaceted approach that includes implementing encryption, managing audit trails, and ensuring adherence to regulations such as GDPR. By establishing robust security controls, monitoring for threats, and utilizing Salesforce's built-in features, administrators can protect sensitive information, maintain a secure environment, and ensure compliance with relevant standards. These practices are essential for safeguarding data, mitigating risks, and supporting the overall integrity of the Salesforce instance.

To ensure ongoing adherence to data security and compliance standards in Salesforce, it is crucial to implement a robust strategy for managing and monitoring security controls. This approach involves not only setting up the right tools and configurations but also continuously assessing and adjusting your security posture as new threats and regulatory requirements emerge.

One key aspect of maintaining data security is conducting regular security reviews and risk assessments. These reviews should include evaluating the effectiveness of current security measures, identifying potential vulnerabilities, and ensuring that all configurations align with best practices and regulatory requirements. Salesforce offers several built-in tools to assist in this process, such as the Security Health Check, which evaluates your organization's security settings against industry benchmarks and Salesforce's security standards. By regularly using these tools, administrators can gain insights into areas needing improvement and take corrective actions to enhance security.

Another important practice is to establish and maintain a

comprehensive data governance framework. Data governance involves creating policies and procedures that dictate how data is managed, accessed, and protected. This framework should address data classification, data ownership, and data stewardship responsibilities. By defining clear roles and responsibilities, organizations can ensure that data security and compliance measures are effectively implemented and enforced.

Data classification is a fundamental component of data governance. It involves categorizing data based on its sensitivity and the level of protection it requires. Salesforce allows administrators to classify data through custom fields and object settings, which can then be used to apply appropriate security controls. For example, highly sensitive data might be subject to stricter access controls and encryption requirements compared to less sensitive information.

Data ownership and stewardship responsibilities should be clearly defined within the organization. Data owners are typically responsible for the accuracy, integrity, and protection of specific data sets. Data stewards are responsible for implementing and enforcing data governance policies. By clearly delineating these roles, organizations can ensure that data is managed effectively and that security measures are consistently applied.

In addition to setting up and maintaining security controls, it is important to stay informed about changes in regulatory requirements and industry standards. Compliance is an ongoing process that requires vigilance and adaptability. For example, the General Data Protection Regulation (GDPR) is a dynamic regulation with evolving guidelines and requirements. Staying up-to-date with GDPR updates and ensuring that Salesforce configurations remain compliant is essential for avoiding potential penalties and maintaining customer trust.

Furthermore, implementing user education and training programs is a critical aspect of data security. Users play a significant role in maintaining data security, and their awareness of best practices and potential threats can greatly impact the overall security posture. Regular training sessions and awareness programs can help users understand their responsibilities regarding data protection, recognize phishing attempts, and follow secure practices for accessing and handling sensitive information.

To further enhance data security, Salesforce administrators should leverage advanced security features such as Salesforce Shield, which provides additional layers of protection beyond the standard security features. Salesforce Shield includes features like Field Audit Trail, which extends the standard audit trail capabilities, and Event Monitoring, which provides detailed insights into user activity and system performance. These tools enable administrators to track user interactions, monitor for unusual activity, and gain a deeper understanding of how data is accessed and used within the Salesforce environment.

Additionally, integrating Salesforce with third-party security solutions can provide a more comprehensive security approach. Security Information and Event Management (SIEM) systems, for example, can aggregate data from various sources, including Salesforce, to provide real-time threat detection and analysis. By integrating Salesforce with these systems, organizations can enhance their ability to detect and respond to potential security incidents more effectively.

Finally, establishing a clear incident response plan is essential for managing potential security breaches and ensuring compliance. This plan should outline the procedures for identifying, reporting, and responding to security incidents.

It should also include steps for communicating with affected parties, conducting investigations, and implementing corrective actions. Regularly testing and updating the incident response plan ensures that the organization is prepared to handle security incidents swiftly and effectively.

In summary, maintaining data security and compliance within Salesforce involves a multifaceted approach that includes implementing robust security controls, conducting regular reviews and assessments, and staying informed about regulatory changes. By establishing a comprehensive data governance framework, leveraging advanced security features, and integrating with third-party solutions, organizations can enhance their security posture and ensure that their Salesforce environment remains secure and compliant. Additionally, user education, incident response planning, and continuous monitoring are essential practices for effectively managing data security and compliance in a dynamic and evolving landscape.

CHAPTER 14: MOBILE SALESFORCE ADMINISTRATION

In the era of ubiquitous mobile technology, effectively managing Salesforce on mobile platforms is crucial for maintaining productivity and accessibility. This exploration into Salesforce Mobile delves into the setup, configuration, and customization needed to optimize Salesforce for mobile use, ensuring that users have a seamless and efficient experience across their devices.

To start, the Salesforce mobile experience begins with the Salesforce Mobile app, available for both iOS and Android devices. Setting up Salesforce Mobile involves several key steps to ensure that the app is properly configured and tailored to meet the needs of your organization. The process starts with the installation of the Salesforce mobile app from the respective app store. Once installed, users must log in with their Salesforce credentials to access the mobile interface.

Configuration of the Salesforce Mobile app requires an understanding of how mobile-specific settings differ from those on the desktop. The Salesforce mobile configuration can be accessed through the Salesforce Setup menu, where administrators can manage various aspects of the mobile experience. This includes setting up and configuring the mobile navigation menu, choosing which tabs and objects should be accessible via mobile, and enabling mobile-specific features such as push notifications and offline access.

One important aspect of mobile configuration is the customization of the mobile layout. The mobile layout can be customized to ensure that users see the most relevant information and have access to the most important features when using Salesforce on their mobile devices. This involves creating mobile-specific page layouts and compact layouts that present information succinctly and are optimized for smaller screens. Customizing the layout helps enhance the user experience by ensuring that key data is visible and accessible without the need for excessive scrolling or navigation.

In addition to layout customization, optimizing Salesforce for mobile access involves configuring mobile settings to improve performance and usability. This includes setting up mobile offline access, which allows users to view and interact with Salesforce data even when they are not connected to the internet. Offline access is particularly useful for users who may need to access data in areas with limited or no connectivity, such as during fieldwork or travel. Administrators should ensure that the offline access settings are properly configured to include the necessary objects and data that users will need while offline.

Another important aspect of mobile optimization is ensuring that custom Salesforce apps and features are compatible with mobile devices. This may involve adapting custom Visualforce pages or Lightning components to ensure that they function correctly and provide a good user experience on mobile devices. It is also essential to test these custom elements thoroughly to ensure they display and perform as expected on different screen sizes and operating systems.

Mobile security is a critical consideration when managing Salesforce on mobile platforms. Salesforce provides several built-in security features to protect data accessed through the mobile app. This includes mobile device management (MDM) integration, which allows administrators to enforce security policies on mobile devices, such as requiring password protection or remote wipe capabilities. Additionally, administrators should configure security settings to control access to Salesforce data and features based on user roles and permissions.

Best practices for mobile Salesforce administration include regularly updating the mobile app to the latest version to take advantage of new features and security improvements. It is also important to provide users with training and support to help them effectively utilize Salesforce on their mobile devices. This training should cover key features and functionality specific to the mobile app, as well as best practices for ensuring data security and performance.

Regular monitoring and feedback collection from mobile users can provide valuable insights into how the mobile experience can be improved. Administrators should actively seek feedback from users regarding their mobile experience and address any issues or concerns that arise. This feedback can help identify areas for further optimization and ensure that the mobile Salesforce experience remains effective and user-friendly.

In summary, managing Salesforce on mobile platforms involves a comprehensive approach to setup, configuration, and customization. By understanding the unique requirements of mobile users and configuring the Salesforce Mobile app accordingly, administrators can ensure that users have access to the data and features they need, regardless of their location. Optimizing mobile layouts, enabling offline access, and ensuring compatibility with custom features are all essential aspects of mobile administration. Additionally, focusing on mobile security, providing user training, and regularly seeking feedback are critical for maintaining a seamless and effective mobile experience. Through these practices, organizations can leverage Salesforce Mobile to enhance productivity and accessibility for their users.

When diving deeper into the management of Salesforce for mobile platforms, it's essential to address how the Salesforce Mobile app integrates with various features and functionalities to provide a cohesive user experience. Central to this integration is the understanding of how mobile devices interact with Salesforce's core elements, ensuring that functionality and performance are optimized for mobile users.

One critical area to consider is the synchronization of data between Salesforce and mobile devices. Salesforce Mobile supports real-time data synchronization, which is vital for ensuring that the information displayed on mobile devices is current and accurate. This synchronization happens through the Salesforce Cloud, which keeps the data up-to-date across all devices accessing the Salesforce environment. Administrators need to configure synchronization settings to balance the need for real-time updates with the performance and data usage considerations of mobile devices.

To enhance the usability of Salesforce on mobile devices, it's also important to leverage Salesforce's built-in features such as the global search and the mobile dashboard. Global search functionality is particularly useful for mobile users who need quick access to information. Administrators can customize search settings to ensure that relevant data appears prominently in search results, improving efficiency and productivity for users on the go. Mobile dashboards, on the other hand, offer a condensed view of key metrics and data visualizations, providing users with critical insights without the need for extensive navigation.

Another key aspect of managing Salesforce Mobile is handling custom objects and fields. Custom objects and fields that have been created in the Salesforce environment need to be appropriately configured for mobile use. This involves ensuring that they are included in the mobile page layouts and that their visibility and accessibility settings are correctly configured. Customizing these elements for mobile use helps maintain consistency and usability across different platforms, ensuring that users can access and interact with the data they need.

Salesforce's Lightning Experience, which is optimized for both desktop and mobile use, plays a significant role in mobile administration. The Lightning Experience includes features designed specifically for mobile users, such as a streamlined interface and touch-friendly navigation elements. Administrators should ensure that Lightning components are properly configured and tested for mobile compatibility to provide a seamless user experience. This involves checking that custom Lightning components function correctly on mobile devices and that they are responsive to different screen sizes.

Integrating Salesforce with mobile device capabilities is another important consideration. Mobile devices come with various built-in features, such as GPS, cameras, and push notifications, which can be leveraged to enhance the Salesforce experience. For instance, Salesforce's mobile app can use GPS to capture location data and associate it with relevant records. Similarly, the camera can be used to upload photos directly to Salesforce, streamlining data entry and record management. Push notifications can keep users informed of important updates and activities, ensuring that they stay engaged with the Salesforce platform.

Security remains a top priority when managing Salesforce on mobile devices. Mobile security settings should be carefully configured to protect sensitive data and ensure compliance with organizational policies. This includes implementing strong authentication methods, such as multi-factor authentication (MFA), to enhance the security of mobile access. Additionally, administrators should configure app-level security settings, such as controlling access to specific features and data based on user roles and permissions. Regular audits and security reviews can help identify potential vulnerabilities and ensure that security measures are up-to-date.

User training and support are also critical components of effective mobile administration. Providing users with training on how to use the Salesforce Mobile app, including its features and functionalities, can help improve their efficiency and satisfaction. Training sessions should cover topics such as mobile navigation, accessing and updating records, and using mobile-specific features like offline access. Additionally, offering ongoing support and resources can help users resolve any issues they encounter and stay informed about new updates and features.

Finally, monitoring and performance optimization are essential for maintaining a high-quality mobile experience. Administrators should regularly review performance metrics, such as app load times and user feedback, to identify areas for improvement. Performance optimization may involve fine-tuning configurations, updating custom components, or addressing any issues related to synchronization and data access. By continuously monitoring and optimizing the mobile Salesforce environment, administrators can ensure that users have a reliable and efficient experience.

In summary, managing Salesforce for mobile platforms involves a multifaceted approach that encompasses data synchronization, customization, integration with mobile device features, security, user training, and performance optimization. By addressing these areas comprehensively, administrators can create a mobile Salesforce experience that enhances productivity and supports users in their dynamic work environments. Ensuring that the Salesforce Mobile app is well-configured, secure, and optimized for mobile use will ultimately contribute to a more effective and satisfying user experience.

When configuring Salesforce for mobile access, it is crucial to understand the role of mobile-specific features in enhancing user experience. One of the most impactful features is offline access, which allows users to view and edit records without an active internet connection. This capability is particularly useful for field representatives and remote workers who may encounter connectivity issues. To set up offline access, administrators must configure the offline settings within the Salesforce Mobile app and ensure that relevant data is included in the offline data cache. This involves selecting which objects and records should be available offline and setting up synchronization rules to manage data updates.

Additionally, the Salesforce Mobile app offers customization options that enable administrators to tailor the mobile experience to meet organizational needs. Customizing the mobile user interface involves configuring mobile-specific page layouts and navigation settings. Administrators can create simplified page layouts that display only the most critical information and actions, making it easier for users to interact with Salesforce on smaller screens. Custom navigation menus can also be set up to streamline access to frequently used features and records. By focusing on mobile-first design principles, administrators can ensure that the mobile interface is intuitive and responsive.

The Salesforce Mobile SDK (Software Development Kit) provides developers with the tools to create custom mobile applications that integrate with Salesforce. This SDK includes libraries and sample code for building native mobile apps that leverage Salesforce data and functionality. Developers can use the SDK to build custom features, such as integrating with device sensors or creating specialized workflows that are optimized for mobile use. When using the Salesforce Mobile SDK, it is important to follow best practices for security and performance to ensure that the custom app provides a seamless user experience while maintaining data integrity and security.

Another critical aspect of mobile administration is managing mobile notifications. Salesforce Mobile supports push notifications, which can be used to alert users about important updates, tasks, or events. Administrators should configure notification settings to balance the need for timely alerts with the risk of overwhelming users with excessive notifications. This involves setting up notification rules and customizing the content of notifications to ensure that they are relevant and actionable. By strategically managing notifications, administrators can enhance user engagement and ensure that important information is communicated effectively.

In addition to configuration and customization, regular testing and feedback collection are essential for maintaining an optimal mobile experience. Administrators should test the mobile app across various devices and operating systems to identify and address any compatibility issues. User feedback can be gathered through surveys or support channels to gain insights into the mobile experience and identify areas for improvement. Continuous testing and feedback collection help ensure that the Salesforce Mobile app remains aligned with user needs and organizational goals.

Finally, it is important to stay informed about updates and new features related to Salesforce Mobile. Salesforce regularly releases updates that may include new functionalities, performance improvements, or security enhancements. Administrators should review release notes and documentation to understand how these updates impact mobile administration and to plan for any necessary adjustments. Keeping abreast of new developments helps ensure that the mobile Salesforce environment remains current and takes advantage of the latest advancements in mobile technology.

In conclusion, effective mobile Salesforce administration involves a comprehensive approach that encompasses offline access, customization, integration with device features, notifications management, and ongoing testing and updates. By addressing these areas thoroughly, administrators can create a mobile Salesforce experience that is both functional and user-friendly, supporting the diverse needs of users who rely on mobile access to Salesforce. Ensuring that the mobile environment is well-configured, secure, and aligned with user expectations contributes to a productive and efficient mobile Salesforce experience.

CHAPTER 15: IMPLEMENTING SALESFORCE EINSTEIN: AI AND ANALYTICS

Salesforce Einstein represents a significant advancement in integrating artificial intelligence and analytics into the Salesforce platform. Implementing Einstein effectively requires understanding its various components and how they can be applied to enhance business operations. To begin, it is essential to grasp the core functionalities of Salesforce Einstein and its impact on predictive analytics, AI-driven insights, and automation tools.

Salesforce Einstein's predictive analytics capabilities are designed to forecast outcomes and trends based on historical data. These predictive models utilize machine learning algorithms to analyze patterns and make predictions about future events. For example, Einstein Discovery is a tool within Salesforce that enables users to uncover insights from their data by automatically identifying trends, anomalies, and key drivers behind business outcomes. To implement Einstein Discovery, you start by selecting the dataset you wish to analyze. The tool then applies machine learning techniques to generate actionable insights, such as predicting which leads are most likely to convert or which customers are at risk of churn. By leveraging these insights, businesses can make data-driven decisions that improve strategic planning and operational efficiency.

AI-driven insights are another critical component of Salesforce Einstein, offering users intelligent recommendations based on their data. Einstein Analytics, now known as Tableau CRM, allows users to build interactive dashboards and reports that are enhanced with AI capabilities. For instance, Einstein Analytics can automatically suggest the most relevant visualizations and metrics based on the data being analyzed. This feature simplifies the process of creating meaningful reports and helps users uncover insights that might not be immediately apparent. To implement AI-driven insights, administrators need to configure and integrate Einstein Analytics with their existing Salesforce environment. This involves setting up data sources, defining metrics, and designing dashboards that present the AI-generated recommendations in a user-friendly manner.

Automation tools provided by Salesforce Einstein are designed to streamline repetitive tasks and improve operational efficiency. Einstein Bots, for example, enable businesses to deploy AI-powered chatbots that can handle routine customer inquiries and support tasks. These bots are capable of understanding natural language and providing relevant responses based on predefined rules and machine learning models. Implementing Einstein Bots involves configuring the chatbot to handle specific types of interactions, such as answering frequently asked questions or guiding users through common processes. This requires setting up conversation flows, training the bot on relevant data, and integrating it with other Salesforce services, such as case management or lead generation.

Another important aspect of Salesforce Einstein is its ability to enhance customer interactions through personalized recommendations. Einstein Recommendations uses machine learning algorithms to suggest products or content that is tailored to individual customer preferences and behavior. By analyzing data such as purchase history, browsing activity, and customer feedback, Einstein Recommendations can provide highly relevant suggestions that drive engagement and increase conversion rates. To implement this feature, administrators must configure recommendation settings, define target audiences, and integrate the recommendations with customer-facing applications, such as email marketing campaigns or e-commerce platforms.

The successful implementation of Salesforce Einstein requires careful planning and configuration to ensure that the AI and analytics tools align with business objectives. This involves setting up data integration processes to ensure that Einstein has access to the relevant datasets, configuring machine learning models to fit specific business needs, and continuously monitoring and refining the AI-driven insights and recommendations. Additionally, it is important to provide training and support to users to help them understand how to leverage Einstein's capabilities effectively. This may include creating documentation, conducting training sessions, and offering ongoing support to address any questions or issues that arise.

In summary, implementing Salesforce Einstein involves leveraging predictive analytics, AI-driven insights, and automation tools to enhance decision-making, improve customer interactions, and drive business intelligence. By understanding and effectively utilizing these components, organizations can gain valuable insights, streamline operations, and deliver personalized experiences that align with their strategic goals. The integration of Salesforce

Einstein into the Salesforce platform represents a powerful opportunity to harness the potential of artificial intelligence and advanced analytics to achieve greater business success.

Implementing Salesforce Einstein involves a deep understanding of how its AI and analytics capabilities can be harnessed to transform business operations. As we continue to explore these functionalities, it becomes clear that integrating Einstein into your Salesforce environment requires both strategic planning and technical proficiency.

One of the significant aspects of Salesforce Einstein is its ability to enhance decision-making through advanced analytics. Einstein Analytics, now branded as Tableau CRM, offers a suite of tools designed to provide actionable insights from complex datasets. This platform enables users to create dynamic dashboards and reports that are powered by AI. For instance, the Einstein Discovery feature within Tableau CRM can automatically analyze your data, identify patterns, and provide recommendations based on its findings. To effectively utilize Einstein Discovery, you need to start by integrating your data sources into Tableau CRM. This involves configuring data connectors to ensure that all relevant data is available for analysis. Once your data is integrated, you can use Einstein Discovery to build predictive models that forecast future trends and outcomes. This predictive capability can be applied to various aspects of your business, such as sales forecasting, customer churn analysis, and inventory management.

Moreover, Einstein's ability to deliver AI-driven insights extends to its natural language processing capabilities. Einstein Language allows users to interact with Salesforce using natural language queries. This feature simplifies the process of extracting insights from data by enabling users to ask questions in plain English and receive immediate, AI-generated responses. Implementing Einstein Language requires setting up language models that are trained on your specific data and business context. This involves configuring natural language understanding (NLU) components and integrating them with your Salesforce environment. Once set up, users can leverage Einstein Language to perform complex data analyses and generate insights without needing to write complex queries or scripts.

The automation capabilities provided by Salesforce Einstein are also pivotal in streamlining business processes. Einstein Bots, for example, can be utilized to handle routine customer interactions, such as answering FAQs, scheduling appointments, or processing simple requests. To implement Einstein Bots, you first need to define the bot's conversational flows and design the interaction pathways. This involves setting up dialog nodes that guide the conversation based on user inputs and predefined rules. You will also need to train the bot using historical interaction data to improve its accuracy and relevance. Once deployed, Einstein Bots can significantly reduce the workload on customer service teams by automating repetitive tasks and providing instant support to users.

Another powerful automation tool within Salesforce Einstein is Einstein Next Best Action. This feature uses AI to analyze customer data and recommend the most appropriate actions for sales and service teams. For instance, Einstein Next Best Action can suggest the best products to offer a customer based on their purchase history or recommend follow-up actions for a sales representative based on a lead's engagement level. Implementing this feature involves configuring the action strategies that align with your business objectives and integrating them into your Salesforce workflows. This setup enables your team to act on data-driven recommendations that enhance customer engagement and drive sales performance.

To fully leverage Salesforce Einstein, it is crucial to ensure that the AI and analytics tools are effectively integrated with your existing Salesforce processes and data. This involves configuring the necessary integrations, such as data connectors, APIs, and third-party applications, to ensure a seamless flow of information. Additionally, it is important to continuously monitor the performance of Einstein's AI models and analytics tools. Regularly reviewing model accuracy, adjusting configurations, and updating data sources are essential steps to maintaining the effectiveness of your Einstein implementation.

Furthermore, user adoption and training play a critical role in the successful implementation of Salesforce Einstein. Providing comprehensive training to users on how to interact with Einstein's features and interpret its insights can help maximize the value derived from the platform. This training should cover the practical applications of Einstein tools, such as creating and using dashboards, interacting with Einstein Bots, and leveraging AI-driven recommendations. Additionally, offering ongoing support and resources can help users stay informed about new features and best practices.

In conclusion, implementing Salesforce Einstein involves a multifaceted approach that integrates predictive analytics, AI-driven insights, and automation tools into your Salesforce environment. By understanding and effectively utilizing these capabilities, organizations can enhance decision-making, streamline operations, and deliver personalized experiences that align with their strategic goals. The successful deployment of Salesforce Einstein requires careful planning, technical expertise, and a focus on user adoption to achieve the full potential of AI and analytics within the Salesforce platform.

To truly harness the power of Salesforce Einstein, it is crucial to delve deeper into the specific functionalities and best practices that will enable effective use of its advanced features. This exploration involves not only understanding the underlying technology but also applying practical strategies to ensure optimal utilization.

A core component of Salesforce Einstein is its predictive analytics capabilities, which significantly enhance the decision-making process by providing forecasts and recommendations based on historical data and AI algorithms. One of the primary tools in this realm is Einstein Prediction Builder. This tool allows users to create custom predictive models without requiring deep expertise in data science or programming. The process begins with identifying a business problem or objective, such as predicting customer churn or sales potential. Users then select relevant data fields and define the outcome they wish to predict. Einstein Prediction Builder uses this information to automatically generate a model that can be integrated into Salesforce processes. For example, if you're aiming to predict which leads are most likely to convert, you would configure Prediction Builder to analyze lead attributes and past conversion data. The model then provides insights into which leads warrant more attention, allowing sales teams to prioritize their efforts effectively.

Another advanced feature of Salesforce Einstein is Einstein Discovery, which provides deeper analytical insights by leveraging machine learning algorithms to identify trends and patterns within your data. To utilize Einstein Discovery, you must first ensure that your data is well-organized and relevant to the problem at hand. Once your data is ready, Einstein Discovery can be used to run analyses that uncover hidden relationships and generate actionable insights. For instance, if your goal is to understand the factors influencing customer satisfaction, Einstein Discovery can analyze feedback and interaction data to reveal underlying drivers. The results are presented in a user-friendly format that highlights key findings and suggests actionable steps, such as adjustments in service practices or product features.

In addition to predictive analytics, Einstein also enhances the Salesforce experience with its AI-driven insights and automation tools. Einstein Bots, for example, automate routine tasks and interactions, providing a more efficient and responsive customer service experience. Implementing Einstein Bots requires designing conversational flows that can handle a variety of customer inquiries and issues. The process involves setting up intents and entities that define how the bot should interpret and respond to user inputs. For example, if a customer inquires about the status of their order, the bot can access relevant data to provide real-time updates without requiring human intervention. Effective implementation of Einstein Bots also involves ongoing monitoring and refinement to ensure that the bot continues to meet user needs and adapts to new scenarios.

Einstein Next Best Action is another critical tool that leverages AI to recommend optimal actions based on customer data and interactions. This feature uses machine learning to analyze historical data and current customer behavior, generating recommendations that align with business goals. To implement Einstein Next Best Action, you must first configure action strategies that reflect your organization's objectives. For instance, if your goal is to increase upsell opportunities, Einstein Next Best Action can suggest products or services that are likely to resonate with individual customers based on their previous purchases and preferences. These recommendations are then integrated into your Salesforce workflows, ensuring that sales and service teams have access to relevant, data-driven suggestions that enhance customer engagement and drive business growth.

Another important consideration when implementing Salesforce Einstein is ensuring data quality and integration. Einstein's effectiveness relies on the accuracy and completeness of the data it analyzes. Therefore, it is essential to establish robust data management practices, including regular data cleansing, validation, and integration with other systems. This ensures that Einstein operates on high-quality data, leading to more accurate predictions and insights. Additionally, seamless integration with other Salesforce tools and third-party applications helps maintain a cohesive ecosystem where Einstein's capabilities can be fully leveraged.

User training and support are also vital for maximizing the benefits of Salesforce Einstein. Providing comprehensive training to users on how to utilize Einstein's features, interpret AI-driven insights, and apply recommendations effectively can significantly impact the success of your implementation. Offering ongoing support and resources, such as documentation, webinars, and help desks, ensures that users can continually enhance their skills and stay updated on new features and best practices.

In summary, implementing Salesforce Einstein involves a multifaceted approach that integrates predictive analytics, AI-driven insights, and automation tools into your Salesforce environment. By understanding and effectively utilizing these capabilities, you can enhance decision-making, streamline operations, and deliver personalized experiences that align with your strategic goals. The successful deployment of Salesforce Einstein requires careful planning, technical expertise, and a focus on user adoption to achieve the full potential of AI and analytics within the Salesforce platform.

CHAPTER 16: SALESFORCE CHATTER: ENHANCING COLLABORATION

Salesforce Chatter represents a dynamic shift in internal collaboration by seamlessly integrating social networking concepts within the Salesforce platform. This tool is designed to foster collaboration, enhance communication, and streamline workflows by leveraging social features to facilitate team interactions. To effectively implement and manage Chatter, it is essential to understand its core features and how they can be utilized to improve team dynamics and operational efficiency.

At the heart of Salesforce Chatter is the concept of feeds, which serve as central hubs for communication within the Salesforce environment. Feeds are akin to social media streams, where users can post updates, share files, and comment on activities. These feeds can be organized around various entities, such as records, people, or groups, allowing for targeted discussions and information sharing. For instance, if a sales team is working on a specific client project, they can create a feed related to that project. Team members can then post updates, share relevant documents, and ask questions, ensuring that all communications are centralized and easily accessible. This approach eliminates the need for scattered email threads and disparate communication channels, leading to more cohesive and efficient teamwork.

Groups within Chatter further enhance collaboration by providing a structured way to organize discussions around specific topics, projects, or departments. Groups can be public, private, or unlisted, offering different levels of visibility and access depending on the nature of the information being shared. Public groups are open to all users within the organization, making them ideal for broad announcements or company-wide discussions. Private groups, on the other hand, are restricted to invited members, which is useful for sensitive projects or departmental conversations. Unlisted groups are hidden from search results and require an invitation to join, providing a high level of confidentiality for discussions that are not intended for a wider audience. Configuring these groups effectively involves setting clear guidelines for their use, defining membership criteria, and ensuring that they align with the organization's communication policies and goals.

User engagement is another critical aspect of leveraging Salesforce Chatter for collaboration. To encourage active participation, it is important to promote a culture of openness and responsiveness. Encouraging users to share their insights, ask questions, and provide feedback fosters an environment where collaboration thrives. Additionally, setting up notifications and alerts for relevant feeds and groups ensures that team members stay informed about important updates and discussions. For example, a user working on a project might receive notifications when someone posts a new update or comment related to that project, enabling them to stay engaged and contribute promptly.

Another valuable feature of Salesforce Chatter is the ability to integrate it with other Salesforce tools and processes. For instance, Chatter can be linked to Salesforce records, allowing users to comment on and discuss specific data entries directly within the record's page. This integration enhances the context of discussions and ensures that all relevant information is readily available to participants. Similarly, Chatter can be used to facilitate approvals and workflows by enabling users to collaborate on tasks and provide input in real time. For example, if a team needs to review and approve a document, they can use Chatter to discuss the document, share feedback, and make decisions without leaving the Salesforce platform.

Implementing Salesforce Chatter also involves addressing governance and administration aspects to ensure that the tool is used effectively and aligns with organizational policies. This includes setting up permissions and access controls to manage who can create, join, and participate in groups and feeds. Administrators can configure these settings to balance openness with security, ensuring that sensitive information is protected while promoting collaboration. Additionally, it is important to monitor Chatter activity and usage to identify any issues or areas for improvement. This can be achieved through regular reports and analytics that provide insights into user engagement, group activity, and overall effectiveness.

To maximize the benefits of Salesforce Chatter, it is also essential to provide training and support to users. Ensuring that team members understand how to use Chatter features, participate in discussions, and access relevant information is crucial for successful adoption. Training sessions, user guides, and ongoing support resources can help users become proficient in using Chatter and address any questions or challenges they may encounter.

In summary, Salesforce Chatter is a powerful tool for enhancing collaboration and communication within organizations. By effectively leveraging its features, such as feeds, groups, and user engagement strategies, teams can improve their workflow, streamline communication, and foster a more collaborative work environment. Proper configuration, governance, and user support are key to ensuring that Chatter delivers its full potential and contributes to the overall success of your Salesforce implementation.

The effective utilization of Salesforce Chatter requires a nuanced understanding of its features and their impact on daily operations. One of the core aspects of Chatter is its ability to integrate with Salesforce records, which enhances its utility beyond just a communication tool. By linking Chatter with Salesforce records, users can directly comment on and discuss specific data points within the context of the record, making interactions more relevant and timely. For instance, if a sales representative wants to discuss a particular opportunity or provide updates about a case, they can do so directly within the opportunity or case record. This integration not only centralizes discussions but also ensures that all related information is easily accessible, reducing the need to switch between different interfaces.

To optimize this integration, it is important to configure Chatter settings to align with your organizational needs. This involves enabling Chatter on specific objects and records where discussions are most relevant. By doing so, you ensure that the right conversations occur in the right context, enhancing the efficiency of information exchange. Additionally, incorporating Chatter's @mentions and hashtags can further streamline communication. By using @mentions, users can directly address colleagues or groups, ensuring that relevant parties are notified and engaged in the discussion. Hashtags, on the other hand, help in categorizing content and making it easier to search and retrieve discussions on specific topics.

Another essential feature of Chatter is the ability to customize and configure Chatter settings to fit the unique needs of different teams or departments. For example, configuring custom Chatter feed filters allows users to focus on the most relevant updates and notifications. This is particularly useful in large organizations where the volume of information can be overwhelming. Customizing feed filters helps users to see the updates that are pertinent to their roles, thereby improving their productivity and ensuring that critical information does not get lost in the noise.

Chatter also supports the creation of external communities, which can be highly beneficial for extending collaboration beyond internal teams. External communities allow organizations to engage with customers, partners, or vendors in a secure environment. For instance, a company might set up a Chatter community for its partners to discuss joint projects, share best practices, and collaborate on strategies. Setting up these communities involves configuring access permissions, ensuring that external users have the appropriate level of access to information and features. It is crucial to establish clear guidelines for interaction and content sharing within these external communities to maintain security and compliance.

Effective management of Chatter involves ongoing monitoring and administration to ensure that it continues to meet organizational needs. Regularly reviewing Chatter activity reports provides insights into user engagement, group participation, and content trends. These reports can help identify areas where Chatter is being used effectively and where improvements might be needed. For instance, if certain groups or feeds have low engagement, it may indicate a need for better promotion or changes in how they are used.

Another aspect of Chatter management is addressing user feedback and making adjustments based on their experiences. Collecting and analyzing user feedback helps to identify any challenges or barriers to effective use of Chatter. This feedback can be gathered through surveys, focus groups, or direct communication with users. By addressing common issues or implementing suggested improvements, you can enhance the overall user experience and ensure that Chatter remains a valuable tool for collaboration.

Training and support are also critical components of successful Chatter implementation. Providing users with comprehensive training on how to use Chatter effectively ensures that they are aware of its features and how to leverage them for their benefit. Training should cover basic functionalities, such as creating posts, joining groups, and using @mentions and hashtags, as well as more advanced features, such as integrating Chatter with Salesforce records and configuring feed filters. Ongoing support should be available to address any questions or issues that arise, ensuring that users can make the most of Chatter.

In conclusion, Salesforce Chatter is a powerful tool that can significantly enhance collaboration and communication within organizations. By integrating Chatter with Salesforce records, customizing settings, managing external communities, and continuously monitoring and improving its use, organizations can maximize the benefits of this tool. Effective implementation and management of Chatter require careful planning, ongoing support, and a commitment to fostering a collaborative culture. When utilized to its full potential, Chatter can transform how teams interact, share information, and work together, ultimately driving greater efficiency and success in achieving organizational goals.

To effectively harness the power of Salesforce Chatter, it's essential to focus on advanced configuration and management techniques. These aspects ensure that Chatter not only serves as a tool for communication but also becomes a central part of the workflow and decision-making processes within your organization.

A key component of Chatter's functionality is its ability to create and manage Chatter groups. Groups in Chatter are used to facilitate discussions among users with common interests or project teams. Configuring these groups to fit the specific needs of your organization involves defining their purpose, setting appropriate access levels, and managing membership. There are two main types of groups in Chatter: public and private. Public groups are accessible to all users within your Salesforce instance, whereas private groups require an invitation to join. Deciding which type of group to use depends on the sensitivity of the information shared and the need for confidentiality.

Public groups are ideal for broad-based discussions and information sharing, where transparency is beneficial. They can serve as a platform for company-wide announcements, best practice sharing, and general discussions. In contrast, private groups are more suitable for sensitive projects or departmental conversations, where access needs to be restricted to a specific set of individuals. Setting up private groups requires careful consideration of who should have access and how to manage invitations and permissions effectively.

In addition to group management, configuring Chatter feeds is crucial for ensuring that users receive relevant updates and notifications. Chatter feeds display posts, comments, and updates related to specific records, groups, or users. Customizing these feeds to highlight important information and filter out less relevant content can greatly enhance user engagement and productivity. For instance, setting up feed filters to prioritize updates from high-priority records or key team members ensures that users see the most critical information first.

Another important aspect of Chatter configuration involves setting up notifications and alerts. Chatter notifications inform users about new posts, comments, or mentions related to their areas of interest. Fine-tuning these notifications helps to prevent information overload while ensuring that users remain informed about important updates. Customizing notification settings allows users to control the frequency and type of alerts they receive, thereby balancing their need to stay updated with the need to avoid distractions.

To further enhance collaboration, leveraging Chatter's integration with Salesforce's automation tools can be highly beneficial. For instance, implementing workflow rules and process builders that trigger Chatter notifications based on specific conditions can automate communication and streamline processes. An example of this is setting up a workflow rule to notify a team via Chatter when a high-value opportunity is created or when a critical support case is escalated. This integration not only ensures timely communication but also helps in aligning team efforts with organizational goals.

Effective management of Chatter also involves monitoring and analyzing its usage to ensure that it continues to meet the needs of users. Salesforce provides various reporting tools that allow administrators to track Chatter activity, such as the number of posts, comments, and group memberships. Analyzing these reports helps identify trends, gauge user engagement, and pinpoint areas for improvement. For example, if a particular group is experiencing low engagement, it may be beneficial to review the group's purpose, content, and membership to determine how to boost activity.

Training and support play a vital role in maximizing the benefits of Chatter. Providing users with training on how to effectively use Chatter features, such as creating posts, joining groups, and using @mentions, can significantly enhance their ability to collaborate. Training sessions should be tailored to different user roles and their specific needs. For instance, sales teams might require training on how to use Chatter for tracking opportunities and sharing updates, while support teams might benefit from training on how to collaborate on case resolutions.

Additionally, offering ongoing support and resources helps users overcome any challenges they may encounter while using Chatter. This support can take the form of help documentation, FAQs, or dedicated support teams that address user questions and issues. Ensuring that users have access to these resources helps maintain a positive experience with Chatter and encourages its continued use.

In summary, implementing and managing Salesforce Chatter involves a comprehensive approach that includes configuring groups and feeds, customizing notifications, leveraging automation, and providing training and support. By focusing on these areas, organizations can enhance collaboration, streamline communication, and ensure that Chatter becomes an integral part of their workflow. Effective use of Chatter not only facilitates better information sharing and teamwork but also drives overall organizational efficiency and success.

CHAPTER 17: CUSTOMIZING SALESFORCE WITH LIGHTNING COMPONENTS

Salesforce Lightning Components represent a transformative approach to customizing the Salesforce platform, offering a modern and efficient way to enhance user interfaces and experiences. To effectively harness the power of Lightning Components, it is essential to understand their architecture, development process, and integration within the Salesforce environment.

The foundational element of Lightning Components is their architecture, which consists of several core components. At the heart of this architecture is the Lightning Component Framework, a UI framework for developing dynamic web apps for mobile and desktop devices. The framework comprises two main parts: Lightning Web Components (LWC) and Aura Components. Understanding the distinctions and applications of both is crucial for effective customization.

Lightning Web Components are a newer addition to the Salesforce development landscape. They leverage modern web standards and provide a more efficient way to build custom components. LWCs are built using standard JavaScript and HTML, which makes them more accessible to developers familiar with contemporary web technologies. They offer improved performance and a streamlined development process compared to Aura Components, owing to their reliance on the browser's native capabilities. For instance, LWCs use the latest JavaScript features, such as modules and classes, which simplifies the development and maintenance of complex components.

On the other hand, Aura Components, introduced earlier, use Salesforce's proprietary Aura framework. While they offer extensive capabilities for creating complex, responsive applications, they involve a steeper learning curve due to their unique syntax and framework-specific concepts. Aura Components are still relevant and necessary for certain scenarios, particularly when dealing with legacy code or components that require functionalities not yet available in LWCs.

To begin creating Lightning Components, one must first set up the Salesforce Developer Environment. This involves configuring Salesforce DX, a set of tools designed to improve the development workflow. Salesforce DX provides a source-driven development approach, which allows for more efficient management of code and metadata. It is essential to establish a Salesforce DX project, set up a scratch org for development, and use tools like Visual Studio Code to write and test Lightning Components.

When building custom components, one starts by defining the component's structure using HTML for the markup, JavaScript for the business logic, and CSS for styling. For Lightning Web Components, the HTML file contains the component's template, while the JavaScript file manages its functionality. CSS is used to apply styles directly to the component. The separation of concerns in LWCs allows for cleaner code and better maintainability.

For Aura Components, the process involves defining the component's markup in an Aura markup file (.cmp), handling its logic in a JavaScript controller file, and applying styles in a CSS file. The component's behavior is controlled through event handling and attributes, which allows for dynamic interactions and data binding.

Integrating Lightning Components into your Salesforce environment involves several steps. First, you must deploy the components to your Salesforce org. This can be done using Salesforce DX commands or through the Salesforce Setup menu, where you can upload component files and configurations. Once deployed, you need to add these components to Salesforce pages, such as Lightning App Builder pages, Record Pages, or Home Pages. The Lightning App Builder provides a drag-and-drop interface for placing components on pages, which facilitates a visual approach to customization.

Additionally, Lightning Components can be integrated with Salesforce data through Apex controllers or Lightning Data Service. Apex controllers allow you to write server-side logic that can be invoked from your components, enabling complex data operations and interactions. Lightning Data Service, on the other hand, provides a simpler way to access and manipulate Salesforce data without the need for custom Apex code. It supports standard CRUD operations and provides a more declarative approach to data handling.

Testing and debugging Lightning Components are crucial steps in the development process. Salesforce provides several tools to assist with this, including the Lightning Inspector extension for Chrome, which helps in debugging Lightning Components by providing insights into their structure, events, and performance. Additionally, Salesforce's built-in testing framework allows for unit testing of LWCs and Aura Components, ensuring that your components function correctly and meet your requirements.

In summary, customizing Salesforce with Lightning Components involves understanding the architecture of both Lightning Web Components and Aura Components, setting up an appropriate development environment, and integrating components into your Salesforce environment. By leveraging the capabilities of these modern tools, you can enhance user interfaces, streamline interactions, and provide a more dynamic and responsive experience within Salesforce.

When diving deeper into customizing Salesforce with Lightning Components, understanding how to effectively build and deploy these components is crucial for maximizing their potential. Building custom Lightning Components involves several considerations, including component design, integration strategies, and performance optimization.

The design of a Lightning Component begins with defining its purpose and functionality. Each component should serve a specific role within the Salesforce ecosystem, whether it's enhancing user experience with a custom interface or facilitating complex data interactions. To create a component, I start by conceptualizing its user interface and functionality, which helps in determining the appropriate structure and technologies to use.

For Lightning Web Components, the development process involves writing HTML, JavaScript, and CSS. The HTML file defines the component's structure and layout, using standard web elements and Salesforce-specific tags. The JavaScript file is where the logic resides, including event handling, data processing, and interaction with Salesforce APIs. CSS is used to style the component, ensuring it aligns with the overall Salesforce design and user interface guidelines.

Aura Components follow a similar approach but with some differences in syntax and structure. The Aura framework uses a component markup file (.cmp) to define the component's layout, a controller file for handling logic, and a helper file for utility functions. Although Aura Components are more flexible in certain scenarios, they are generally more complex due to the framework's unique syntax and event-handling model.

Integrating Lightning Components into Salesforce requires a clear understanding of the Salesforce user interface and how components interact with other elements within the platform. Once components are developed, they need to be added to Salesforce pages, such as Lightning App Builder pages, Record Pages, or Home Pages. The Lightning App Builder provides a user-friendly interface to drag and drop components, making it easier to customize the Salesforce user interface without extensive coding.

For more advanced integration, I can use Apex controllers or Lightning Data Service. Apex controllers enable server-side logic and data manipulation, allowing components to perform complex operations and interact with Salesforce's database. When using Apex, it's important to ensure that the code is optimized for performance and security, adhering to Salesforce's best practices.

Lightning Data Service, on the other hand, provides a more declarative approach to data access. It simplifies CRUD operations by handling data transactions directly within the component, reducing the need for custom Apex code. This service provides built-in features for record data management and caching, which enhances performance and user experience.

To ensure that custom Lightning Components meet user needs and function correctly, thorough testing is essential.

Salesforce offers several tools and methods for testing components. For Lightning Web Components, unit tests can be written using the Jest framework, which allows for JavaScript code testing in isolation. For Aura Components, Salesforce provides a testing framework that supports component testing and debugging.

Additionally, I use Salesforce's built-in developer tools, such as the Lightning Inspector for Chrome, to debug and analyze components. This tool provides insights into component performance, events, and data interactions, helping identify and resolve issues efficiently.

Performance optimization is a critical aspect of working with Lightning Components. Poorly optimized components can lead to slow page load times and a suboptimal user experience. To enhance performance, I focus on optimizing component code, minimizing server calls, and leveraging client-side caching. Proper use of Salesforce's caching mechanisms and efficient data handling practices can significantly improve component performance.

Lastly, ensuring that custom Lightning Components adhere to Salesforce's security and compliance standards is paramount. Components should be designed with security best practices in mind, such as validating user inputs, handling data securely, and following Salesforce's security guidelines. Regular security reviews and audits help maintain the integrity and safety of the components.

By focusing on these aspects—design, integration, testing, performance optimization, and security—I can effectively leverage Lightning Components to customize Salesforce, enhance user interfaces, and provide a more dynamic and responsive experience. This approach not only improves the functionality of Salesforce but also ensures that the components meet the highest standards of performance and security.

Continuing with the customization of Salesforce through Lightning Components, another vital aspect is ensuring that components are reusable and maintainable. This practice not only improves efficiency but also contributes to a consistent user experience across different Salesforce applications.

When creating Lightning Components, I start by following best practices for component design. Reusability is a key consideration, meaning that components should be designed in a modular way, so they can be easily incorporated into various parts of the Salesforce environment. This involves creating components that are generalized and configurable, allowing them to adapt to different use cases without significant changes to the underlying code.

One way to enhance reusability is by employing component attributes effectively. Attributes serve as variables within components, allowing for customization based on the context in which the component is used. By defining attributes, I can make components more flexible and adaptable to different requirements. For example, a component designed for displaying records might include attributes for specifying which record type to display, how to filter the records, and what layout to use.

Another important consideration is the use of events in Lightning Components. Events facilitate communication between components, enabling them to interact and exchange information. There are two main types of events: application events and component events. Application events are used for broader communication across multiple components within the same application, while component events are more localized, designed for communication between a parent component and its child components. Proper use of events allows for a more cohesive and interactive user experience, as components can respond dynamically to user actions and data changes.

For effective component management and maintenance, it is essential to implement a consistent and organized approach to naming conventions, code structure, and documentation. Naming conventions should be clear and descriptive, helping to identify the purpose and function of each component at a glance. A well-structured codebase, with logical organization of HTML, JavaScript, and CSS files, simplifies debugging and future modifications.

Documentation plays a critical role in maintaining components. Comprehensive documentation should include information about the component's purpose, attributes, events, and any dependencies. This documentation not only aids in the development process but also serves as a valuable resource for other team members who may work with the components in the future. Using inline comments within the code can also improve understanding and facilitate easier updates.

Testing and validation of Lightning Components are crucial for ensuring their functionality and reliability. In addition to unit testing and integration testing, user acceptance testing (UAT) is an important step. UAT involves end-users interacting with the components in a real-world scenario to ensure that they meet the expected requirements and provide a satisfactory user experience. Feedback from UAT can highlight areas for improvement and ensure that the components align with user needs and expectations.

Performance considerations must also be taken into account. While Lightning Components offer powerful customization capabilities, inefficient code or excessive server requests can impact performance. Techniques such as lazy loading, where components or data are loaded only when needed, can help mitigate performance issues. Additionally, optimizing the component's rendering process and minimizing the use of expensive operations can contribute to a smoother and faster user experience.

Security is a fundamental aspect of developing Lightning Components. Components should be designed with security in mind, following Salesforce's security best practices. This includes validating user inputs to prevent injection attacks, using secure methods for handling sensitive data, and ensuring that components adhere to Salesforce's security model. Regular security reviews and adherence to Salesforce's security guidelines are essential for maintaining the integrity and protection of the Salesforce environment.

Finally, it is important to stay current with Salesforce's updates and new features related to Lightning Components. Salesforce continuously evolves its platform, introducing new tools and enhancements that can impact component development. Keeping abreast of these changes ensures that components remain compatible with the latest Salesforce releases and can take advantage of new capabilities.

In summary, customizing Salesforce with Lightning Components involves a thoughtful approach to design, integration, reusability, testing, performance, and security. By adhering to best practices and focusing on these key areas, I can create powerful and flexible components that enhance the Salesforce experience and drive greater value for users.

CHAPTER 18: ADVANCED REPORTING AND ANALYTICS

When diving into advanced reporting and analytics within Salesforce, the focus shifts from basic report creation to crafting intricate and powerful analytical tools that can drive strategic business decisions. This segment is essential for leveraging Salesforce's full analytical capabilities, providing deeper insights into organizational data.

The first step in advanced reporting is to understand the underlying data model and how it influences report creation. Salesforce's data model is built around objects, fields, and relationships, which are crucial for designing reports that are both comprehensive and insightful. As you explore advanced reporting, the emphasis is on leveraging this model to its fullest extent. This involves not only selecting the right objects and fields but also understanding how different objects relate to each other through lookups and master-detail relationships.

Creating sophisticated reports begins with mastering report types. Standard report types may not always meet the requirements for complex reporting needs, so custom report types often come into play. Custom report types allow you to define new relationships between objects, providing a tailored data structure that suits specific analytical needs. This customization ensures that reports can pull data from multiple objects in a way that reflects the true complexity of business processes.

Once the report type is established, configuring the report itself involves advanced features such as cross-filters, bucket fields, and custom formulas. Cross-filters enable you to refine data further by applying filters based on related objects. For example, if you need to analyze opportunities associated with certain accounts that have specific characteristics, cross-filters can isolate this data effectively. Bucket fields allow for categorizing report data into predefined ranges or groups, making it easier to analyze data trends without complex formula calculations. Custom formulas, on the other hand, provide a way to perform calculations directly within the report, offering dynamic insights based on the data presented.

Data visualization is another critical component of advanced reporting. Salesforce offers a variety of visualization tools, including charts, graphs, and dashboards. To enhance the clarity and impact of data presentations, it's essential to select the appropriate visualization type based on the nature of the data and the insights you wish to convey. For instance, bar charts are effective for comparing discrete categories, while line graphs are ideal for showing trends over time. Advanced dashboards allow for the integration of multiple reports into a single view, providing a holistic picture of key metrics and performance indicators. These dashboards can be customized with components such as charts, tables, and gauges, allowing users to interact with the data and drill down into specifics.

The use of dynamic dashboards adds another layer of sophistication. Dynamic dashboards enable personalized views based on the logged-in user's data, ensuring that each user sees information pertinent to their role or department.

This personalization is achieved through the use of dashboard filters and user-specific settings, enhancing the relevance and impact of the data presented.

Advanced analytics in Salesforce extends beyond standard reporting into the realm of predictive and prescriptive analytics. Predictive analytics uses historical data and statistical algorithms to forecast future trends and outcomes. Salesforce's Einstein Analytics (now known as Tableau CRM) provides tools for building predictive models that can identify patterns and predict future performance. These models can be integrated into reports and dashboards, offering actionable insights that can drive decision-making.

Prescriptive analytics, on the other hand, goes a step further by recommending specific actions based on the analytical insights. This involves using AI and machine learning to suggest optimal strategies or interventions. For example, prescriptive analytics can recommend the best approach for addressing customer churn or optimizing sales strategies, providing a proactive approach to business challenges.

To implement these advanced analytics techniques effectively, it's crucial to have a robust data governance strategy in place. Data governance ensures that data quality, consistency, and security are maintained, which is essential for reliable reporting and analysis. This involves establishing data management practices, defining data ownership, and implementing policies for data accuracy and security.

Moreover, integrating external data sources into Salesforce reports can enhance the depth of analysis. Salesforce's integration capabilities allow for the incorporation of data from external systems, such as ERP or CRM systems, providing a more comprehensive view of business operations. This integration can be achieved through tools like Salesforce Connect, which enables real-time data access, or through custom integrations that bring external data into Salesforce reports and dashboards.

In summary, advanced reporting and analytics in Salesforce require a deep understanding of the platform's data model, sophisticated report configurations, and effective data visualization techniques. By leveraging these capabilities, you can create insightful reports and dashboards that support strategic decision-making, drive business performance, and provide a comprehensive view of organizational data. As you delve into these advanced features, remember that the goal is to transform raw data into actionable insights that can propel your business forward.

To further delve into advanced reporting and analytics within Salesforce, we need to explore the nuances of creating complex report configurations and utilizing sophisticated analytics features. This aspect of Salesforce reporting focuses on refining data presentations and extracting deeper insights through advanced techniques.

Starting with complex report configurations, one of the key elements is mastering the use of joined reports. Joined reports enable the combination of data from multiple report types into a single view, which is particularly useful when you need to analyze related data from different sources. For example, you might create a joined report that combines opportunities with related activities, such as tasks and events, to provide a comprehensive view of sales performance and associated actions. This method requires a good understanding of how different objects and their relationships impact the data displayed in the report.

Another advanced feature is the use of matrix reports, which allow for multi-dimensional data analysis. Matrix reports enable you to group and summarize data along both rows and columns, making them ideal for analyzing data trends and patterns across different dimensions. For instance, if you need to analyze sales performance across different regions and time periods, a matrix report can present this information in a clear, comparative format, helping to identify trends and outliers.

Custom summary formulas further enhance the analytical power of reports. These formulas allow for the calculation of custom metrics and KPIs directly within the report. For example, you might create a formula to calculate the average deal size or to measure the percentage of closed-won opportunities. These custom metrics provide additional layers of insight, enabling more nuanced data analysis and reporting.

In addition to advanced reporting configurations, effective data visualization is crucial for communicating insights clearly and effectively. Salesforce offers various visualization tools, such as charts and graphs, which can be customized to fit specific reporting needs. One important consideration when choosing visualization types is the nature of the data and the message you want to convey. For instance, pie charts are useful for showing proportional data, while bar charts are more effective for comparing discrete categories. Combining multiple visualization types in a single dashboard can provide a more comprehensive view of the data, making it easier to interpret and act upon.

Dynamic dashboards are another powerful feature for enhancing data visualization. Unlike static dashboards, dynamic dashboards allow users to view data that is relevant to their individual roles or permissions. This personalized approach ensures that each user sees information pertinent to their specific needs, improving the relevance and impact of the data presented. Setting up dynamic dashboards involves configuring dashboard filters and user-specific settings, which requires an understanding of user roles and data access permissions.

The role of predictive analytics and artificial intelligence in advanced reporting cannot be overstated. Salesforce Einstein, now integrated into Salesforce's analytics tools, provides predictive insights that leverage historical data to forecast future trends. Implementing predictive analytics involves setting up models that analyze past data to predict outcomes such as sales forecasts or customer behavior. These models can be integrated into reports and dashboards, providing actionable insights that drive decision-making. For instance, a predictive model might forecast the likelihood of an opportunity closing based on historical patterns, allowing sales teams to prioritize their efforts more effectively.

Prescriptive analytics, which builds on predictive insights, recommends specific actions to optimize outcomes. Salesforce's AI-driven tools can suggest strategies or interventions based on the predictive data. For example, prescriptive analytics might recommend targeted actions to reduce customer churn or optimize sales strategies. These recommendations are derived from advanced algorithms and machine learning models that analyze data trends and suggest the best course of action to achieve desired results.

Integrating external data sources into Salesforce reports can further enhance the depth and breadth of your analytics. Salesforce Connect and custom integrations enable the incorporation of data from external systems, such as ERP or CRM systems, into Salesforce reports and dashboards. This integration provides a more comprehensive view of business operations, allowing for more informed decision-making. For example, integrating financial data from an ERP system with Salesforce sales data can offer a holistic view of financial performance and sales effectiveness.

Effective data governance is critical for ensuring the accuracy and reliability of advanced reporting and analytics. This involves implementing policies and practices for data management, including data quality, consistency, and security. Establishing clear data governance practices helps to maintain the integrity of the data used in reports and ensures that the insights derived from the data are reliable and actionable.

In summary, advanced reporting and analytics within Salesforce involve a range of sophisticated techniques and tools. By mastering complex report configurations, leveraging dynamic dashboards, and utilizing predictive and prescriptive analytics, you can create powerful reports and dashboards that provide deeper insights and support strategic decision-making. Integrating external data sources and implementing robust data governance practices further enhance the effectiveness of your reporting and analytics efforts, enabling you to drive business performance and achieve your strategic objectives.

As we continue our exploration of advanced reporting and analytics within Salesforce, it's essential to delve into the practical aspects of implementing and utilizing these sophisticated techniques. We've touched upon the fundamental features, but the real value lies in how these tools can be employed to address specific business needs and drive strategic outcomes.

A crucial aspect of advanced reporting is understanding how to effectively use and manage custom report types. Custom report types are designed to provide a tailored view of your Salesforce data, beyond the standard report types offered by Salesforce. By defining custom report types, you can include specific objects and fields that are not available in standard report types, allowing for more granular and relevant reporting. For example, if you need to create a report that combines data from custom objects, such as project milestones and customer feedback, a custom report type can be configured to include these objects and their relationships, giving you a comprehensive view of project performance and customer satisfaction.

Once custom report types are established, it is important to focus on the design and layout of your reports to maximize their effectiveness. Advanced reporting techniques often involve creating summary and matrix reports that aggregate and present data in a meaningful way. For example, summary reports can group data by various criteria and provide subtotals, making it easier to analyze performance by different segments or categories. Matrix reports, on the other hand, allow for more complex data analysis by displaying data in a grid format with both row and column groupings. This format is particularly useful for analyzing trends and patterns across multiple dimensions.

Another critical aspect is the use of Salesforce's advanced dashboard features to enhance data visualization and accessibility. Dashboards in Salesforce are not just visual representations of data; they are interactive tools that can provide real-time insights and support dynamic decision-making. By incorporating various components such as charts, tables, and gauges into dashboards, you can create a comprehensive view of key performance indicators (KPIs) and other critical metrics. Additionally, dashboard filters allow users to view data relevant to their specific roles or interests, enhancing the dashboard's utility and relevance.

Dynamic dashboards, which update in real time based on user interactions and data changes, are particularly valuable for providing up-to-date insights. For instance, a sales manager might use a dynamic dashboard to monitor live sales performance metrics, adjusting filters to focus on different regions or time periods as needed. This flexibility ensures that the dashboard remains a relevant and powerful tool for making informed decisions.

Advanced analytics features, such as Einstein Analytics,

further enhance your ability to derive insights from your data. Einstein Analytics integrates with Salesforce to provide AI-driven insights and predictive analytics. By leveraging machine learning algorithms, Einstein Analytics can identify patterns and trends that might not be immediately apparent through traditional reporting methods. For example, Einstein's predictive models can forecast future sales trends based on historical data, helping sales teams to proactively adjust their strategies and target their efforts more effectively.

Incorporating external data sources into Salesforce reports and dashboards can also provide a more holistic view of your business. Salesforce Connect and various integration tools allow you to pull data from external systems and incorporate it into your Salesforce environment. This capability is especially useful for organizations that rely on data from multiple systems, such as ERP or marketing automation platforms. By integrating this data, you can create unified reports and dashboards that offer a comprehensive perspective on your business performance.

Data governance and quality control play a crucial role in ensuring the accuracy and reliability of your advanced reports and analytics. Establishing robust data governance practices helps to maintain data integrity and consistency, which is essential for making informed decisions. This involves implementing policies and procedures for data management, including regular data audits, validation rules, and user access controls. Ensuring that your data is accurate and up-to-date is fundamental to the effectiveness of your reporting and analytics efforts.

Finally, it is important to continually assess and refine your reporting and analytics strategies to align with evolving business needs and objectives. Regularly reviewing and updating your reports and dashboards ensures that they remain relevant and valuable as your business grows and changes. Soliciting feedback from end users and stakeholders can provide insights into how reports and dashboards can be improved to better meet their needs and support their decision-making processes.

In conclusion, advanced reporting and analytics within Salesforce offer powerful tools for gaining deeper insights and making data-driven decisions. By mastering custom report types, utilizing advanced dashboard features, and leveraging predictive and AI-driven analytics, you can enhance your organization's ability to analyze and interpret data. Integrating external data sources and maintaining strong data governance practices further strengthen the effectiveness of your reporting efforts. As you continue to refine your reporting and analytics strategies, you'll be better equipped to drive strategic decision-making and achieve your business goals.

CHAPTER 19: AUTOMATING BUSINESS PROCESSES WITH FLOW

Salesforce Flow is a transformative tool designed to automate and streamline business processes within the Salesforce ecosystem. As an integral part of Salesforce's automation capabilities, Flow allows administrators and developers to create sophisticated workflows that eliminate repetitive tasks, enforce business rules, and enhance operational efficiency. This exploration into Salesforce Flow will focus on the foundational concepts of Flow, its various types, and practical use cases to help you effectively design and implement automated solutions tailored to your organization's needs.

To begin, understanding the core concept of Flow is essential. Salesforce Flow is an automation tool that enables users to build custom workflows using a visual interface. This tool simplifies the creation of complex automation processes without the need for extensive coding knowledge. Flows can be used to automate a wide range of business processes, from updating records to collecting user input and orchestrating multi-step operations.

There are two primary types of flows in Salesforce: Screen Flows and Auto-Launched Flows. Screen Flows are interactive and involve user input. They are typically used in scenarios where a user needs to complete a series of steps or provide information through a user interface. For example, a Screen Flow could be designed to guide a user through a multi-step data entry process, ensuring that all required information is captured and validated before proceeding to the next step.

Auto-Launched Flows, on the other hand, are designed to run in the background without user interaction. They are often used for backend processes such as updating records based on specific triggers or performing calculations. Auto-Launched Flows can be invoked through various means, including process builders, Apex code, or other automation tools within Salesforce. These flows are ideal for scenarios where you need to automate tasks such as sending notifications, updating related records, or executing batch operations.

When designing a flow, it is important to consider its structure and components. The Flow Builder, Salesforce's visual interface for creating flows, offers a range of elements that can be used to define the flow's logic and behavior. Key elements include:

- Screen Elements: Used in Screen Flows to create user interfaces and collect input from users. Screen elements can include text fields, picklists, checkboxes, and other input components.
- Decision Elements: Allow you to implement branching logic based on conditions. Decisions help determine the path the flow will take based on user input or record values.
- Assignment Elements: Used to set or update variable values within the flow. This is useful for storing and manipulating data as the flow progresses.
- Record Create, Update, and Delete Elements: Enable the flow

to interact with Salesforce records. These elements are used to create new records, update existing ones, or delete records based on specific criteria.

- Loop Elements: Facilitate the processing of multiple records or values by iterating through them in a defined sequence. Loops are helpful for scenarios where you need to perform actions on a set of records.

A well-designed flow begins with a clear understanding of the business process you aim to automate. Start by mapping out the process steps, identifying the data inputs and outputs, and determining the decision points that will drive the flow's logic. This initial planning phase is crucial for ensuring that the flow meets the intended objectives and delivers the desired outcomes.

Once you have defined the process, you can begin building the flow using the Flow Builder. The Flow Builder's drag-and-drop interface makes it easy to add and configure elements, define their properties, and establish connections between them. As you build the flow, you can test and debug it using the built-in simulation tools to ensure that it behaves as expected and handles various scenarios correctly.

For effective management of flows, it is important to establish best practices for deployment, maintenance, and monitoring. Ensure that flows are thoroughly tested in a sandbox environment before deploying them to production. This helps identify and resolve any issues that may arise in a controlled setting, minimizing the risk of disruptions in your live environment.

Additionally, keep track of flow performance and monitor for any errors or issues. Salesforce provides monitoring tools that can help you review flow execution logs and identify potential problems. Regularly reviewing and optimizing flows based on performance metrics and user feedback will help maintain their effectiveness and ensure they continue to meet evolving business needs.

In summary, Salesforce Flow offers a powerful means of automating business processes and enhancing operational efficiency. By understanding the types of flows available, mastering the Flow Builder's components, and adhering to best practices for design and management, you can leverage Salesforce Flow to streamline operations, reduce manual tasks, and drive greater productivity within your organization. As you explore and implement flows, consider the unique needs of your business and tailor your automation solutions accordingly to achieve optimal results.

In designing and implementing Salesforce Flow to automate business processes, it is essential to delve deeper into the nuances of flow configuration and practical application. This exploration will include a closer look at advanced configuration options, best practices for ensuring successful automation, and real-world use cases that illustrate the versatility and impact of Salesforce Flow.

To begin with, advanced configuration options within Salesforce Flow offer a range of powerful features that can significantly enhance the functionality of your automation. One of these features is the use of variables, which are critical for storing and manipulating data within a flow. Variables can hold values temporarily and pass them between different elements of the flow, enabling dynamic interactions and complex data handling. Understanding how to define and use variables effectively is crucial for creating flows that are not only functional but also adaptable to varying business scenarios.

Another important aspect of advanced configuration is the use of collection variables and data elements. Collection variables allow you to manage and process multiple records or values at once, making them ideal for scenarios where batch processing is required. For instance, if you need to update a set of records based on a specific condition, collection variables can simplify this task by allowing you to loop through and perform actions on each record in the collection. Similarly, data elements, such as Get Records, Update Records, and Delete Records, provide the capability to interact with Salesforce data directly within the flow, enabling complex data operations and integrations.

When designing flows, it's also crucial to consider flow triggers and invocation methods. Flows can be triggered in various ways, such as through a user action, a process builder, or an Apex class. Understanding how to configure these triggers and the conditions under which flows should be executed is key to ensuring that your automation aligns with your business requirements. For example, a flow can be set to run when a record is created or updated, or it can be invoked manually by users through a button or link. Each method has its use cases and implications, and selecting the appropriate trigger is vital for optimizing flow performance and user experience.

In addition to configuration, best practices for building and managing flows are essential for maintaining efficiency and reliability. One such best practice is to document your flows thoroughly. Detailed documentation helps ensure that the logic and purpose of the flow are clear, facilitating easier maintenance and troubleshooting. Documentation should include descriptions of each element, the flow's purpose, any specific configurations or settings, and any dependencies or related processes. This practice not only aids in future updates but also supports team collaboration and knowledge transfer.

Another best practice is to design for scalability and performance. As your organization grows and processes evolve, the flows you create must be able to handle increased complexity and data volume. To achieve this, consider optimizing flow performance by minimizing the number of elements and operations within the flow. Avoid excessive use of loops or complex branching logic that could impact execution speed. Additionally, testing flows thoroughly in a sandbox environment before deployment helps identify performance issues and ensures that the flow behaves as expected under different scenarios.

Moreover, leveraging error handling and debugging tools within Salesforce Flow is crucial for managing and resolving issues that may arise during flow execution. Salesforce provides built-in tools for debugging flows, such as the Debug Flow feature, which allows you to simulate flow execution and review its behavior step by step. Implementing error handling mechanisms, such as fault paths and custom error messages, can also help manage exceptions and provide users with meaningful feedback when something goes wrong. This approach enhances the reliability of your flows and improves the overall user experience.

Practical use cases for Salesforce Flow highlight its versatility and potential impact on business operations. For instance, a common use case is automating the lead qualification process. A flow can be designed to evaluate incoming leads based on predefined criteria, such as lead source, industry, or potential revenue. The flow can then automatically assign leads to the appropriate sales representative, send notifications, and update lead statuses based on the evaluation results. This automation not only streamlines the lead management process but also ensures that leads are handled consistently and efficiently.

Another example is automating employee onboarding. A flow can guide new hires through the onboarding process by collecting necessary information, setting up user accounts, and provisioning access to required resources. By automating these tasks, organizations can reduce manual effort, minimize errors, and provide a smoother onboarding experience for new employees.

In summary, Salesforce Flow offers powerful capabilities for automating and optimizing business processes. By mastering advanced configuration options, adhering to best practices, and applying flows to practical use cases, you can enhance operational efficiency, reduce manual tasks, and drive meaningful improvements in your organization's workflow. As you continue to explore and implement Salesforce Flow, focus on creating well-documented, scalable, and performance-optimized solutions that align with your business objectives and support your automation goals.

In exploring the advanced aspects of Salesforce Flow, it is important to understand the diverse ways in which flows can be optimized and managed to achieve robust automation solutions. This part will delve into the nuances of flow optimization, integration with other Salesforce features, and practical considerations for maintaining and scaling flows within your organization.

One critical area of focus is the optimization of flow performance. As the complexity of flows increases, so does the potential impact on system performance. To mitigate this, it is essential to adopt strategies that enhance flow efficiency. One such strategy involves minimizing the number of elements used within a flow. Each element in a flow, such as decisions, loops, or data operations, contributes to the overall processing time. By consolidating elements and reducing unnecessary steps, you can streamline the flow's execution. For instance, combining multiple data updates into a single operation rather than executing them separately can significantly enhance performance.

Another important optimization technique is using efficient query practices. When flows interact with Salesforce data, such as through "Get Records" elements, the way queries are constructed can impact performance. To optimize queries, avoid retrieving excessive data or using overly broad criteria. Instead, refine your queries to fetch only the necessary records and fields. Implementing selective filters and indexed fields can also improve query speed and efficiency.

To further enhance performance, utilize bulk processing where applicable. Salesforce Flow supports bulk processing through features like Collection Variables and Looping. By processing multiple records in bulk rather than individually, you can reduce the number of operations performed and decrease the overall execution time. For example, if a flow needs to update a set of records, processing them in a bulk operation can be more efficient than updating each record individually.

Integrating Salesforce Flow with other Salesforce features can also amplify its effectiveness. One such integration is with Salesforce Process Builder. While Salesforce Flow provides advanced automation capabilities, Process Builder offers a user-friendly interface for creating simple automation rules. By combining these tools, you can leverage Process Builder to trigger flows based on specific criteria or events. For instance, you might use Process Builder to initiate a flow that handles complex data processing or updates based on certain conditions.

Apex code integration is another powerful way to extend the functionality of Salesforce Flow. Apex can be used to execute complex logic or interact with external systems that might not be directly achievable through flows alone. For instance, if a flow needs to perform calculations or data manipulations beyond its native capabilities, Apex can be invoked to handle these tasks. Integrating Apex with flows requires careful planning and testing to ensure that the code and flow operate seamlessly together.

Furthermore, utilizing Flow Subflows can enhance the

modularity and reusability of your flows. Subflows allow you to break down complex flows into smaller, manageable components. By creating reusable subflows, you can encapsulate common logic or operations and call them from multiple flows. This approach not only simplifies the design of individual flows but also promotes consistency and reduces duplication of effort.

Effective management and maintenance of flows are essential to ensure their continued effectiveness and relevance. Regular review and testing of flows are crucial practices. As business processes and requirements evolve, flows may need to be updated or adjusted. Regularly reviewing flows helps identify any outdated elements or inefficiencies, and testing ensures that changes do not introduce new issues. Salesforce provides tools for debugging and error handling, which are valuable for identifying and resolving issues during flow execution.

In addition to reviewing and testing, maintaining proper version control for flows is important. Version control allows you to track changes, manage different versions of flows, and revert to previous versions if necessary. Salesforce's versioning features, along with best practices such as maintaining documentation and change logs, can support effective version management.

Scaling flows to accommodate growing data volumes or increased complexity requires careful consideration. As flows are deployed and used in larger environments, they may need to handle more data or integrate with additional systems. Monitoring flow performance and usage metrics is essential for identifying potential scalability issues. Additionally, leveraging best practices for optimizing flow performance, such as efficient query practices and bulk processing, can help ensure that flows continue to operate effectively as they scale.

In summary, mastering the advanced aspects of Salesforce

Flow involves not only creating effective automation solutions but also optimizing performance, integrating with other Salesforce features, and managing flows for ongoing effectiveness. By focusing on performance optimization, leveraging integrations, and maintaining robust management practices, you can build and sustain flows that drive efficiency, streamline processes, and support the dynamic needs of your organization. Through thoughtful design, careful testing, and continuous improvement, Salesforce Flow can be a powerful tool for automating and enhancing business operations.

CHAPTER 20: SALESFORCE GOVERNANCE AND BEST PRACTICES

In establishing a robust Salesforce environment, the importance of governance and best practices cannot be overstated. Effective governance frameworks and adherence to best practices are fundamental to ensuring that Salesforce instances are not only well-managed but also align with organizational goals and compliance requirements. This discussion will delve into the critical aspects of governance, policy development, and best practices that form the cornerstone of successful Salesforce administration.

The first step in developing a governance framework is understanding the necessity for clear and structured policy development. Policies act as guidelines that govern how Salesforce is utilized, ensuring consistency and adherence to organizational standards. Developing comprehensive policies involves addressing several key areas, such as data management, security, customization, and user access. Each policy should be designed to address the specific needs of the organization while aligning with industry standards and regulations.

For instance, a data management policy should outline how

data is collected, stored, and utilized within Salesforce. This includes specifying data quality standards, data retention policies, and procedures for data cleansing and validation. Proper data management ensures that the data within Salesforce is accurate, up-to-date, and reliable, which is crucial for making informed business decisions and maintaining operational efficiency.

Similarly, a security policy should address how to protect sensitive information within Salesforce. This includes defining user roles and permissions, implementing access controls, and establishing protocols for monitoring and responding to security incidents. A robust security policy helps safeguard against unauthorized access, data breaches, and other security threats, ensuring that the Salesforce environment remains secure and compliant with relevant regulations.

Effective governance also involves the establishment of change management processes. Change management is crucial for handling modifications to the Salesforce environment, whether they involve updates, new customizations, or changes to existing configurations. A structured change management process includes procedures for requesting, reviewing, and approving changes, as well as for testing and deploying these changes in a controlled manner. This process helps prevent unintended disruptions and ensures that changes are implemented smoothly and with minimal risk.

In addition to policy development, adhering to best practices is essential for maintaining a well-managed Salesforce environment. Best practices encompass a range of guidelines and techniques that contribute to effective Salesforce administration and management. One such best practice is regular system audits. Conducting periodic audits helps identify potential issues, assess compliance with policies, and evaluate system performance. Audits provide valuable insights into areas that may require improvement and help ensure that the Salesforce environment operates optimally.

Another key best practice is establishing clear documentation for all aspects of Salesforce management. Documentation serves as a reference for users and administrators, providing detailed information about configurations, customizations, and processes. Well-maintained documentation ensures that knowledge is shared across the organization and helps facilitate training, troubleshooting, and ongoing system maintenance.

User training and support are also integral to successful Salesforce governance. Providing comprehensive training for users ensures that they are familiar with Salesforce functionalities, policies, and best practices. Ongoing support helps address any issues or questions that arise, promoting efficient use of the system and reducing the likelihood of errors or misuse. Investing in user training and support fosters a positive user experience and enhances overall system adoption and utilization.

Moreover, implementing performance monitoring practices is crucial for maintaining a high-performing Salesforce environment. Regularly monitoring system performance, including response times, data processing speeds, and user interactions, helps identify potential bottlenecks or issues. Performance monitoring allows administrators to proactively address performance-related concerns and optimize the system to meet evolving business needs.

A key component of governance is the establishment of a review and feedback mechanism. This mechanism involves regularly soliciting feedback from users and stakeholders about their experiences with Salesforce and any challenges they may encounter. Gathering feedback helps administrators understand user needs, identify areas for improvement, and make informed decisions about system enhancements or changes.

Finally, maintaining a strategic vision for Salesforce management is essential for long-term success. This involves aligning Salesforce initiatives with organizational goals and continuously assessing how the platform can support business objectives. A strategic approach ensures that Salesforce remains a valuable asset, contributing to overall business growth and success.

In summary, effective governance and adherence to best practices are critical for maintaining a well-managed Salesforce environment. Developing comprehensive policies, adhering to best practices, and implementing robust change management and performance monitoring processes are essential components of successful Salesforce administration. By fostering a structured approach to Salesforce management and aligning initiatives with organizational goals, organizations can ensure the long-term success and sustainability of their Salesforce environment.

Continuing from the foundation laid in the initial discussion, we delve deeper into the intricacies of implementing effective governance frameworks within Salesforce. Governance frameworks are pivotal in establishing a structured approach to managing Salesforce environments. They provide a set of guidelines and principles that ensure the platform is used effectively, efficiently, and in alignment with organizational objectives. Crafting a governance framework involves several key components, each contributing to the overall management and success of Salesforce.

A critical aspect of any governance framework is defining roles and responsibilities. Clearly delineating who is responsible for various aspects of Salesforce management helps ensure accountability and proper oversight. This includes assigning roles such as system administrators, developers, data stewards, and business users. Each role should have defined responsibilities and access levels, which align with their functions and expertise. Establishing these roles and responsibilities helps streamline operations and ensures that each component of the Salesforce environment is managed by the appropriate individual or team.

Another integral component is the development of governance policies and procedures. These policies should cover various facets of Salesforce usage, including data management, security, and change management. Policies should be comprehensive, addressing how data is handled, how security measures are implemented, and how changes to the system are managed. Procedures should be clearly documented, outlining the steps to follow for different processes such as data entry, user access management, and system updates. Well-defined policies and procedures provide a consistent approach to managing Salesforce and help mitigate risks associated with mismanagement or non-compliance.

Implementing regular review and audit processes is essential for maintaining the effectiveness of governance practices. Regular audits help assess compliance with established policies and procedures, identify potential issues or areas for improvement, and ensure that the Salesforce environment operates as intended. These reviews should be conducted periodically and may involve examining system configurations, user access logs, and data quality. The findings from audits should be documented and used to inform any necessary adjustments or enhancements to governance practices.

To support the governance framework, change management processes must be robust and well-defined. Change management involves planning, testing, and implementing modifications to the Salesforce environment in a controlled manner. This process includes submitting change requests, evaluating their impact, and obtaining necessary approvals before implementation. A structured change management process helps prevent disruptions, ensures that changes are made systematically, and minimizes the risk of unintended consequences.

Communication and training are also critical elements of successful governance. Ensuring that all users are aware of governance policies and procedures is essential for compliance and effective system usage. Regular training sessions can help users understand their roles, responsibilities, and the importance of adhering to governance practices. Effective communication channels should be established to keep stakeholders informed about changes, updates, and other relevant information.

In addition to these components, data governance plays a crucial role in maintaining data integrity and compliance. Data governance involves defining data standards, establishing data stewardship roles, and implementing processes for data quality management. Ensuring that data is accurate, complete, and consistent is vital for making informed business decisions and maintaining the reliability of the Salesforce system. This includes setting up data validation rules, conducting data cleansing activities, and monitoring data quality metrics.

Moreover, security governance is a key focus area, addressing how sensitive information is protected within Salesforce. Security governance involves implementing access controls, defining user permissions, and establishing protocols for data encryption and protection. Regularly reviewing and updating security measures helps safeguard against potential threats and ensures that sensitive information remains secure.

Another essential aspect of governance is performance

management. Monitoring the performance of the Salesforce environment helps identify any issues that may affect system efficiency or user experience. Performance management involves tracking key performance indicators (KPIs), such as system response times and user adoption rates. By analyzing these metrics, administrators can make informed decisions about system optimization and improvements.

Finally, maintaining alignment with organizational goals is crucial for effective governance. Salesforce governance should support the broader objectives of the organization and contribute to its overall success. This involves regularly reviewing the governance framework to ensure that it aligns with evolving business needs and strategic priorities. By ensuring that Salesforce initiatives are aligned with organizational goals, administrators can maximize the value of the platform and support the organization's long-term success.

In conclusion, implementing a comprehensive governance framework is essential for managing Salesforce effectively. By defining roles and responsibilities, developing policies and procedures, conducting regular reviews and audits, and focusing on key areas such as data and security governance, organizations can ensure that their Salesforce environment is well-managed and aligned with their strategic objectives. Effective communication, training, and performance management further contribute to the success of Salesforce governance, supporting a structured and sustainable approach to platform management.

As we conclude our exploration into Salesforce governance and best practices, it's crucial to address the role of continuous improvement within the governance framework. Maintaining a well-managed Salesforce environment is not a one-time endeavor but an ongoing process that requires regular evaluation and adaptation. By embracing a culture of continuous improvement, organizations can ensure that their Salesforce implementation remains effective, relevant, and aligned with evolving business needs.

To facilitate continuous improvement, it is important to establish a systematic approach for gathering feedback and assessing performance. This involves soliciting input from various stakeholders, including users, administrators, and executives. Feedback mechanisms such as surveys, focus groups, and one-on-one interviews can provide valuable insights into the effectiveness of the governance framework and identify areas for enhancement. By actively seeking and addressing feedback, organizations can make informed decisions about necessary adjustments and improvements.

Performance metrics and KPIs play a vital role in monitoring and evaluating the effectiveness of governance practices. Establishing relevant metrics allows organizations to track progress, measure success, and identify potential issues. Key performance indicators may include user adoption rates, system performance metrics, data quality scores, and compliance with governance policies. Regularly reviewing these metrics helps ensure that the Salesforce environment is meeting organizational goals and provides a basis for making data-driven improvements.

Change management remains a critical component of governance, particularly when it comes to implementing improvements. A structured change management process ensures that modifications to the Salesforce environment are carefully planned, tested, and communicated. This includes evaluating the impact of changes, obtaining necessary approvals, and documenting the process. By following a structured approach to change management, organizations can minimize disruptions and maintain the stability of their Salesforce environment.

In addition to performance metrics, best practices play a significant role in guiding effective governance. Adhering to industry best practices helps organizations avoid common pitfalls and leverage proven strategies for success. This includes following established guidelines for data management, security, user access, and system configuration. Staying informed about industry trends and updates to Salesforce features can also help organizations incorporate best practices into their governance framework.

Documentation is another key aspect of effective governance. Comprehensive documentation provides a clear record of governance policies, procedures, and decisions. This includes documenting roles and responsibilities, policies for data management and security, change management processes, and any other relevant information. Well-maintained documentation serves as a valuable reference for current and future administrators, ensuring consistency and continuity in governance practices.

Furthermore, training and education are essential for maintaining a well-managed Salesforce environment. Providing ongoing training for users, administrators, and stakeholders helps ensure that everyone is aware of governance policies and best practices. Training programs should be regularly updated to reflect changes in Salesforce features, governance practices, and organizational needs. By investing in education, organizations can enhance user proficiency, improve adherence to governance policies, and maximize the value of their Salesforce implementation.

Risk management is another important consideration in governance. Identifying and mitigating potential risks helps protect the Salesforce environment from potential threats and ensures its stability. Risk management involves assessing potential vulnerabilities, implementing preventive measures, and developing contingency plans. This includes addressing risks related to data security, system performance, and compliance with regulatory requirements.

As organizations evolve and their needs change, the governance framework should be reviewed and updated accordingly. Regularly revisiting the governance framework helps ensure that it remains aligned with organizational goals and adapts to new challenges and opportunities. This may involve revising policies, updating procedures, and incorporating feedback from stakeholders.

In conclusion, effective governance and best practices are fundamental to maintaining a well-managed Salesforce environment. By embracing a culture of continuous improvement, monitoring performance metrics, adhering to industry best practices, and investing in documentation and training, organizations can ensure the long-term success and sustainability of their Salesforce implementation. A structured approach to governance, combined with proactive risk management and regular reviews, supports a robust and resilient Salesforce environment that meets organizational objectives and drives business success.

CHAPTER 21: MANAGING CHANGE IN SALESFORCE

Managing change effectively is a cornerstone of successful Salesforce administration. As organizations evolve, so too must their Salesforce environments adapt to new requirements, features, and improvements. Properly managing these changes ensures that enhancements are integrated smoothly, user experience remains positive, and disruptions are minimized.

At the heart of change management in Salesforce is a well-structured change management process. This process begins with planning. Before initiating any changes, it is essential to conduct a thorough assessment of the proposed modifications. This includes understanding the scope of the change, its potential impact on the existing system, and the resources required for implementation. Planning involves creating a detailed change request, which outlines the objectives, benefits, risks, and dependencies associated with the change.

An effective change management plan should also include a change schedule. Scheduling is crucial to ensure that changes are implemented at a time that minimizes impact on business operations. This involves coordinating with various stakeholders to select an optimal time for deployment, considering factors such as peak usage periods and other ongoing projects. A well-defined schedule helps prevent conflicts and ensures that the change process aligns with organizational priorities.

Once planning is complete, the next step is communicating the change. Clear and transparent communication is vital for gaining stakeholder buy-in and ensuring a smooth transition. Effective communication involves not only informing users about the upcoming changes but also providing them with relevant information on how these changes will affect their work. This can be achieved through various channels such as email announcements, internal newsletters, and training sessions. It is important to address any concerns or questions that users may have and to provide them with the support they need during the transition.

Stakeholder engagement plays a significant role in the success of change management. Engaging stakeholders early in the process helps in understanding their needs and expectations, and allows for their input to be considered in the change plan. Stakeholders may include end-users, administrators, developers, and executives. Their feedback can provide valuable insights into potential issues and help in fine-tuning the change strategy. Engaging stakeholders also fosters a sense of ownership and acceptance, which can facilitate a smoother transition.

Testing is another critical component of change management. Before deploying changes to the production environment, it is essential to conduct thorough testing in a staging or sandbox environment. Testing helps identify any potential issues or conflicts that may arise from the change. This includes functional testing to ensure that the change works as intended, as well as performance testing to assess its impact on system performance. Involving end-users in the testing process can also provide additional validation and help in identifying any usability concerns.

Following testing, the implementation phase involves deploying the change to the production environment. It is important to have a detailed implementation plan that includes specific steps, responsibilities, and timelines. During implementation, close monitoring is essential to address any issues that may arise promptly. Having a rollback plan in place is also crucial in case the change needs to be reverted due to unforeseen problems.

After the change has been implemented, conducting a post-implementation review is necessary to evaluate its effectiveness and address any issues that may have surfaced. The review should assess whether the change met its objectives, whether it has introduced any new issues, and how it has impacted users. Gathering feedback from users and stakeholders during this review can provide valuable insights for future changes and help in refining the change management process.

Training and support are vital for ensuring that users can effectively adapt to changes. Providing training sessions, user guides, and support resources helps users understand how to use new features or adjustments. Ongoing support is also important for addressing any questions or issues that users may encounter after the change has been implemented. By offering comprehensive training and support, organizations can enhance user satisfaction and reduce resistance to change.

Documentation is a key aspect of change management. Documenting the change management process, including planning, communication, testing, implementation, and post-implementation reviews, provides a clear record of the change process. This documentation serves as a reference for future changes and helps ensure consistency in change management practices.

In summary, managing change in Salesforce requires a

structured approach that includes careful planning, effective communication, stakeholder engagement, rigorous testing, and thorough documentation. By following these practices, organizations can ensure that changes are smoothly integrated into their Salesforce environment, enhancing the overall user experience and supporting business objectives.

When navigating the complexities of change management in Salesforce, a key aspect I focus on is the alignment of changes with organizational goals and user needs. This alignment ensures that any modifications made to the Salesforce environment are not only technically sound but also strategically beneficial. To achieve this, I engage in detailed discussions with stakeholders to understand their requirements and expectations. By integrating their feedback into the planning process, I can design changes that meet their needs while also aligning with the broader objectives of the organization.

Another critical component of managing change is the development and execution of a comprehensive testing strategy. Testing is crucial for identifying potential issues before changes are rolled out to the entire user base. I start by creating a testing plan that includes various types of tests, such as unit testing, integration testing, and user acceptance testing (UAT). Unit testing focuses on individual components or features to ensure they work correctly in isolation. Integration testing, on the other hand, examines how new changes interact with existing components and workflows. User acceptance testing involves end-users testing the changes in a controlled environment to ensure that they meet their expectations and requirements.

To effectively manage the testing process, I establish a test environment that mirrors the production environment as closely as possible. This allows for accurate testing of changes without affecting the live system. During testing, I closely monitor the results and address any issues that arise. This iterative process helps to refine the changes and ensure they are robust before they are deployed to the production environment.

As I prepare for deployment, I also focus on creating a rollback plan. A rollback plan outlines the steps to revert changes if something goes wrong during deployment. This plan is crucial for minimizing disruptions and ensuring that the system remains stable. I document the rollback procedures and ensure that all team members are familiar with them. This preparation allows for a quick response in case of any unforeseen issues during deployment.

Deployment itself is carried out in a structured manner to minimize risk and ensure a smooth transition. I typically use deployment tools and processes that automate and streamline the deployment process. For instance, using Salesforce Change Sets or deployment tools like Salesforce DX can help manage the deployment of changes across different environments. These tools allow for version control, automate repetitive tasks, and provide visibility into the deployment process.

During deployment, I closely monitor the system for any immediate issues and maintain open communication with stakeholders. This ensures that any problems are addressed promptly and that users are kept informed about the status of the deployment. I also provide support resources to help users navigate any changes and address any questions or concerns they may have.

After deployment, the focus shifts to monitoring and support. I continue to track the performance of the changes and gather feedback from users. This ongoing monitoring helps identify any issues that may not have been apparent during testing. I also remain available to provide support and address any issues that users encounter. This support is essential for ensuring a positive user experience and for resolving any issues that may arise post-deployment.

Additionally, I conduct a post-implementation review to assess the success of the changes. This review involves evaluating whether the changes met their objectives, analyzing any issues encountered, and gathering feedback from users. The insights gained from this review are valuable for informing future change management efforts and for continuous improvement.

In summary, managing change in Salesforce involves a multifaceted approach that includes planning, testing, deployment, and post-implementation support. By aligning changes with organizational goals, engaging in thorough testing, creating a rollback plan, and maintaining open communication with stakeholders, I can effectively manage changes and ensure their successful integration into the Salesforce environment. This comprehensive approach not only minimizes disruptions but also maximizes the benefits of the changes, contributing to a more efficient and effective Salesforce system.

As I move through the process of managing change in Salesforce, it becomes apparent that communication plays a pivotal role in ensuring the success of any changes implemented. Effective communication with stakeholders throughout the change management process helps to build trust, manage expectations, and address concerns proactively. I prioritize creating a detailed communication plan that outlines how and when information about changes will be shared with different groups, including end-users, project managers, and executive sponsors.

The communication plan typically includes a schedule for regular updates, key messages to be conveyed, and channels for delivering information. For instance, I might use email newsletters, internal memos, and team meetings to provide updates on the progress of changes. Additionally, I establish feedback mechanisms, such as surveys or discussion forums, to allow stakeholders to voice their opinions and ask questions. This two-way communication ensures that I stay informed about any issues or concerns that arise and can address them promptly.

Another critical aspect of change management is managing user training and support. I recognize that changes to Salesforce can impact users' workflows and require them to adapt to new processes or features. To facilitate a smooth transition, I develop training materials and conduct training sessions tailored to the needs of different user groups. These sessions might include hands-on workshops, instructional videos, or detailed user guides, depending on the complexity of the changes and the audience's familiarity with Salesforce.

I also make sure to provide ongoing support after the changes are implemented. This support includes setting up a helpdesk or support team to assist users with any issues they encounter and offering additional training or resources as needed. By being responsive to user needs and providing timely assistance, I can help users adapt more quickly to the changes and minimize disruptions to their work.

In addition to managing user training and support, I focus on measuring the impact of the changes on business processes and performance. I define key performance indicators (KPIs) that align with the objectives of the changes and use them to assess whether the changes are achieving the desired outcomes. For example, if the goal of a change is to improve sales reporting, I might measure improvements in report accuracy, the time taken to generate reports, and user satisfaction with the reporting process. By analyzing these metrics, I can determine whether the changes are effective and identify areas for further improvement.

Post-implementation reviews are an essential part of this process. I conduct these reviews to evaluate the overall success of the changes and to gather insights for future change management efforts. During the review, I assess whether the changes met their objectives, analyze any issues or challenges encountered, and gather feedback from users. This feedback helps to identify lessons learned and best practices that can be applied to future changes.

I also document the outcomes of the review and share them with relevant stakeholders. This documentation serves as a reference for future projects and helps to ensure that successful strategies and practices are maintained. It also provides an opportunity to acknowledge the contributions of team members and stakeholders, reinforcing their involvement and support in the change process.

Finally, I consider the importance of continuous improvement in change management. The landscape of Salesforce and the needs of the organization are always evolving, and it is essential to stay adaptable and responsive to these changes. I regularly review and update change management processes and practices to incorporate new insights, technologies, and methodologies. This proactive approach helps to ensure that change management remains effective and aligned with the organization's goals and needs.

In summary, managing change in Salesforce requires a comprehensive approach that includes effective communication, user training and support, impact measurement, post-implementation reviews, and continuous improvement. By focusing on these aspects, I can ensure that changes are smoothly integrated, accepted by users, and aligned with organizational objectives. This thorough and strategic approach to change management not only facilitates successful transitions but also enhances the overall effectiveness and efficiency of the Salesforce environment.

CHAPTER 22: ADVANCED DATA MANAGEMENT TECHNIQUES

In the realm of Salesforce, managing data efficiently becomes increasingly complex as the volume and diversity of data grow. To address these challenges, advanced data management techniques are essential. This section focuses on three key areas: data partitioning, data archiving, and advanced deduplication methods. Each technique plays a crucial role in maintaining data integrity and optimizing system performance.

When discussing data partitioning, it is vital to understand that partitioning involves dividing a large dataset into smaller, more manageable subsets. This strategy improves performance and makes data management more efficient. In Salesforce, data partitioning can be particularly beneficial for organizations dealing with extensive records or complex datasets. By segmenting data based on certain criteria—such as geographical regions, business units, or data types—I can enhance query performance and reduce the load on system resources.

For instance, if a company operates in multiple regions, partitioning data by geographic location allows for more efficient data retrieval and reporting. Each region's data is isolated, which can streamline operations and improve the speed of searches and reports. In Salesforce, this can be achieved by using custom fields or objects to categorize data, and by leveraging Salesforce's data storage options to keep these subsets separate.

Data archiving is another crucial aspect of advanced data management. Over time, Salesforce environments accumulate vast amounts of historical data that may no longer be actively used but still need to be retained for compliance or reference purposes. Archiving involves moving this less frequently accessed data from the main system into a separate storage solution. This helps to keep the primary database uncluttered and improves overall system performance.

To implement an effective data archiving strategy, I first identify the criteria for determining which data should be archived. This might include data that has not been accessed for a certain period or data related to completed projects or closed deals. Once the criteria are established, I can use Salesforce's data export tools or third-party solutions to extract and store this data securely. It's also important to ensure that archived data remains accessible for audits or compliance checks, which can be achieved by maintaining a well-documented archiving process and implementing appropriate retrieval mechanisms.

Advanced deduplication methods are essential for ensuring data integrity and optimizing database performance. Duplicate records can lead to inaccurate reporting, inefficient workflows, and increased storage costs. Salesforce provides built-in tools for identifying and merging duplicate records, but for more complex scenarios, advanced techniques are required. These techniques may involve custom deduplication algorithms or integrating with third-party applications that offer more sophisticated deduplication capabilities.

When implementing advanced deduplication methods, I start by defining the criteria for identifying duplicates. This might involve matching records based on multiple fields or using fuzzy matching algorithms to account for variations in data. Once duplicates are identified, I carefully review and merge them to avoid data loss. It's also important to establish processes for ongoing deduplication to prevent new duplicates from entering the system. Regularly scheduled data quality audits and employing data cleansing tools can help maintain a clean and accurate database.

Combining these advanced techniques—data partitioning, data archiving, and deduplication—provides a comprehensive approach to managing Salesforce data effectively. Each technique addresses specific challenges and contributes to a more organized and performant system. By implementing these strategies, I can ensure that Salesforce remains responsive and scalable, even as data volumes and complexity increase.

In practice, the successful application of these techniques requires a thorough understanding of the organization's data needs and usage patterns. I work closely with stakeholders to identify their requirements and tailor the data management strategies accordingly. This collaborative approach helps to ensure that the solutions implemented are both practical and aligned with the organization's overall objectives.

By focusing on these advanced data management techniques, I can maintain data integrity, optimize system performance, and support the organization's evolving needs. This approach not only improves the efficiency of data handling but also enhances the reliability and accuracy of the information used for decision-making and operational processes.

When addressing advanced data management techniques in Salesforce, it is essential to delve deeper into how these strategies not only address immediate data challenges but also contribute to long-term system health and operational efficiency.

To elaborate further on data partitioning, this technique is not merely about splitting data into smaller chunks; it involves a thoughtful design to ensure that each partition serves a specific purpose and optimizes system performance. In Salesforce, effective data partitioning often requires a clear understanding of the data's use cases and access patterns. For instance, if the data involves customer interactions, partitioning by business units or regions can significantly enhance performance by reducing the search space for queries.

A practical example of implementing data partitioning in Salesforce could involve setting up multiple custom objects to handle different types of data or using record types to segregate data within a single object. For instance, if an organization deals with customer support cases, partitioning these cases based on urgency or status can streamline the process of tracking and resolving them. This approach also helps in maintaining a cleaner database by ensuring that each partition only contains relevant data, which in turn improves the performance of both data retrieval and reporting.

Transitioning to data archiving, it's important to implement a robust strategy for managing historical data. The archiving process involves more than just moving data to a different location; it requires establishing policies and procedures for how data is archived, retrieved, and maintained. For example, an effective data archiving strategy might involve creating a separate data warehouse or using cloud storage solutions specifically designed for long-term data retention.

When archiving data, I first define the criteria for what constitutes archival-worthy data. This could be based on data age, relevance, or regulatory requirements. Once the criteria are set, I utilize Salesforce's built-in tools or third-party solutions to export and store this data securely. It is crucial to ensure that the archived data is easily retrievable if needed for future reference or compliance purposes. Implementing a clear indexing and metadata system helps in quickly locating and accessing archived data without impacting the primary system's performance.

Advanced deduplication methods require a strategic approach to maintain data quality. While Salesforce provides native tools for deduplication, more sophisticated scenarios necessitate additional strategies. Advanced deduplication involves not only identifying and merging duplicates but also preventing their recurrence. This can be achieved by setting up validation rules, employing advanced algorithms, or integrating with specialized deduplication tools.

In practice, I often begin by analyzing the data to identify common sources of duplication. This analysis might reveal patterns or conditions under which duplicates are created, such as during data imports or integrations. Based on this analysis, I implement custom deduplication logic or leverage external tools that offer more granular control over the deduplication process. For example, a third-party deduplication service might provide fuzzy matching capabilities that can detect duplicates even when there are slight variations in the data.

To ensure ongoing data quality, I establish regular data cleansing routines and monitor for new duplicates. This proactive approach helps to maintain a high level of data accuracy and reliability. By integrating deduplication processes into regular data maintenance schedules, I can prevent data quality issues from escalating and ensure that the database remains clean and efficient.

Advanced data management techniques in Salesforce are not

just about applying these strategies in isolation but about integrating them into a holistic data management framework. This framework should include best practices for data governance, quality assurance, and continuous improvement. By adopting a comprehensive approach, I can effectively manage large volumes of data, support complex data requirements, and optimize system performance.

Ultimately, these advanced techniques are about more than just technical implementation; they are about aligning data management practices with the organization's goals and ensuring that the data infrastructure supports both current and future needs. By focusing on data partitioning, archiving, and deduplication, I can enhance the efficiency, accuracy, and scalability of Salesforce data management, thereby supporting the organization's success and growth.

As I continue exploring advanced data management techniques in Salesforce, it's crucial to consider how these methods can be integrated into a broader data management strategy that addresses both current and future needs. To maintain data integrity and optimize performance effectively, one must understand and apply these techniques in a nuanced way.

A significant aspect of managing Salesforce data involves addressing the challenges posed by growing data volumes and evolving business requirements. Implementing data partitioning helps alleviate performance issues by distributing data across different segments, but it's also essential to ensure that these partitions are designed to scale as the data grows. For instance, in a scenario where a company manages sales data from multiple regions, partitioning the data by region ensures that queries related to specific regions do not suffer from performance degradation due to excessive data volume. However, it's important to continuously evaluate and adjust the partitioning strategy as the data and business needs evolve.

To achieve this, I regularly review data access patterns and usage statistics to determine if the existing partitioning strategy remains effective. This involves analyzing query performance and identifying any bottlenecks that may indicate a need for re-partitioning or adjustments in the existing partition scheme. Additionally, I employ tools like Salesforce's Analytics Cloud or third-party performance monitoring solutions to gather insights into data usage and performance metrics.

When it comes to data archiving, the primary goal is to efficiently manage historical data without compromising on accessibility and compliance. Beyond the initial setup of an archiving strategy, ongoing management is key to ensuring that archived data remains relevant and accessible. This includes establishing a clear process for handling data retrieval requests and ensuring that archived data is indexed and searchable.

In practice, I implement data retention policies that align with legal and regulatory requirements, as well as business needs. For example, if an organization needs to retain customer interaction data for several years for compliance reasons, I create an archiving plan that includes both automated and manual processes for data retention. This plan often involves periodic reviews of the archived data to ensure that it meets the required standards and that retrieval processes are functioning correctly.

Advanced deduplication is another critical aspect of maintaining data integrity. While native deduplication tools in Salesforce provide a solid foundation, handling more complex scenarios often requires additional measures. For example, duplicate records might arise from data imports, integrations, or user errors. To address this, I implement custom deduplication logic using Salesforce's Apex code or external tools that offer advanced matching algorithms.

A practical approach involves creating a comprehensive deduplication strategy that includes both real-time and batch processes. For instance, I set up real-time deduplication rules to prevent the creation of duplicates at the point of data entry. Simultaneously, I schedule regular batch processes to identify and merge existing duplicates. This dual approach ensures that new duplicates are prevented while existing data remains clean and accurate.

Furthermore, I integrate deduplication processes into data import and integration workflows to ensure that duplicate records are identified and handled before they enter the system. This might involve using data integration tools that include built-in deduplication features or developing custom solutions to handle specific deduplication requirements.

As part of a comprehensive data management strategy, it's also essential to consider data governance practices. Data governance encompasses the policies and procedures that ensure data is managed effectively and remains accurate, secure, and compliant with regulations. By implementing strong data governance practices, I ensure that advanced data management techniques are applied consistently and that data quality is maintained across the organization.

This includes defining clear data ownership and stewardship roles, establishing data quality metrics, and creating processes for data validation and cleansing. Additionally, I ensure that data management practices are documented and communicated to all relevant stakeholders to support transparency and accountability.

By integrating data partitioning, archiving, and deduplication techniques with robust data governance practices, I create a data management framework that not only addresses current challenges but also prepares the organization for future growth. This holistic approach ensures that Salesforce data remains reliable, accessible, and optimized for performance, ultimately supporting the organization's operational efficiency and strategic goals.

CHAPTER 23: SALESFORCE APPEXCHANGE: FINDING AND IMPLEMENTING APPS

Salesforce AppExchange is an invaluable resource for expanding the capabilities of your Salesforce environment. With thousands of third-party applications available, it provides solutions that can enhance functionality, streamline processes, and drive greater efficiency within your organization. To effectively utilize AppExchange, it is crucial to understand how to find, evaluate, and implement these applications in a way that aligns with your business needs and objectives.

The process of finding the right app begins with a clear understanding of your organizational requirements and the specific challenges you aim to address. The AppExchange marketplace offers a variety of applications, ranging from simple tools that enhance existing features to complex solutions that integrate new functionalities into Salesforce. To start, I first identify the key areas where enhancements are needed. This might involve improving data management, automating workflows, or integrating with other systems.

Navigating the AppExchange requires a strategic approach. The marketplace provides several filters and search options to narrow down the selection based on categories, such as sales, service, marketing, and more. Additionally, I use keywords related to the specific problem or need that I am addressing. For example, if my goal is to enhance customer service capabilities, I might search for apps that offer advanced ticketing systems or customer support integrations.

Once potential apps are identified, the next step is to evaluate their suitability. This evaluation process involves examining several key factors. First, I review the app's description, features, and benefits as outlined on its AppExchange listing. This includes understanding the specific functionality it offers, how it integrates with Salesforce, and the overall value it can add to the organization.

User reviews and ratings are also instrumental in this evaluation process. They provide insights into other customers' experiences with the app, including its reliability, ease of use, and customer support quality. I pay close attention to reviews that mention similar use cases to mine, as they can offer valuable perspectives on how well the app performs in real-world scenarios.

Another critical aspect is the app's vendor. Assessing the credibility and reputation of the vendor can help determine the app's reliability and the level of support you can expect. I review the vendor's history, their other available apps, and any available support documentation. Vendors with a track record of successful deployments and active support teams are generally more reliable.

After selecting an app, the next phase is installation and configuration. The AppExchange offers detailed installation guides and support resources for most applications. I follow these guides carefully to ensure a smooth installation process.

This typically involves adding the app to your Salesforce environment, configuring settings, and integrating it with existing Salesforce features and data.

Configuration might require tailoring the app to meet specific organizational needs. This could include setting up custom fields, adjusting workflows, or defining user permissions. During this phase, I work closely with key stakeholders to ensure that the app's configuration aligns with their requirements and that any necessary training is provided.

Integration is a crucial part of the implementation process. Many apps need to interact with existing Salesforce objects and processes. I use Salesforce's integration tools and APIs to facilitate seamless communication between the app and the Salesforce platform. This might involve configuring data synchronization, setting up automated triggers, or integrating with other systems.

Ensuring that the app aligns with business objectives is an ongoing process. Post-implementation, I continuously monitor the app's performance and gather feedback from users. This feedback helps identify any issues or areas for improvement. Regular reviews ensure that the app continues to meet organizational needs and adapts to any changes in business processes.

Lastly, I establish a process for managing updates and upgrades. Many apps receive periodic updates that introduce new features or enhancements. Keeping the app up-to-date is essential for maintaining compatibility with Salesforce and taking advantage of the latest functionalities. I follow best practices for managing app updates, including testing updates in a sandbox environment before deploying them to production.

By carefully selecting, evaluating, and implementing apps from the AppExchange, I can significantly enhance the capabilities of my Salesforce environment. This process not only improves operational efficiency but also ensures that the solutions adopted are well-integrated and aligned with the strategic goals of the organization.

Finding the right applications on Salesforce AppExchange is just the beginning of a successful integration process. Once you have identified a potential app, the next critical step involves a thorough evaluation to ensure that it meets your needs and integrates seamlessly with your existing Salesforce environment.

My approach to evaluating an app starts with a detailed examination of its documentation. Each app on AppExchange comes with a range of resources, including user guides, feature lists, and demo videos. These resources offer insight into how the app functions and its key benefits. By reviewing these materials, I can determine whether the app's features align with the specific requirements of my organization.

Next, I delve into the app's compatibility with our current Salesforce setup. This includes checking its compatibility with our Salesforce edition, understanding any additional system requirements, and verifying that it integrates with the customizations and configurations already in place. For example, if our Salesforce environment uses custom objects or workflows, I ensure that the app can interact with these elements without causing conflicts.

A crucial part of this evaluation is assessing the app's performance and scalability. I look for information about how the app handles large volumes of data and whether it scales efficiently as our needs grow. Performance metrics and benchmarks provided by the vendor or gathered from user reviews help in understanding how well the app will perform under different conditions.

User feedback is another significant factor in the evaluation process. AppExchange provides user reviews and ratings that can offer a glimpse into the real-world experiences of others who have used the app. I carefully analyze these reviews, paying attention to recurring themes, such as ease of use, support quality, and the app's impact on productivity. Reviews that highlight specific issues or challenges are particularly valuable, as they can help anticipate and address potential problems before implementation.

The vendor's support and maintenance practices are also critical considerations. I research the vendor's reputation and track record in providing timely updates, bug fixes, and customer support. An app's support structure is vital for addressing any issues that arise during and after implementation. I check for available support channels, such as online forums, direct customer service, and detailed documentation.

Once I have thoroughly evaluated an app and determined that it aligns with our needs, the next step is the installation and configuration process. Installation typically begins with adding the app to our Salesforce environment via the AppExchange interface. This process is usually straightforward, but it's essential to follow the installation guide provided by the vendor to ensure that all necessary components are correctly installed.

After installation, configuring the app to fit our specific requirements is crucial. Configuration involves setting up the app to work seamlessly with our existing Salesforce data and processes. This may include customizing settings, creating user profiles, and defining data access permissions. I collaborate with relevant stakeholders to gather input and ensure that the configuration aligns with their needs and expectations.

Integration with existing Salesforce features and other

systems is another key aspect of the implementation process. Many apps require integration with Salesforce objects, workflows, or external systems. I use Salesforce's integration tools and APIs to facilitate this process, ensuring that data flows smoothly between the app and Salesforce. This may involve setting up data synchronization, configuring automated processes, or integrating with third-party applications.

Monitoring the app's performance and user feedback post-implementation is essential for ensuring ongoing success. I track key performance indicators, such as system uptime, user satisfaction, and the app's impact on operational efficiency. Gathering feedback from users helps identify any issues or areas for improvement, allowing for timely adjustments and enhancements.

Managing updates and upgrades is a final, but ongoing, aspect of maintaining the app's effectiveness. Vendors frequently release updates that introduce new features, enhancements, or bug fixes. It's important to stay informed about these updates and plan for their implementation. I typically test updates in a sandbox environment before deploying them to the production system to minimize potential disruptions.

By carefully evaluating, installing, configuring, and integrating apps from the AppExchange, I ensure that these tools enhance our Salesforce environment effectively and align with our strategic goals. This methodical approach helps maximize the value of our investments in Salesforce applications and supports our broader organizational objectives.

To ensure that applications from the Salesforce AppExchange are fully integrated and utilized effectively, it's crucial to have a structured approach to their deployment and ongoing management. Following the installation and initial configuration, attention must turn to how these applications are adopted and leveraged within the organization.

One key aspect is user training and onboarding. As new applications are introduced into our Salesforce environment, I prioritize educating users on their functionalities and benefits. Effective training sessions cover both the basics of the application and more advanced features that could enhance their workflows. Providing users with comprehensive training materials, such as user guides, video tutorials, and FAQs, ensures they are well-equipped to use the new tools efficiently. Regular training sessions and refreshers help maintain proficiency and adapt to any updates or changes in the application.

Additionally, I develop a support plan to assist users as they transition to using the new app. This involves setting up a helpdesk or support team that can address any questions or issues that arise. An effective support plan also includes creating a feedback loop where users can report problems and suggest improvements. This feedback is invaluable for refining the application's use and addressing any unexpected challenges.

Performance monitoring of the app is another critical component of the management process. After implementation, I closely monitor the app's impact on system performance and user productivity. This involves tracking metrics such as load times, error rates, and system integration efficiency. Utilizing Salesforce's built-in analytics tools, I can assess how well the app is performing and identify any areas where optimization may be required.

Regular performance reviews and system audits are conducted to ensure that the app continues to meet its intended objectives. During these reviews, I analyze the app's effectiveness in addressing the needs it was designed to meet and evaluate whether it has contributed to achieving business goals. These reviews help in identifying any adjustments needed to enhance the app's performance or to address any issues that may have arisen.

In parallel, I manage the lifecycle of the app by keeping track of its updates and changes. Vendors frequently release new versions of their applications, which may include bug fixes, new features, or performance improvements. Staying up-to-date with these releases ensures that our environment benefits from the latest advancements and maintains compatibility with other system components. I typically test new versions in a controlled environment before deploying them to production to mitigate any risks of disruption.

Furthermore, I engage in periodic reviews of the app's integration with other systems and processes. This ensures that any changes in our Salesforce environment or related systems do not negatively impact the app's functionality. Maintaining robust integration involves updating configurations and addressing any compatibility issues that arise from system changes or upgrades.

In cases where the app no longer meets the organization's needs or where a more suitable solution is identified, I manage the transition process for removing or replacing the app. This includes decommissioning the application in a manner that preserves data integrity and ensures a smooth handover to new systems. It's important to follow a structured decommissioning plan that includes data migration or backup procedures, updating system documentation, and communicating with stakeholders about the changes.

Throughout the lifecycle of an app, maintaining alignment with business objectives is crucial. I regularly revisit the goals and objectives that led to the app's selection and assess whether it continues to contribute value. This strategic alignment ensures that our investments in applications support overall business goals and adapt to any changes in organizational priorities.

By focusing on these aspects, I ensure that applications from the AppExchange are not only successfully integrated but also continually optimized to deliver maximum value. This comprehensive approach to deployment, management, and ongoing evaluation helps in leveraging these tools effectively, ultimately enhancing our Salesforce environment and supporting our organizational objectives.

CHAPTER 24: INTEGRATING SALESFORCE WITH EXTERNAL SYSTEMS

Integrating Salesforce with external systems is a crucial aspect of modern business operations, allowing for a unified and streamlined approach to managing data across diverse platforms. To achieve effective integration, it is important to understand the various integration options available, including APIs, middleware, and data connectors. This section delves into these integration methods, offering a comprehensive understanding of how to set up and manage these connections to ensure seamless communication between Salesforce and other business applications.

Salesforce's robust API capabilities are central to its integration strategy. The Salesforce API allows for programmatic access to Salesforce data, enabling other systems to read, write, and update Salesforce records. To begin, it's essential to familiarize oneself with Salesforce's API offerings, including REST API, SOAP API, and Bulk API. Each API serves different purposes and scenarios. The REST API is ideal for web and mobile applications that require access to Salesforce data, while the SOAP API is suited for enterprise-level integrations where strong data typing is necessary. The Bulk API is designed for handling large volumes of data efficiently.

Setting up an API integration involves several key steps. Initially, I configure the API settings within Salesforce, including creating a connected app to obtain the necessary credentials such as client ID and client secret. Next, I develop the integration code using the appropriate API endpoints and methods, ensuring that it adheres to Salesforce's security and data handling standards. It's crucial to handle authentication properly, often through OAuth, to secure the data exchanged between systems.

In addition to direct API integrations, middleware solutions offer a powerful way to connect Salesforce with external systems. Middleware platforms, such as MuleSoft, Dell Boomi, and Jitterbit, act as intermediaries that facilitate data exchange between Salesforce and other applications. Middleware can simplify complex integrations by providing pre-built connectors, transformation capabilities, and centralized management of integration workflows.

When using middleware, I start by configuring the integration flows within the middleware platform. This involves mapping fields between Salesforce and the external system, setting up transformation rules to ensure data consistency, and establishing error-handling mechanisms. Middleware platforms often come with dashboards and monitoring tools that allow me to track the performance of integrations and troubleshoot any issues that arise.

Data connectors also play a significant role in integrating Salesforce with external systems. These connectors are pre-built solutions that facilitate the integration process by providing ready-to-use connections between Salesforce and popular business applications such as ERP systems, marketing platforms, and financial software. Data connectors can significantly reduce the time and effort required to implement integrations, as they come with built-in functionalities tailored to specific applications.

Implementing data connectors involves selecting the appropriate connector for the external system and configuring it to work with Salesforce. I need to ensure that the connector settings are properly aligned with the requirements of both Salesforce and the external application. This typically includes configuring authentication credentials, defining data synchronization rules, and mapping data fields.

To ensure seamless integration, it's important to address several key considerations. Data consistency and accuracy are paramount, as discrepancies between systems can lead to significant issues. I implement data validation and error-checking mechanisms to ensure that data exchanged between Salesforce and external systems remains accurate and consistent.

Monitoring and managing the performance of integrations is another critical aspect. I utilize Salesforce's integration monitoring tools and middleware platform dashboards to track the status of integration processes. This includes monitoring for failed transactions, latency issues, and data synchronization errors. Regularly reviewing integration logs and reports helps in identifying and addressing potential issues proactively.

Security is also a major concern when integrating Salesforce with external systems. I ensure that all data exchanges are encrypted and that access controls are in place to protect sensitive information. Properly configuring authentication methods and adhering to Salesforce's security guidelines helps in mitigating potential security risks associated with data integration.

Finally, I conduct thorough testing before deploying integrations to a production environment. This involves running test scenarios to validate the integration's functionality and performance under various conditions. Testing helps in identifying any potential issues and ensures that the integration meets the desired business requirements.

By following these practices and leveraging Salesforce's integration capabilities, I can effectively connect Salesforce with external systems, enhancing its functionality and ensuring seamless data flow across business applications. This comprehensive approach to integration enables organizations to achieve greater efficiency and cohesion in their operations.

To effectively integrate Salesforce with external systems, one must delve into the technical and strategic aspects of data exchange and system interoperability. Building on the fundamentals of API and middleware integration, it is important to explore how these components work together to create a cohesive data ecosystem.

When setting up API-based integrations, I often start by defining the requirements for the data exchange. This involves identifying which external systems need to communicate with Salesforce and what data needs to be exchanged. The next step is to design the integration architecture, ensuring that it aligns with both Salesforce's and the external system's data models and security requirements. This includes mapping out the data flow and defining the endpoints for the API calls.

Salesforce provides robust tools for managing API connections. For instance, Salesforce's Developer Console and Workbench are invaluable for testing API requests and responses. These tools allow me to simulate API calls, validate responses, and troubleshoot issues before fully implementing the integration. It's also crucial to adhere to API best practices, such as implementing efficient query mechanisms and handling rate limits to avoid performance bottlenecks.

In many scenarios, using middleware platforms becomes

necessary to handle complex integrations involving multiple systems or when dealing with systems that do not offer robust API support. Middleware solutions act as a bridge, enabling seamless data transfer and synchronization between Salesforce and other applications. They provide features such as data transformation, orchestration, and error handling that simplify the integration process.

One effective strategy is to leverage pre-built connectors offered by middleware platforms. These connectors are designed to integrate with popular third-party systems like ERP solutions, marketing automation tools, and customer service platforms. By using these connectors, I can streamline the integration process, reduce development time, and ensure compatibility with industry standards.

When configuring middleware, I start by setting up integration flows that define how data moves between systems. This often involves specifying triggers and actions, such as how data should be pushed from Salesforce to an external CRM system or how customer information should be pulled from an ERP system into Salesforce. Middleware platforms usually offer visual design tools that make it easier to map data fields and configure data transformations.

Another important consideration is data synchronization. Ensuring that data remains consistent across systems is crucial for maintaining data integrity. I use synchronization mechanisms provided by middleware platforms to regularly update records and handle conflicts. For example, I can configure the system to update Salesforce records in real-time whenever changes occur in the external system or vice versa.

Data connectors are another key tool in the integration toolkit, providing out-of-the-box solutions for connecting Salesforce with external systems. These connectors are particularly useful for integrating with applications that have established interfaces and standardized data formats. For instance, connectors for financial systems can facilitate the exchange of transaction data, while connectors for marketing platforms can synchronize lead and campaign information.

Implementing data connectors involves configuring the connector settings to match the requirements of both Salesforce and the external system. This typically includes setting up authentication credentials, defining data mapping rules, and scheduling data transfer intervals. Many data connectors come with user-friendly interfaces that simplify configuration and management.

As with any integration effort, security remains a top priority. I ensure that all data exchanged between Salesforce and external systems is encrypted, both in transit and at rest. Implementing robust authentication mechanisms, such as OAuth or API keys, helps protect against unauthorized access. Additionally, I review and follow best practices for securing integration endpoints and managing access controls.

Monitoring and maintaining integrations is an ongoing task. I use Salesforce's built-in monitoring tools, along with those provided by middleware and data connector platforms, to track the performance and health of integrations. Regularly reviewing logs, performance metrics, and error reports allows me to identify and address potential issues before they impact operations.

Testing is a critical phase in the integration process. Before going live, I conduct extensive testing to ensure that the integration works as expected and meets business requirements. This includes functional testing to verify that data flows correctly between systems, as well as performance testing to ensure that the integration can handle expected data volumes and load.

In summary, integrating Salesforce with external systems

involves a thorough understanding of various integration methods, including APIs, middleware, and data connectors. By carefully planning and executing these integrations, I can enhance Salesforce's functionality, improve data flow, and ensure that the system works seamlessly with other business applications. This comprehensive approach enables organizations to maximize the value of their Salesforce investment and achieve greater operational efficiency.

In the integration process, ensuring that data remains accurate and synchronized across systems is vital for maintaining operational efficiency and data integrity. A key aspect of this is dealing with data consistency issues that can arise when integrating Salesforce with external systems. To address these issues, I employ various strategies and best practices to ensure that data remains reliable and up-to-date.

One approach I use is to implement data validation rules and error handling mechanisms both in Salesforce and within the external systems. By setting up these rules, I can catch inconsistencies or errors in data as it is transferred between systems. For example, if an external system sends data to Salesforce that does not meet the predefined criteria, the integration process can be configured to flag this data and either correct it automatically or notify the relevant personnel for manual review.

Additionally, implementing automated data reconciliation processes helps to identify and resolve discrepancies between Salesforce and external systems. This involves setting up regular data checks and comparisons to ensure that records match across all integrated platforms. Automated tools can facilitate this reconciliation by comparing data sets and generating reports on any discrepancies, which I can then address accordingly.

Another critical consideration in integration is handling different data formats and structures between Salesforce and external systems. Data transformation tools and middleware solutions play a crucial role in this regard. They allow me to map data fields between systems, convert data formats as needed, and ensure that data is accurately translated during the integration process. This transformation capability is particularly important when dealing with systems that use different data schemas or encoding methods.

As I work through the integration process, I also pay close attention to the performance and scalability of the integration solutions. This involves evaluating how well the integration handles various data volumes and how it impacts the performance of Salesforce and the external systems. To optimize performance, I use techniques such as batching large data transfers, implementing efficient query mechanisms, and monitoring integration performance metrics to identify and address any potential bottlenecks.

Testing remains a fundamental part of the integration process. I conduct extensive testing to validate that the integration behaves as expected under different scenarios. This includes unit testing individual components of the integration, integration testing to ensure that different systems work together seamlessly, and user acceptance testing to verify that the integration meets the end users' needs. Each of these testing phases helps to identify and resolve any issues before the integration goes live.

Post-implementation, ongoing support and maintenance are essential for ensuring the long-term success of the integration. I establish a regular maintenance schedule to review the performance of the integration, address any issues that arise, and make updates as necessary. This proactive approach helps to prevent integration problems from escalating and ensures that the integration continues to function smoothly as systems and business requirements evolve.

Moreover, user training and support are critical to the successful adoption of integrated systems. I provide training sessions for users to familiarize them with the new workflows and functionalities introduced by the integration. Additionally, I set up support channels to assist users with any questions or issues they may encounter. By ensuring that users are well-informed and supported, I can facilitate a smoother transition and maximize the benefits of the integration.

Documentation is another important aspect of managing integrations. I maintain comprehensive documentation that includes details on the integration architecture, data mappings, configuration settings, and troubleshooting procedures. This documentation serves as a valuable resource for understanding the integration setup and for addressing any issues that may arise in the future.

In summary, successfully integrating Salesforce with external systems involves a multi-faceted approach that includes addressing data consistency, handling different data formats, optimizing performance, and ensuring ongoing support and maintenance. By carefully planning, implementing, and managing these integrations, I can enhance Salesforce's capabilities, improve data flow, and achieve seamless communication between Salesforce and other business applications. This meticulous approach not only maximizes the value of Salesforce but also supports overall business efficiency and effectiveness.

CHAPTER 25: MANAGING SALESFORCE USERS AND PERMISSIONS

In managing Salesforce users and permissions, I find that establishing a structured approach is essential to ensure both security and operational efficiency. The foundation of effective user and permissions management lies in understanding the various components that control access within Salesforce: user roles, profiles, and permission sets. Each of these components plays a distinct role in defining what users can and cannot do within the system.

Starting with user roles, these define the hierarchy and reporting structure within Salesforce. Roles are essential for controlling data access at a broad level, primarily through role hierarchy and sharing settings. In Salesforce, the role hierarchy determines the visibility of records and the level of access users have to data based on their position within the organizational structure. For instance, a user in a higher role within the hierarchy can typically view and access records owned by users in lower roles. This hierarchy must be carefully planned to reflect the organizational structure and ensure that data access is aligned with business needs.

Profiles are another critical component in managing user

access. Each user profile specifies the objects and fields a user can view, create, edit, or delete. Profiles also control access to various Salesforce functionalities, including tabs, applications, and record types. For instance, a Sales Manager's profile might grant access to all sales-related objects and fields, whereas a Customer Support Agent's profile would restrict access to those related to customer service. By creating and assigning appropriate profiles, I can tailor access levels to fit different job functions, ensuring that users have access to the tools and data they need without unnecessary permissions.

Permission sets offer a more flexible way to manage user permissions compared to profiles. While profiles define the base level of access for a user, permission sets allow for the addition of specific permissions on top of what is granted by the profile. This flexibility is particularly useful when users require additional access for specific projects or tasks without changing their base profile. For instance, if a user's role involves temporary access to a new module or feature, a permission set can be assigned to provide this access without altering the user's primary profile. This granular control helps in managing access dynamically and ensures that users have just the right level of permissions.

When managing user access, it is crucial to adhere to the principle of least privilege. This principle dictates that users should be granted only the permissions necessary to perform their job functions. By applying this principle, I can minimize the risk of data breaches and ensure that users do not have access to sensitive information beyond their needs. Regularly reviewing and updating user permissions is also vital to maintaining security. As roles and responsibilities change, it is important to adjust access levels accordingly to reflect these changes and prevent unauthorized access.

Another important aspect of user and permissions management is auditing and monitoring. Salesforce provides tools and reports to track user activities and changes to permissions. By leveraging these tools, I can monitor who has accessed or modified data and ensure that permissions are being used appropriately. This oversight helps in identifying and addressing any potential security issues or misconfigurations promptly.

User training is an often overlooked but essential element of managing Salesforce users and permissions. Ensuring that users understand their roles, the scope of their access, and how to use Salesforce effectively can significantly impact productivity and security. I provide training sessions and resources to help users navigate the system and understand their permissions, which in turn helps in reducing errors and enhancing overall system use.

Additionally, implementing a clear change management process for permissions is crucial. Any modifications to user roles, profiles, or permission sets should be managed through a structured process that includes proper documentation, testing, and communication. This ensures that changes are made systematically, reducing the risk of unintended access issues or disruptions in the system.

In summary, managing Salesforce users and permissions involves a comprehensive approach that includes defining and assigning user roles, profiles, and permission sets, adhering to the principle of least privilege, and implementing robust auditing and monitoring practices. By focusing on these areas, I can create a secure and efficient Salesforce environment that supports organizational goals and protects sensitive data.

Managing Salesforce users and permissions effectively extends beyond the initial setup of roles, profiles, and permission sets. It involves an ongoing process of adjustment and refinement to ensure that security and efficiency are maintained as the organization evolves.

One of the most critical tasks in user management is configuring role hierarchies accurately. The role hierarchy not only determines the visibility of records but also impacts how data is shared across the organization. When setting up the role hierarchy, it is essential to map it closely to the organizational structure, reflecting both reporting lines and data access needs. I pay careful attention to avoid over-permissioning; for example, a Sales Director should be able to view all sales data across their team but should not necessarily have access to data outside their department unless specifically required. Ensuring that roles are well-defined helps in maintaining a balance between necessary access and security.

Profiles, as foundational elements of access control, need to be crafted with precision. Each profile defines the baseline permissions for a group of users. While Salesforce offers several standard profiles, customizing these profiles to align with specific job functions is often necessary. This customization process involves selecting the appropriate object-level and field-level permissions, as well as configuring access to applications and features. For instance, a Marketing Analyst might require detailed access to campaign and lead objects but should have limited access to financial records. By tailoring profiles to job functions, I ensure that users have the tools they need to perform their duties efficiently without unnecessary access.

Permission sets enhance the granularity of access management by allowing additional permissions to be assigned on top of the base profile. This flexibility is particularly beneficial for scenarios where users need temporary or role-specific access. For example, if a user in the Customer Service department needs to access a new feature or data set temporarily for a project, I can assign a permission set to grant this access without altering the user's primary profile. This approach simplifies permissions management and reduces the risk of inadvertently providing excessive access.

Effective management of user permissions also involves regular reviews and updates. As users change roles or as business processes evolve, their access needs may change. Regularly auditing user permissions helps ensure that access levels remain appropriate. During these reviews, I check for any discrepancies or outdated permissions and make necessary adjustments to align with current job functions and business requirements. This proactive approach is crucial for maintaining security and ensuring that users only have access to the data they need.

In addition to role, profile, and permission management, leveraging Salesforce's built-in tools for monitoring and reporting on user activities is essential. Salesforce provides various audit logs and reports that help track user actions, permission changes, and access patterns. By analyzing these reports, I can identify any unusual activities or potential security issues and address them promptly. This continuous monitoring is an integral part of maintaining a secure Salesforce environment.

Training and communication play a significant role in ensuring effective user and permissions management. Educating users about their roles, access levels, and best practices for using Salesforce helps minimize errors and enhances overall system utilization. I make it a point to provide clear documentation and training resources that explain how permissions work and how they should use Salesforce within the scope of their access. Clear communication also extends to informing users about any changes to their access or roles, ensuring that they understand the reasons behind these adjustments.

Managing user permissions also involves implementing and adhering to a robust change management process. Any changes to user roles, profiles, or permission sets should be documented, tested, and communicated effectively. I follow a structured process for making changes, which includes creating a change request, obtaining necessary approvals, testing changes in a sandbox environment, and finally implementing them in production. This approach helps ensure that changes are made systematically, reducing the risk of errors and disruptions.

In conclusion, effective management of Salesforce users and permissions requires a combination of strategic planning, ongoing oversight, and clear communication. By carefully configuring roles, profiles, and permission sets, regularly reviewing access levels, and leveraging Salesforce's monitoring tools, I can maintain a secure and efficient environment. This ongoing management process ensures that users have the appropriate access to perform their roles effectively while protecting sensitive data and supporting organizational goals.

In managing Salesforce users and permissions, another critical aspect is ensuring that the principles of least privilege and segregation of duties are consistently applied. The principle of least privilege means that users should only be granted the minimum level of access necessary for them to perform their job functions. This approach minimizes the risk of unauthorized access and potential data breaches. For instance, a customer service representative does not need access to the financial data or administrative settings of Salesforce. By adhering to this principle, I ensure that users have access only to the resources they need and nothing more.

Similarly, the segregation of duties involves distributing tasks and responsibilities to ensure that no single individual has control over all aspects of a critical process. This helps prevent fraud and errors. In Salesforce, this principle can be implemented by assigning different roles and permissions to individuals who handle different stages of a process. For example, one user might be responsible for entering data into Salesforce, while another user might handle the approval and review process. By separating these duties, I reduce the risk of errors and enhance the overall integrity of the data.

Another essential practice in managing Salesforce users and permissions is implementing effective access reviews and audits. Periodic access reviews involve systematically evaluating user permissions to ensure they align with current job responsibilities. These reviews help identify any discrepancies or excess permissions that may have accumulated over time. I use Salesforce's built-in reporting and auditing tools to generate reports on user access and permission changes. By regularly reviewing these reports, I can address any issues promptly and make necessary adjustments to maintain a secure environment.

When configuring permissions and access, it's crucial to consider the potential impact of integrating third-party applications or customizations within Salesforce. Third-party applications often require additional permissions to function correctly, and it's essential to understand how these permissions might affect overall security. Before installing any third-party app from the AppExchange, I carefully review its permission requirements and assess how it will interact with existing user roles and profiles. This helps ensure that the app does not inadvertently grant excessive access or conflict with existing permissions.

Similarly, customizations and development within Salesforce can also impact user permissions. Custom objects, fields, and workflows can introduce new data access requirements or change existing access levels. When implementing customizations, I ensure that they are thoroughly tested in a sandbox environment before deploying them to production. This testing process includes verifying that the new customizations do not interfere with existing user permissions and that they comply with security policies.

Managing user permissions also involves being prepared for organizational changes such as mergers, acquisitions, or departmental restructures. These changes often necessitate adjustments to user roles, profiles, and permissions. When faced with such changes, I follow a structured approach to assess the impact on user access and make the necessary modifications. This might involve creating new roles or profiles, adjusting existing permissions, or reassigning users to different roles. By planning and executing these changes carefully, I ensure that user access remains appropriate and secure during periods of organizational change.

User onboarding and offboarding processes are also integral to effective permissions management. During the onboarding process, I ensure that new users are assigned the correct roles and permissions based on their job functions. This involves creating and configuring profiles and permission sets that align with their responsibilities. Conversely, during the offboarding process, I promptly revoke access for departing employees to prevent any unauthorized access to Salesforce. Implementing a standardized onboarding and offboarding procedure helps maintain security and operational efficiency.

Finally, fostering a culture of security awareness among Salesforce users is crucial for effective permissions management. Users should be educated about the importance of data security and the role they play in maintaining it. Providing training on best practices for using Salesforce, understanding their permissions, and recognizing potential security threats helps users make informed decisions and adhere to security policies. Regularly updating training materials and conducting refresher courses can reinforce security practices and keep users informed of any changes to the Salesforce environment.

In summary, managing Salesforce users and permissions involves applying principles of least privilege and segregation of duties, conducting regular access reviews and audits, carefully managing third-party integrations and customizations, preparing for organizational changes, and implementing effective onboarding and offboarding processes. By adhering to these best practices and fostering a culture of security awareness, I can ensure that the Salesforce environment remains secure, efficient, and aligned with organizational goals.

CHAPTER 26: OPTIMIZING SALESFORCE PERFORMANCE

Effective performance optimization is essential for maintaining a smooth and responsive Salesforce environment. The performance of a Salesforce instance can be influenced by various factors, including data storage, query efficiency, and system configuration. By understanding and applying techniques to enhance these aspects, I can ensure that the Salesforce system operates at its best, providing a seamless user experience and supporting organizational productivity.

A critical starting point for performance optimization is monitoring the Salesforce environment. Salesforce provides various tools and features to help track system performance and identify potential issues. The Salesforce Lightning Experience includes the Lightning Performance Overview dashboard, which offers insights into the performance of different components and transactions within the Salesforce environment. By regularly reviewing this dashboard, I can identify trends and areas where performance may be lagging. Additionally, Salesforce's Event Monitoring and Debug Logs provide more granular details about specific events and transactions, helping to pinpoint performance bottlenecks and issues.

Data storage optimization is another crucial aspect of performance management. As Salesforce instances grow, the volume of data can impact system performance, particularly if the data is not managed effectively. One approach to optimizing data storage is to implement data archiving strategies. By archiving older or less frequently accessed data, I can reduce the amount of data stored in active tables, improving query performance and overall system responsiveness. Salesforce offers several tools for data archiving, including data export options and third-party applications available through AppExchange that can help automate the archiving process.

Additionally, efficient data model design plays a significant role in performance optimization. A well-designed data model with appropriate indexing and relationships can enhance query performance and reduce the time required to retrieve data. When designing the data model, I focus on creating indexed fields for frequently queried data and optimizing the relationships between objects to minimize the complexity of queries. Regularly reviewing and refining the data model ensures that it continues to support performance goals as the Salesforce instance evolves.

Query performance is another area where optimization can have a substantial impact. Salesforce uses SOQL (Salesforce Object Query Language) for querying data, and inefficient queries can lead to performance issues. To improve query performance, I follow best practices for writing efficient SOQL queries. This includes selecting only the necessary fields, using appropriate filters to reduce the volume of returned data, and avoiding complex queries with multiple nested subqueries. Salesforce's Query Plan Tool can help analyze the performance of SOQL queries, providing insights into potential inefficiencies and suggestions for improvement.

System efficiency is also influenced by the configuration and customization of Salesforce. Over-customization can lead to performance issues, as custom code, triggers, and workflows can increase the complexity of operations and data processing. To optimize system efficiency, I review and manage customizations regularly. This involves evaluating custom code for performance issues, optimizing Apex triggers to ensure they are not executing unnecessary operations, and streamlining workflows to avoid excessive processing overhead. Salesforce's built-in tools, such as the Apex Governor Limits and the Salesforce Optimizer, provide valuable information about system performance and help identify areas for improvement.

Monitoring and managing system resources is another aspect of performance optimization. Salesforce operates within a multi-tenant architecture, and system resources are shared among multiple organizations. This means that resource usage can impact performance, particularly during peak usage times. I monitor system resource usage, such as CPU time and memory consumption, to ensure that it remains within acceptable limits. Salesforce provides resource usage reports and tools to help track and manage system resources, allowing me to take proactive measures to prevent performance degradation.

Another important consideration is user experience. Performance issues can often be linked to user interactions, such as slow page load times or delays in data retrieval. To enhance user experience, I focus on optimizing the user interface and ensuring that it is responsive and efficient. This includes optimizing Lightning pages, minimizing the use of resource-intensive components, and implementing best practices for page layouts and user interactions. Regular user feedback and performance testing help identify areas where the user experience can be improved.

Finally, staying informed about Salesforce updates and best practices is essential for ongoing performance optimization. Salesforce continuously releases updates and enhancements that can impact performance. By staying up-to-date with Salesforce release notes and participating in the Salesforce community, I can learn about new features and improvements that may enhance system performance. Additionally, leveraging resources such as Salesforce's Performance Best Practices documentation and webinars provides valuable insights into optimizing the Salesforce environment.

In conclusion, optimizing Salesforce performance involves a comprehensive approach that includes monitoring system performance, managing data storage, enhancing query efficiency, optimizing system configuration and customizations, monitoring resource usage, and improving user experience. By implementing these techniques and staying informed about best practices, I can ensure that the Salesforce environment operates at peak performance, supporting the organization's goals and providing a seamless user experience.

Optimizing Salesforce performance is a multi-faceted process that requires a deep understanding of both the technical and functional aspects of the system. One of the key strategies for enhancing Salesforce performance involves managing and optimizing data storage. As Salesforce data grows, it becomes increasingly important to ensure that the system can handle large volumes of data efficiently. One effective approach to managing data storage is to implement data partitioning. By segmenting data into different partitions based on criteria such as date ranges or data categories, I can reduce the amount of data that needs to be processed in any single query, which can significantly improve performance.

Additionally, data archiving is another critical technique

for optimizing data storage. Regularly archiving older or less frequently accessed data helps keep the active data set manageable and improves query performance. Salesforce offers various tools and features for data archiving, such as the Data Export service, which allows for scheduled exports of data to external storage. Implementing an archiving strategy requires careful planning to ensure that archived data remains accessible when needed, and that the archiving process does not impact system performance.

Efficient data model design is essential for optimizing query performance. The way data is structured within Salesforce can greatly affect how quickly and efficiently queries are executed. To optimize the data model, I focus on creating well-indexed fields for frequently queried data and organizing relationships between objects to minimize query complexity. For example, using custom indexes on fields that are often used in search filters can enhance query speed. Additionally, I review and refine the data model regularly to ensure that it continues to meet performance requirements as the Salesforce instance evolves.

Another crucial aspect of performance optimization is managing query performance. Salesforce uses SOQL (Salesforce Object Query Language) for querying data, and poorly optimized queries can lead to significant performance issues. To optimize SOQL queries, I follow best practices such as selecting only the necessary fields, using appropriate filters to narrow down the data, and avoiding complex queries with multiple nested subqueries. Salesforce provides tools like the Query Plan Tool to help analyze the performance of SOQL queries. By using these tools, I can identify and address inefficiencies in query execution.

The performance of Apex code also plays a critical role in overall system performance. Apex code, particularly if not well-optimized, can lead to issues such as excessive processing time or governor limit errors. To improve Apex performance, I regularly review and optimize custom code. This includes techniques such as bulkifying code to handle large volumes of records efficiently, minimizing the use of nested queries, and ensuring that code is well-structured and follows best practices. Additionally, I use Salesforce's debugging tools and governor limit monitoring to identify and address performance issues related to Apex code.

System configuration and customizations can significantly impact performance. Over-customization can lead to complex processes that may affect system efficiency. To manage customizations effectively, I conduct regular reviews of custom code, triggers, and workflows to ensure they do not adversely affect performance. For example, I optimize Apex triggers to ensure they are not executing unnecessary operations and streamline workflows to avoid excessive processing overhead. Salesforce's built-in tools, such as the Salesforce Optimizer, provide valuable insights into system performance and help identify areas for optimization.

Monitoring system resources is another important aspect of performance optimization. Salesforce operates in a multi-tenant environment, where system resources are shared among different organizations. Resource usage, such as CPU time and memory consumption, can impact performance, particularly during peak usage periods. I monitor system resource usage through Salesforce's resource usage reports and tools. By keeping an eye on these metrics, I can take proactive measures to prevent performance degradation and ensure that the system remains responsive.

User experience is also closely tied to performance. Slow page load times or delays in data retrieval can negatively impact user satisfaction and productivity. To enhance the user experience, I focus on optimizing the user interface and ensuring that it is responsive and efficient. This includes optimizing Lightning pages by minimizing the use of resource-intensive components, implementing best practices for page layouts, and conducting regular performance testing. User feedback is invaluable in identifying areas where the user experience can be improved.

Lastly, staying informed about Salesforce updates and best practices is essential for ongoing performance optimization. Salesforce regularly releases updates and new features that can impact performance. By staying up-to-date with release notes, attending webinars, and participating in the Salesforce community, I can learn about new features and improvements that may enhance system performance. Leveraging resources such as Salesforce's Performance Best Practices documentation also provides valuable guidance for optimizing the Salesforce environment.

In summary, optimizing Salesforce performance involves a comprehensive approach that includes managing data storage, refining the data model, optimizing query performance, reviewing customizations, monitoring system resources, enhancing user experience, and staying informed about updates. By applying these strategies, I can ensure that the Salesforce environment operates efficiently and continues to meet the needs of the organization.

The continuous monitoring of Salesforce performance is vital to maintaining and improving the overall efficiency of the system. Effective monitoring begins with establishing a baseline for normal performance metrics. This baseline helps in identifying deviations and potential issues as they arise. To achieve this, I leverage Salesforce's built-in monitoring tools, such as the Performance and Security Dashboard. This tool provides insights into various aspects of system performance, including API call usage, user activity, and system resource consumption.

An essential aspect of performance monitoring involves

tracking system logs. Salesforce provides detailed logs for Apex executions, batch processes, and scheduled jobs. By reviewing these logs, I can pinpoint performance bottlenecks or issues that might not be apparent through other monitoring methods. For instance, Apex execution logs can reveal long-running operations or inefficient queries that may be affecting performance. Regularly analyzing these logs allows me to proactively address potential issues before they escalate into major problems.

Another important factor in performance optimization is understanding and managing governor limits. Salesforce imposes governor limits to ensure that no single organization can monopolize shared resources. These limits include restrictions on the number of database operations, API calls, and CPU time per transaction. To optimize performance while staying within these limits, I carefully design Apex code and data processing tasks to minimize resource consumption. For example, using efficient algorithms and avoiding excessive nested loops can help stay within CPU time limits. Additionally, I monitor governor limit usage through Salesforce's Developer Console to ensure that I am not approaching any limits that could impact performance.

Data skew is another factor that can affect performance. Data skew occurs when a disproportionate amount of data is associated with a single record or value, leading to performance degradation, particularly in related records. To mitigate data skew, I use strategies such as distributing data more evenly across records and avoiding large numbers of child records associated with a single parent record. Regular data reviews and adjustments can help maintain a balanced data distribution, thereby improving query and transaction performance.

Custom reports and dashboards can sometimes cause performance issues if they are not optimized properly.

Complex reports with numerous filters, joins, or large data sets can lead to slow performance. To enhance report performance, I ensure that reports are designed with efficiency in mind. This includes limiting the number of fields included, using indexed fields for filters, and avoiding overly complex formulas. Additionally, leveraging Salesforce's reporting tools to create summary reports instead of detailed, real-time reports can improve performance. Regularly reviewing and optimizing reports and dashboards helps ensure that users receive timely and accurate information without sacrificing system performance.

Efficiently managing integration points with external systems also plays a critical role in optimizing overall system performance. External integrations, such as data synchronization with third-party applications or systems, can impact Salesforce performance if not properly managed. I carefully design and monitor integrations to ensure that they are efficient and do not overwhelm the Salesforce instance. This involves setting up appropriate batch sizes for data processing, using asynchronous operations where possible, and regularly reviewing integration logs for performance issues. Effective integration management ensures that data flows smoothly between Salesforce and external systems without causing performance degradation.

User training and best practices can also contribute to performance optimization. Users play a crucial role in system performance through their interactions with Salesforce. Providing training on best practices for using the system, such as avoiding inefficient search queries or excessive data uploads, can help improve overall performance. I also encourage users to report any performance issues they encounter, as their feedback can provide valuable insights into areas that may need optimization.

In addition to these strategies, Salesforce continuously

updates its platform with new features and performance enhancements. Staying informed about these updates and incorporating them into the Salesforce environment can help maintain and improve performance. I regularly review Salesforce release notes and participate in community forums to stay up-to-date with the latest best practices and performance optimization techniques.

In summary, optimizing Salesforce performance involves a comprehensive approach that includes monitoring system metrics, managing governor limits, addressing data skew, optimizing reports and dashboards, managing external integrations, and educating users. By implementing these strategies and staying informed about platform updates, I can ensure that the Salesforce environment operates at peak efficiency and continues to meet the needs of the organization. This ongoing commitment to performance optimization is essential for maintaining a high-performing Salesforce instance and delivering a positive user experience.

CHAPTER 27: SALESFORCE DATA MIGRATION AND IMPORT

Effective data migration and import are fundamental to ensuring that Salesforce remains a reliable and accurate repository of business information. These processes involve several critical steps, including data mapping, transformation, and the use of appropriate import tools. Each phase of data migration must be carefully managed to handle large volumes of data, maintain accuracy, and preserve data integrity.

The first step in data migration is understanding and defining the data mapping process. Data mapping involves aligning data fields from the source system to the corresponding fields in Salesforce. This requires a thorough analysis of both the source and target data structures. I start by creating a detailed data mapping document that outlines how each field in the source system translates to a field in Salesforce. This document serves as a blueprint for the migration process and ensures that all necessary data is captured accurately. It is crucial to include considerations for custom fields and objects in Salesforce that may not have a direct counterpart in the source system.

Data transformation is the next critical step. Data

transformation involves converting data from the source format to a format compatible with Salesforce. This step is essential when dealing with data that requires formatting adjustments, data type conversions, or cleaning to meet Salesforce's standards. For example, dates and numeric values often require specific formats, and textual data may need to be cleansed of unwanted characters or inconsistencies. I use tools such as Excel or specialized data transformation software to perform these tasks, ensuring that the data aligns with Salesforce's requirements before import.

Handling large volumes of data presents its own set of challenges. To manage this effectively, I employ several strategies to ensure smooth migration. One key strategy is to break the data into manageable chunks or batches. Salesforce imposes limits on the number of records that can be processed in a single transaction, so dividing the data into smaller batches helps to avoid hitting these limits and ensures that the import process runs efficiently. Additionally, I schedule data imports during off-peak hours to minimize the impact on system performance and user activity.

To ensure data accuracy, I conduct rigorous data validation before and after the import. Before importing data, I perform a series of validation checks to confirm that the data meets Salesforce's requirements and that all necessary fields are correctly mapped. During the import process, I monitor for any errors or warnings that may arise, addressing issues as they occur. After the import, I conduct post-migration validation by comparing the data in Salesforce with the source data to ensure that it has been accurately transferred and that no records were lost or incorrectly updated.

Data integrity is a critical concern throughout the migration process. To maintain data integrity, I implement several best practices. First, I ensure that all data relationships are preserved during the migration. This involves mapping lookup and master-detail relationships accurately to maintain the connections between related records. Additionally, I perform integrity checks to verify that no data duplication occurs and that all records are correctly linked. Regular backups of the data before starting the migration process are also essential to safeguard against any potential issues or data loss.

Salesforce provides several tools and resources to facilitate data import and migration. The Data Import Wizard, for example, is a user-friendly tool that allows for the import of standard and custom objects. It supports both simple and complex data imports and provides an interface for mapping fields and setting import options. For more complex data migration scenarios, I use the Data Loader, which offers more advanced features for handling large data volumes, including the ability to schedule regular imports and exports. Data Loader also provides detailed error logs that can be reviewed to troubleshoot any issues that arise during the import process.

In addition to these tools, I also leverage Salesforce's APIs for integrating data from external systems. The REST and SOAP APIs provide programmatic access to Salesforce data, allowing for automated data imports and updates. When using APIs, I ensure that API calls are optimized and that error handling is implemented to manage any issues that occur during data transfer.

To conclude, effective data migration and import require careful planning and execution to ensure that data is accurately and efficiently transferred into Salesforce. By following best practices for data mapping, transformation, and import, and by utilizing Salesforce's tools and resources, I can manage large volumes of data while maintaining data accuracy and integrity. This thorough approach helps to ensure that Salesforce remains a robust and reliable system for managing business information.

When undertaking data migration and import into Salesforce,

it's crucial to focus on the methodologies that ensure both precision and efficiency. A central aspect of this process is managing data quality before, during, and after the migration. This includes not only the transformation and import of data but also the validation and reconciliation phases that follow.

Firstly, data quality management begins with an initial audit of the source data. This involves reviewing the data to identify any inconsistencies, duplicates, or errors that could affect the migration process. I start by assessing the completeness of the data and ensuring that all required fields are populated. This initial audit helps in pinpointing areas where data may need to be cleaned or standardized. For example, if the source data includes inconsistent date formats or varying terminologies for similar categories, these issues must be addressed to align with Salesforce's data standards.

Data cleansing is an integral part of preparing data for migration. This step involves correcting or removing inaccurate, corrupted, or irrelevant data from the source system. Tools such as data quality software or scripts can be used to automate parts of this process, such as identifying and merging duplicate records or standardizing field values. During cleansing, it's essential to maintain a balance between correcting errors and preserving data integrity, ensuring that the changes do not introduce new issues.

Once the data is cleaned and standardized, transformation processes are implemented. Transformation entails converting data from its original format to one that is compatible with Salesforce's structure. This may involve changing data types, reformatting fields, or aggregating information to meet Salesforce's requirements. For instance, if the source data contains customer addresses in different formats, these must be reformatted to align with Salesforce's address fields. Transformations are typically managed using tools like ETL (Extract, Transform, Load) platforms or data transformation scripts.

During the data import process, attention must be given to the selection and configuration of the appropriate tools. Salesforce provides various options for importing data, including the Data Import Wizard and Data Loader. The Data Import Wizard is suitable for simpler import tasks and is accessible directly from the Salesforce user interface. It allows for importing data into standard and custom objects and offers a guided process for mapping fields and handling errors.

For more complex migrations, especially those involving large volumes of data or requiring automation, the Data Loader is often preferred. The Data Loader supports bulk data operations and allows for detailed control over the import process. It enables scheduling of data imports, managing data relationships, and handling large data sets more efficiently. With Data Loader, I also have access to detailed logs that provide insights into any issues encountered during the import, which aids in troubleshooting and ensuring successful data transfer.

Data validation post-import is another critical phase in the migration process. After data is imported into Salesforce, I perform a series of checks to ensure that the data appears as expected and meets the criteria defined during the mapping phase. This involves verifying that all records have been correctly imported and that relationships between objects have been accurately maintained. For instance, if a migration involved importing contacts and their associated accounts, I would validate that all contacts are linked to the correct accounts and that no data has been lost or corrupted during the import.

Furthermore, reconciliation is performed to compare the data in Salesforce with the source data. This process involves cross-checking key metrics and records between the source system and Salesforce to confirm that the migration was accurate. Reconciliation can be facilitated through automated reports or manual checks, depending on the complexity and volume of the data. Any discrepancies found during reconciliation need to be addressed promptly to maintain data integrity.

In addition to these processes, it's important to establish a robust data governance framework. This framework should include guidelines and protocols for ongoing data management, ensuring that data remains accurate and relevant over time. This involves regular audits, data quality checks, and updating data management practices as the Salesforce environment evolves.

Lastly, documenting the entire data migration process is essential. Comprehensive documentation provides a record of the migration strategy, data mappings, transformation rules, and any issues encountered. This documentation serves as a valuable reference for future migrations or data management activities and ensures that best practices are adhered to in subsequent projects.

By focusing on these critical areas—data quality management, cleansing, transformation, import, validation, and reconciliation—I ensure that the data migration process into Salesforce is thorough and effective. Each step is carefully executed to maintain data accuracy and integrity, ultimately supporting a reliable and high-performing Salesforce environment.

In managing large-scale data migrations into Salesforce, it's essential to consider the handling of data volumes to ensure a smooth transition. When dealing with extensive datasets, several best practices can significantly enhance the effectiveness of the migration process. These practices involve optimizing data handling techniques and carefully planning the import phases to minimize disruptions and maximize data accuracy.

One of the primary challenges with large data volumes is managing performance during the import process. To address this, I focus on breaking down the data into manageable batches. Instead of attempting to import the entire dataset in one go, which can overwhelm the system and lead to timeouts or errors, I divide the data into smaller chunks. This batching approach not only helps in better monitoring the import process but also reduces the likelihood of encountering system performance issues. Tools such as Salesforce Data Loader facilitate batch processing by allowing me to configure the size of the batches and manage import jobs more effectively.

Another important consideration is to implement and test the import process in a sandbox environment before executing it in the production environment. By conducting a trial migration in a sandbox, I can identify and resolve potential issues without affecting live data. This practice involves performing a full-scale test migration using a subset of data to simulate the import process. The insights gained from this testing phase are invaluable in refining data mappings, transformation rules, and import configurations. Additionally, it helps in validating that the data structure, relationships, and business rules are correctly applied.

Data mapping is a critical step in ensuring that data is imported accurately and effectively. During this phase, I meticulously align source data fields with the corresponding Salesforce fields. This mapping process involves not only matching field names but also understanding data types and formats to ensure compatibility. For example, if the source data contains dates in a different format than what Salesforce expects, I must apply appropriate transformations to align the data. I use data mapping tools or spreadsheets to document and verify these mappings, which serves as a reference during the actual import process.

The transformation of data plays a pivotal role in ensuring that the data fits the structure and requirements of Salesforce. Transformations may include converting data types, aggregating information, or applying business rules. For instance, if the source data includes fields that need to be split or combined to match Salesforce's schema, I handle these transformations during the pre-import phase. Additionally, transformation processes should account for data validation rules set up in Salesforce, such as picklist values or mandatory fields. This ensures that the data being imported adheres to Salesforce's data integrity constraints.

Data integrity management is crucial throughout the migration process to maintain the accuracy and consistency of data. To safeguard data integrity, I implement validation checks both before and after the import. Pre-import checks include verifying that the source data meets the required quality standards and that transformation rules are correctly applied. Post-import, I conduct thorough validation to confirm that the data in Salesforce matches the source data and that no records have been lost or altered unexpectedly. This involves running reports and comparing key metrics to ensure consistency.

Handling errors and exceptions is another key aspect of the migration process. During the import, errors can arise due to data quality issues, format mismatches, or system constraints. It's essential to have a robust error-handling strategy in place. I utilize the error logs provided by Salesforce Data Loader or other import tools to identify and address issues. For example, if certain records fail to import due to validation errors, I review the error messages to understand the root cause and make necessary corrections to the data or mapping configurations.

Additionally, it's important to establish a clear

communication plan with stakeholders throughout the migration process. This includes providing regular updates on the progress of the migration, addressing any concerns or issues that arise, and ensuring that users are aware of any changes or impacts on their workflows. Effective communication helps manage expectations and facilitates a smoother transition for all parties involved.

Post-migration, I focus on monitoring the performance of Salesforce and validating that the imported data is being utilized correctly by the system. This involves checking for any performance issues that may have arisen due to the new data, such as slow queries or system lag. I also ensure that reports, dashboards, and workflows that rely on the migrated data are functioning as expected. If any issues are detected, I take prompt action to address them and ensure that the system operates efficiently.

In summary, managing data migration and import into Salesforce requires careful planning and execution. By focusing on best practices such as batching data, conducting sandbox testing, meticulous data mapping, transformation, and error handling, I ensure a successful migration process. Each step, from preparation through to post-migration monitoring, is designed to maintain data integrity, optimize performance, and achieve a seamless integration of new data into the Salesforce environment.

CHAPTER 28: DEVELOPING CUSTOM APPLICATIONS ON SALESFORCE

Salesforce offers a powerful platform for developing custom applications that can be tailored to meet specific business requirements. Understanding the development environment and the various tools available is essential for building applications that enhance functionality and address unique business needs. This section will guide you through the development tools and techniques in Salesforce, focusing on Apex code, Visualforce pages, and Lightning Web Components, and will provide insights into how to build and deploy custom applications effectively.

To begin, the Salesforce development environment is designed to facilitate the creation of custom solutions through a range of tools and languages. Apex, Salesforce's proprietary programming language, is a core component of this environment. Apex is an object-oriented language that allows for server-side logic execution, enabling developers to create complex business processes and automate tasks. It is particularly useful for operations that require a high level of customization and integration with Salesforce's data model. By using Apex, developers can write triggers, classes, and asynchronous code to handle various business logic scenarios. For instance, if you need to automatically update related records when a particular field is changed, you would use Apex triggers to execute this logic in response to data changes.

Alongside Apex, Visualforce is a framework for building custom user interfaces on the Salesforce platform. Visualforce allows developers to create custom pages that integrate seamlessly with Salesforce data and functionality. This framework is based on a tag-based markup language, similar to HTML, which provides a flexible way to design user interfaces. Visualforce pages can be combined with Apex controllers to handle complex business logic and interactions. For example, if a custom application requires a specialized input form or a unique display of data that standard Salesforce pages cannot accommodate, Visualforce can be used to build these pages, providing a tailored experience for users.

However, with the evolution of Salesforce's platform, Lightning Web Components (LWC) have emerged as a modern and efficient way to build custom applications. LWC is a JavaScript framework that leverages the latest web standards to create reusable and high-performance components. Unlike Visualforce, which is server-side rendered, LWC components are client-side, resulting in faster and more responsive user interfaces. LWC allows developers to build interactive and dynamic components that can be embedded in Lightning Experience and Salesforce mobile apps. For instance, if you need a highly interactive dashboard or a complex custom component that integrates with Salesforce data, LWC provides the tools and flexibility to build these components efficiently.

Developing custom applications involves more than just coding; it also requires understanding the Salesforce data model and ensuring that your application integrates smoothly with existing Salesforce features. This means that developers must be familiar with Salesforce objects, fields, relationships, and security models. When designing a custom application, it is crucial to align with Salesforce's data architecture to maintain data integrity and leverage Salesforce's built-in features effectively. For example, if your application needs to interact with Salesforce records, you must consider how to handle CRUD (Create, Read, Update, Delete) operations and ensure that your code adheres to Salesforce's governor limits and best practices.

Deploying custom applications on Salesforce involves several steps to ensure that the application functions correctly in the production environment. First, thorough testing is essential to identify and resolve any issues before deployment. Salesforce provides tools such as the Developer Console, Debug Logs, and automated testing frameworks to facilitate this process. Writing unit tests for Apex code is particularly important, as Salesforce requires a minimum code coverage percentage before allowing deployment to production. Additionally, using sandboxes for staging and testing allows developers to simulate the production environment and validate the application's performance and behavior under real-world conditions.

Once testing is complete, deployment can be managed through Salesforce's change sets or tools like Salesforce DX. Change sets are a user-friendly way to deploy metadata changes between Salesforce environments, whereas Salesforce DX offers a more sophisticated approach, enabling version control and continuous integration/continuous deployment (CI/CD) practices. Both methods require careful management of dependencies and configurations to ensure a smooth transition from development to production.

Throughout the development process, adherence to Salesforce best practices is crucial. This includes following coding standards, optimizing performance, and ensuring that custom solutions are maintainable and scalable. For instance, using bulk-safe Apex code helps prevent issues with governor limits, while adopting a modular approach to LWC development promotes reusability and easier maintenance.

In conclusion, developing custom applications on Salesforce requires a comprehensive understanding of the platform's development tools and techniques. By leveraging Apex, Visualforce, and Lightning Web Components, developers can build robust solutions tailored to specific business needs. Ensuring that applications are well-integrated with Salesforce's data model and following best practices for testing and deployment will result in high-quality applications that enhance Salesforce's functionality and meet business objectives effectively.

Building custom applications on Salesforce is a powerful way to extend the platform's capabilities and address specific business requirements. To effectively utilize Salesforce for custom development, it is essential to understand the distinct components of the Salesforce development environment, including Apex, Visualforce, and Lightning Web Components. Each of these tools serves a unique purpose and offers different advantages depending on the needs of the application.

Apex code is integral to custom development within Salesforce. As a strongly typed, object-oriented programming language, Apex allows developers to create complex business logic and execute server-side operations. Apex is particularly valuable for automating business processes, such as custom calculations, data validations, and integration tasks. When developing with Apex, it is crucial to design code that adheres to Salesforce's governor limits, which are designed to ensure efficient resource usage and maintain system stability. These limits impose restrictions on factors such as the number of database operations and the amount of memory consumed during transaction processing. Efficiently managing these limits involves using techniques such as bulk processing, which handles multiple records in a single transaction, and optimizing queries to reduce resource consumption.

In addition to writing Apex code, developers often need to create custom user interfaces to provide a tailored experience for users. This is where Visualforce comes into play. Visualforce is a framework that allows for the creation of custom pages with a unique user interface. Unlike standard Salesforce pages, Visualforce pages are built using a markup language similar to HTML, combined with Apex controllers to handle server-side logic. Visualforce pages are particularly useful when a more customized layout or functionality is required that goes beyond what standard Salesforce page layouts can provide. For example, a custom order management system might require a specialized interface for managing complex order processes, which can be designed using Visualforce.

Despite its robustness, Visualforce is gradually being supplemented by Lightning Web Components (LWC), which offer a more modern approach to developing custom user interfaces. LWC leverages contemporary web standards, including JavaScript and web components, to build reusable and high-performance UI elements. One of the key advantages of LWC over Visualforce is its client-side rendering, which improves performance and responsiveness by handling more interactions in the browser rather than relying on server-side processing. This client-side approach enables developers to create dynamic, interactive components that provide a seamless user experience. For example, if a custom application requires a dynamic dashboard with real-time data updates, LWC provides the tools to build such components efficiently.

When integrating these development tools into a custom application, it is essential to consider the overall architecture and design principles. A well-designed custom application should ensure data integrity, maintain performance, and provide a user-friendly experience. This involves designing a robust data model that aligns with Salesforce's architecture, creating scalable code, and implementing best practices for security and performance.

Effective data management is critical when developing custom applications. This includes ensuring that the application's data interactions, such as CRUD (Create, Read, Update, Delete) operations, are handled efficiently and securely. Apex triggers and asynchronous operations, such as batch Apex and future methods, are commonly used to manage data changes and background processing. It is important to test these operations thoroughly to avoid issues such as data inconsistencies or performance bottlenecks.

Deployment of custom applications involves several key steps to ensure that changes are correctly transitioned from development to production environments. Salesforce provides tools such as change sets, Salesforce DX, and the Metadata API to manage deployments. Change sets are useful for transferring metadata between related Salesforce environments, while Salesforce DX offers a more comprehensive approach, supporting version control and CI/CD practices. Testing is an integral part of the deployment process. Developers should use unit tests for Apex code and leverage sandbox environments to validate functionality and performance before moving to production. Testing ensures that the custom application performs as expected and does not introduce issues in the production environment.

As custom applications evolve, ongoing maintenance and updates are necessary to address changes in business requirements, platform updates, and user feedback. Implementing a maintenance strategy that includes monitoring application performance, managing technical debt, and incorporating user feedback helps ensure that the application remains effective and aligned with business goals.

In conclusion, developing custom applications on Salesforce requires a deep understanding of the platform's development tools and techniques. Apex, Visualforce, and Lightning Web Components each play a critical role in creating tailored solutions that meet specific business needs. By leveraging these tools effectively, adhering to best practices for data management and deployment, and committing to ongoing maintenance, developers can build powerful applications that enhance Salesforce's capabilities and drive business success.

To develop custom applications effectively on Salesforce, it is essential to focus not only on the tools and technologies but also on the methodologies and strategies that ensure successful implementation. This entails understanding the lifecycle of custom application development, from initial planning and design through to deployment and ongoing maintenance.

The initial phase of custom application development involves thorough planning and requirement gathering. This stage is critical for defining the scope of the application, understanding the business needs, and outlining the specific functionalities required. Engaging with stakeholders and users during this phase helps identify their needs and expectations, ensuring that the application aligns with business objectives. Documentation plays a key role in this process, as it provides a clear blueprint for the development team to follow.

Once the requirements are established, the next step is to design the application's architecture. This involves creating a data model that supports the application's functionality and ensures data integrity. Salesforce's schema builder and data modeling tools can assist in visualizing and designing the data model, which includes objects, fields, relationships, and validation rules. It is crucial to design a data model that not only meets current needs but also accommodates future growth and changes.

Following the design phase, the development phase begins, where you will leverage Apex, Visualforce, and Lightning Web Components to build the custom application. Apex code enables you to implement complex business logic and automation. Writing efficient and scalable Apex code is essential, as it directly impacts the application's performance and maintainability. It is advisable to follow best practices such as writing test classes to cover your Apex code and adhering to governor limits to prevent performance issues.

Visualforce pages are used to create custom user interfaces, especially when the standard Salesforce pages do not meet the requirements. When designing Visualforce pages, focus on creating a user-friendly and intuitive interface that enhances the user experience. Use Visualforce controllers to handle server-side logic and ensure that the pages integrate seamlessly with the rest of the Salesforce environment.

As you move forward with development, Lightning Web Components offer a modern approach to building user interfaces. They provide enhanced performance and a more responsive user experience compared to Visualforce. LWC allows for the creation of reusable components that can be easily integrated into Salesforce pages and applications. Ensure that your components follow Salesforce's Lightning Design System guidelines to maintain consistency and usability across the application.

Testing is a crucial aspect of custom application development. It involves validating that the application functions as intended and meets all specified requirements. Unit tests for Apex code, along with integration and user acceptance tests, help identify and resolve issues before deployment. Testing should be comprehensive, covering various scenarios and edge cases to ensure the application's robustness and reliability.

Deployment of custom applications involves moving the application from the development environment to production. Salesforce provides several tools and methodologies for deployment, including change sets, Salesforce DX, and the Metadata API. Change sets are suitable for transferring metadata between Salesforce environments, while Salesforce DX supports advanced development practices such as version control and continuous integration. Using these tools effectively ensures a smooth transition and minimizes the risk of deployment-related issues.

Post-deployment, the focus shifts to monitoring and maintaining the custom application. This involves tracking performance metrics, addressing user feedback, and implementing necessary updates or enhancements. Salesforce's monitoring tools, such as the debug logs and performance monitoring dashboards, can help identify and address performance issues. Regular maintenance ensures that the application remains functional, secure, and aligned with evolving business needs.

Security is a critical consideration throughout the development and deployment process. Ensure that the custom application adheres to Salesforce's security best practices, including proper handling of sensitive data, implementing appropriate access controls, and conducting security reviews. Protecting the application from potential vulnerabilities helps safeguard your data and maintain user trust.

In conclusion, developing custom applications on Salesforce involves a comprehensive approach that encompasses planning, design, development, testing, deployment, and ongoing maintenance. By leveraging Salesforce's development tools—Apex, Visualforce, and Lightning Web Components

—you can create powerful applications tailored to your organization's specific needs. Adhering to best practices and focusing on aspects such as performance, security, and user experience will contribute to the success and longevity of your custom applications.

CHAPTER 29: IMPLEMENTING AND MANAGING SALESFORCE COMMUNITIES

Salesforce Communities offer a robust platform for creating digital spaces where businesses can interact with external stakeholders, including customers, partners, and employees. Implementing and managing these communities involves several key processes: setting up the community, configuring its features, managing user access, and customizing the community to align with business needs. Each of these aspects plays a crucial role in enhancing engagement, fostering collaboration, and achieving organizational goals.

To start, the setup of a Salesforce Community begins with defining its purpose and objectives. Communities can serve various functions such as customer support, partner collaboration, or internal employee engagement. Identifying the primary goal of the community will guide the configuration process and help tailor the experience to meet the needs of the target audience. Salesforce offers various templates to facilitate community creation, including Customer Service, Partner Central, and Employee Central templates. Each template is designed with specific features and layouts suited to different community purposes.

Once the template is selected, the next step involves configuring the community settings. This includes defining the community's name, URL, and branding elements such as logos and color schemes. Customizing these elements ensures that the community aligns with your company's brand identity and provides a cohesive experience for users. Additionally, setting up the community's structure involves creating and organizing pages and components. Salesforce provides a drag-and-drop interface that simplifies the process of adding and arranging elements like dashboards, discussion forums, and knowledge articles.

One critical aspect of community configuration is setting up the necessary permissions and access controls. Salesforce Communities leverage the same robust security model as Salesforce's core platform, allowing you to manage user access based on profiles, roles, and permission sets. For external users, such as customers and partners, you'll need to configure profiles and permission sets that grant appropriate levels of access to community resources. This ensures that users can view and interact with the content and features relevant to their needs while maintaining the security and integrity of the system.

Managing user access is a dynamic process that requires ongoing attention. As users join or leave the community, or as their roles within the organization change, their access rights may need to be adjusted. Salesforce Communities provide tools for managing user membership and permissions. You can create and manage public and private groups, assign users to specific groups, and define access levels for each group. Additionally, you can use Salesforce's automation tools to streamline user management tasks, such as automatically assigning new users to groups based on their roles or attributes.

Customizing the community to enhance user engagement and collaboration involves leveraging various Salesforce features and components. For example, you can integrate Chatter, Salesforce's enterprise social network, into the community to facilitate real-time communication and collaboration. Chatter allows users to post updates, share files, and participate in discussions, creating an interactive and engaging environment. Similarly, incorporating Salesforce's knowledge base functionality enables users to access a repository of articles and resources, helping them find answers to common questions and issues.

Another important customization aspect is setting up community analytics and reporting. Salesforce provides built-in reporting and dashboard capabilities that allow you to track community performance metrics such as user activity, engagement levels, and content utilization. Analyzing these metrics helps identify areas for improvement and measure the effectiveness of community initiatives. For example, if you notice a decline in user engagement, you might need to adjust the content or features offered in the community to better meet user needs.

Integration with other Salesforce features and external systems can further enhance the functionality of your community. For instance, integrating with Salesforce's Service Cloud can streamline case management and support processes, enabling community users to create and track support cases directly within the community. Similarly, integrating with marketing automation tools can help manage campaigns and track the effectiveness of community-driven marketing efforts.

To ensure that the community remains effective and aligned with business objectives, regular monitoring and maintenance are essential. This includes updating content, reviewing user feedback, and making necessary adjustments based on performance data. Engaging with community members and soliciting their feedback can provide valuable insights into their needs and preferences, allowing you to continually refine and improve the community experience.

In summary, implementing and managing Salesforce Communities involves a multi-faceted approach that includes setting up the community, configuring its features, managing user access, and customizing the experience to enhance engagement and collaboration. By leveraging Salesforce's tools and capabilities, you can create a dynamic and effective community that supports your organization's goals and fosters meaningful interactions with external stakeholders.

Implementing and managing Salesforce Communities requires a nuanced approach that ensures the platform is both functional and engaging for its users. After establishing the basic setup and configuration, the focus must shift towards optimizing user interaction and maintaining a high level of engagement. This involves a range of strategies from refining the user experience to employing advanced community management features.

To begin, it is essential to dive deeper into the customization of community portals. Tailoring the community to meet the specific needs of its users enhances its usability and effectiveness. Salesforce Communities offer extensive customization options, including the ability to design unique page layouts and themes that reflect the organization's branding. Utilizing the Lightning Community Builder, one can create a personalized and visually appealing interface. This drag-and-drop tool simplifies the addition of components such as news feeds, calendar events, or custom forms, enabling users to tailor the community experience without extensive coding knowledge.

In addition to visual customization, it is crucial to focus on functional enhancements. Salesforce provides a range of components and features that can be added to communities to support various use cases. For example, integrating Salesforce Knowledge allows community members to access a repository of articles, FAQs, and guides. This self-service capability reduces the need for direct support and empowers users to find solutions independently. Similarly, incorporating Salesforce's case management functionality within the community portal enables users to create, track, and manage support cases directly from the community interface.

Effective community management also involves setting up and configuring advanced features to drive user engagement. One such feature is the use of Chatter, Salesforce's collaboration tool. By integrating Chatter into the community, organizations can facilitate discussions, share updates, and collaborate on projects in real-time. Chatter groups can be tailored to specific topics or user interests, fostering a more focused and relevant exchange of information. This integration supports enhanced interaction and ensures that users remain actively engaged with the community content.

Another important aspect of managing Salesforce Communities is the use of analytics to monitor and improve community performance. Salesforce provides robust reporting and dashboard tools that enable administrators to track various metrics such as user activity, content engagement, and overall community health. By analyzing these metrics, administrators can gain insights into user behavior and identify areas for improvement. For instance, if certain topics or discussion threads show high engagement levels, it may be beneficial to create additional content or resources related to those topics. Conversely, if there is a noticeable drop in user activity, it may signal the need for content refreshment or the introduction of new features.

User feedback plays a critical role in community management. Regularly soliciting input from community members through surveys, feedback forms, or direct interactions can provide valuable insights into their needs and preferences. Implementing user feedback not only enhances the community experience but also demonstrates a commitment to meeting user expectations. This feedback loop helps in making data-driven decisions regarding content updates, feature enhancements, and overall community strategy.

Security and compliance are also vital considerations when managing Salesforce Communities. Ensuring that the community adheres to organizational policies and regulatory requirements involves setting up proper access controls and data protection measures. Salesforce Communities utilize the same robust security model as Salesforce's core platform, allowing for detailed control over who can access specific content and features. Regularly reviewing and updating security settings, permissions, and compliance protocols is essential to maintaining a secure and compliant community environment.

Managing community growth and scalability is another key aspect. As the community expands, it is important to ensure that the platform can handle increased user volumes and content. Salesforce offers tools to monitor system performance and scalability, helping administrators to identify potential bottlenecks and address them proactively. Planning for scalability includes optimizing community configuration, implementing efficient data management practices, and ensuring that the underlying infrastructure can support growing demands.

Integrating external systems with Salesforce Communities can further enhance functionality and user experience. For example, integrating with third-party applications or services can provide additional features such as advanced analytics, marketing automation, or customer relationship management capabilities. These integrations allow for a more seamless and connected experience, ensuring that the community supports various aspects of business operations.

Overall, implementing and managing Salesforce Communities involves a comprehensive approach that balances customization, engagement, analytics, security, and scalability. By focusing on these areas, organizations can create a dynamic and effective community platform that not only meets the needs of its users but also supports broader business objectives. Through continuous refinement and optimization, Salesforce Communities can serve as a powerful tool for engagement, collaboration, and business growth.

Managing Salesforce Communities involves not only setting up the initial configuration but also continually evolving the platform to meet the needs of its users and align with organizational goals. A pivotal aspect of this ongoing process is ensuring that the community remains dynamic and adaptable, responding effectively to changes in user requirements and business priorities.

One of the core elements of maintaining a successful community is regular content management. Content within Salesforce Communities must be consistently updated to keep users engaged and informed. This involves not only publishing new articles, updates, and announcements but also periodically reviewing and archiving outdated content. Keeping the content relevant and up-to-date enhances the user experience, promotes active participation, and supports the community's overall objectives. Leveraging tools such as Salesforce Knowledge, administrators can streamline content management by categorizing and tagging articles, making it easier for users to find information and ensuring that the most pertinent content is readily accessible.

Equally important is the management of user access and permissions. As the community evolves and grows, the need to periodically review and adjust user roles and access levels becomes crucial. Salesforce Communities allow for detailed control over user permissions, which helps in tailoring the community experience to different user groups. For instance, you might have different access levels for internal employees, external partners, and customers. Ensuring that each group has access to the appropriate resources and functionality without compromising security is essential for maintaining an effective community. Regular audits of user permissions help in identifying and addressing any potential security risks or access issues.

Another critical area is community moderation. Managing user interactions and content within the community is vital for maintaining a positive and professional environment. Salesforce provides tools to set up moderation workflows, which can include features like flagging inappropriate content, reviewing user-generated posts before they go live, and implementing community guidelines. Effective moderation ensures that the community remains a constructive space for interaction and prevents the spread of misinformation or inappropriate content.

In addition to content and access management, ongoing user engagement is a key focus. One effective way to keep users engaged is by implementing gamification strategies. Salesforce Communities support various gamification features such as badges, leaderboards, and points systems. These elements can motivate users to participate more actively by rewarding them for their contributions, whether it's through posting content, answering questions, or participating in discussions. Gamification not only boosts engagement but also fosters a sense of achievement and community among users.

Tracking and analyzing community performance is another crucial component of effective management. Salesforce provides comprehensive analytics tools that allow administrators to monitor various metrics related to user activity, content engagement, and overall community health. By setting up dashboards and reports, administrators can gain insights into how users are interacting with the community, identify popular topics or areas of interest, and uncover potential issues. For example, if certain posts or topics are generating high levels of engagement, it may be beneficial to create more content around those themes. Conversely, if user activity drops, it may indicate the need for a fresh approach or new initiatives to re-engage the community.

Feedback collection is an integral part of continuous improvement. Regularly soliciting feedback from community members helps in understanding their needs, preferences, and pain points. This feedback can be gathered through surveys, suggestion forms, or direct conversations. Acting on this feedback not only improves the community experience but also demonstrates that the organization values user input and is committed to making ongoing enhancements.

In terms of system performance and scalability, it's important to regularly review and optimize the community's technical infrastructure. As the community grows, ensuring that the underlying systems can handle increased user volumes and data loads is essential. Salesforce provides tools for monitoring system performance and identifying potential bottlenecks. Regular performance reviews, coupled with proactive optimization measures, help in maintaining a smooth and responsive user experience.

Finally, it's essential to align the community's objectives with broader organizational goals. The community should support the organization's strategic initiatives and contribute to overall business success. This involves regularly assessing the community's impact on key performance indicators, such as customer satisfaction, partner collaboration, or employee engagement. By ensuring that the community's activities and features are in sync with organizational objectives, administrators can maximize its value and effectiveness.

In summary, managing Salesforce Communities requires a multifaceted approach that encompasses content management, user access, moderation, engagement, performance tracking, feedback integration, and alignment with organizational goals. By focusing on these areas, organizations can create a vibrant and effective community platform that fosters engagement, collaboration, and support. Through continuous refinement and adaptation, Salesforce Communities can evolve to meet the changing needs of its users and contribute to the organization's success.

CHAPTER 30: DISASTER RECOVERY AND DATA BACKUP STRATEGIES

Ensuring the continuity and resilience of a Salesforce environment is paramount, and effective disaster recovery and data backup strategies are fundamental to achieving this goal. In this section, we will delve into the critical aspects of disaster recovery planning and data backup for Salesforce, focusing on strategies to protect your data and maintain system integrity in the face of potential disruptions.

Disaster recovery planning begins with understanding the potential risks and threats that could impact your Salesforce environment. These risks can range from natural disasters, such as floods or earthquakes, to technical failures, cyberattacks, or human errors. Identifying these risks and assessing their potential impact on your Salesforce instance is the first step in developing a robust disaster recovery plan.

Once risks have been identified, it is crucial to establish clear objectives for disaster recovery. This includes defining the Recovery Time Objective (RTO) and Recovery Point Objective (RPO). The RTO refers to the maximum acceptable amount of time that the Salesforce system can be down before it adversely affects the business. The RPO indicates the maximum acceptable amount of data loss measured in time, which helps determine how frequently data backups should be performed. Setting these objectives provides a framework for planning and implementing appropriate recovery solutions and ensures that you can meet business continuity requirements.

In Salesforce, data backup strategies are central to disaster recovery planning. Salesforce provides built-in backup options, but understanding how to leverage these effectively is crucial. The Salesforce Data Export feature allows for manual backups of your Salesforce data in a format that can be used for recovery purposes. While useful, this approach is limited in frequency and may not fully meet the needs of a comprehensive backup strategy.

For more robust backup solutions, consider utilizing third-party backup tools and services. These tools often offer automated and incremental backups, allowing for more frequent data protection and quicker recovery times. Third-party solutions can provide additional features, such as automated backups, granular data recovery, and improved management of backup schedules. When selecting a backup tool, evaluate factors such as ease of integration with Salesforce, backup frequency, and the ability to perform full and partial restorations.

Alongside data backups, it is important to have a well-defined recovery plan that outlines the steps to be taken in the event of a disaster. This plan should include procedures for data restoration, system reconfiguration, and communication protocols. Documenting these procedures ensures that all stakeholders know their roles and responsibilities during a recovery situation. Regular testing of the recovery plan is essential to verify its effectiveness and identify any gaps or areas for improvement. Conducting simulations and drills helps ensure that the recovery process can be executed smoothly and that all personnel are familiar with their tasks.

Additionally, consider implementing version control and change management practices as part of your disaster recovery strategy. Salesforce environments are subject to frequent changes, including customizations, new features, and configuration updates. Maintaining version control of these changes ensures that you can revert to previous states if needed, which is especially important when recovering from incidents that affect custom code or configurations.

To further enhance data protection, ensure that your backup and recovery processes comply with relevant data protection regulations and standards. This includes considerations for data encryption, access controls, and audit trails. Encrypting backup data ensures that it remains secure during storage and transmission, while access controls help prevent unauthorized access to backup files. Maintaining detailed audit trails provides visibility into backup activities and supports compliance with regulatory requirements.

In summary, disaster recovery and data backup strategies are critical for safeguarding your Salesforce environment and ensuring business continuity. By identifying potential risks, setting recovery objectives, and implementing effective backup solutions, you can protect your data and minimize the impact of disruptions. A well-defined recovery plan, coupled with regular testing and version control practices, further strengthens your disaster recovery capabilities. Ensuring compliance with data protection regulations and incorporating encryption and access controls enhances the security and integrity of your backup processes. Through these measures, you can build a resilient Salesforce environment capable of withstanding and recovering from unforeseen challenges.

In continuing with disaster recovery and data backup strategies for Salesforce, it is essential to focus on practical implementation and ongoing management to ensure that the strategies are both effective and sustainable. The intricacies of these processes involve not only selecting appropriate tools but also integrating them into your organization's overall IT framework.

One crucial aspect of implementing backup solutions involves choosing the right frequency and type of backups. Automated backups are highly recommended for their convenience and reliability. These backups can be scheduled at intervals that align with your RTO and RPO objectives. Depending on your data's criticality and the volume of changes, you might choose daily, weekly, or even more frequent backups. Incremental backups, which capture only the changes made since the last backup, can be particularly effective for minimizing data loss while optimizing storage usage.

It is also beneficial to use a combination of full and incremental backups. Full backups provide a complete snapshot of your data at a specific point in time, whereas incremental backups capture changes made since the last backup. This hybrid approach ensures comprehensive data protection while maintaining efficient use of storage resources.

Data transformation and migration processes can often be complex, and having a solid backup strategy in place ensures that data can be recovered if issues arise. For instance, when performing large-scale data migrations, a robust backup of the existing Salesforce data is crucial. This precaution allows you to revert to a stable state if the migration introduces any errors or issues.

Additionally, ensuring that your backup data is securely stored is of paramount importance. Data encryption both in transit and at rest safeguards against unauthorized access and potential breaches. Implementing encryption practices guarantees that backup data remains confidential and protected from any external threats. Coupled with encryption, establishing secure access controls ensures that only authorized personnel can access and manage backup data. Regularly reviewing and updating access permissions helps mitigate the risk of accidental or intentional data breaches.

A significant component of disaster recovery planning involves testing and validating the recovery process. It is not enough to merely create a recovery plan; this plan must be regularly tested to ensure its effectiveness. Conducting periodic recovery drills simulates disaster scenarios and verifies that the recovery steps can be executed promptly and accurately. These tests reveal any potential weaknesses in the recovery process and allow for adjustments before an actual incident occurs. Documenting the results of these tests and updating the recovery plan based on findings helps maintain a high level of preparedness.

In addition to internal testing, consider engaging with external experts or consultants who specialize in disaster recovery and data protection. These professionals can provide valuable insights and recommendations based on industry best practices and emerging trends. Their expertise can help you refine your disaster recovery strategy and ensure it remains aligned with current technological advancements and regulatory requirements.

Another aspect to consider is the integration of your Salesforce backup and recovery strategy with broader organizational disaster recovery plans. Salesforce is often one component of a larger IT ecosystem, and its recovery strategy should be aligned with other systems and applications. Coordinating with your IT department to ensure that Salesforce recovery efforts are integrated into the overall disaster recovery framework ensures that all aspects of the organization's IT infrastructure are addressed in a cohesive manner.

Moreover, maintaining accurate and up-to-date documentation is vital for effective disaster recovery and data backup management. Detailed records of backup schedules, data locations, recovery procedures, and contact information for key personnel should be readily accessible. This documentation not only supports recovery efforts but also serves as a reference during audits and compliance checks.

Finally, continuous improvement of your disaster recovery and backup strategies is necessary to keep pace with changes in your Salesforce environment and evolving business needs. Regularly reviewing and updating your backup and recovery procedures in response to changes such as new Salesforce features, updates, or organizational shifts ensures that your strategies remain effective and relevant.

In summary, effective implementation and management of disaster recovery and data backup strategies require careful planning, robust tools, and ongoing evaluation. By choosing appropriate backup frequencies, ensuring secure data storage, testing recovery processes, and integrating with broader IT plans, you can build a resilient Salesforce environment capable of withstanding and recovering from potential disruptions. Continuous improvement and up-to-date documentation further support the long-term effectiveness of your disaster recovery efforts, ultimately safeguarding your Salesforce data and maintaining business continuity.

Implementing a comprehensive disaster recovery strategy and effective data backup solutions involves addressing several key considerations to ensure that your Salesforce environment remains resilient and operational under various circumstances. Beyond just the technical aspects, it is crucial to foster a culture of preparedness and proactive management within your organization.

One of the primary concerns in disaster recovery and data

backup is ensuring the reliability of your backup systems. To achieve this, it is imperative to choose a backup solution that aligns with your organizational needs and Salesforce's architecture. Salesforce provides its own backup options through the Data Export feature, which allows for manual exports of data. However, for more automated and robust solutions, third-party tools and services can offer enhanced capabilities, such as incremental backups, real-time data replication, and cloud storage options. Selecting a solution that integrates seamlessly with Salesforce and supports your specific data protection requirements is vital.

It is also essential to establish a clear and detailed recovery plan that outlines the steps and procedures to be followed in the event of a disaster. This plan should include defined roles and responsibilities, communication protocols, and a step-by-step guide for data recovery. Having this plan documented and readily accessible ensures that, in the event of an issue, all team members know their roles and can act quickly to restore operations. Regularly reviewing and updating the recovery plan to reflect changes in your Salesforce environment and business processes will help maintain its effectiveness.

Data integrity and consistency during backup and recovery operations are crucial. As you implement backup solutions, it is important to verify that data is not only being backed up correctly but also that it remains intact and accurate. Performing periodic checks and validations of backup data helps ensure that it is complete and usable. Additionally, understanding the potential impact of different types of data loss scenarios—such as accidental deletions, corruption, or unauthorized modifications—can guide you in developing more targeted backup strategies and recovery procedures.

Addressing the scalability of your backup and recovery solutions is another key consideration. As your Salesforce data grows and your organization evolves, your backup strategies must be able to scale accordingly. This involves not only accommodating increasing data volumes but also adapting to changes in data types and structures. Ensuring that your backup solutions can handle these changes without compromising performance or reliability is crucial for long-term data protection.

The geographic distribution of backup data is another aspect to consider. Storing backups in multiple locations, such as different data centers or geographic regions, can help mitigate the risk of data loss due to localized disasters, such as natural disasters or regional outages. This strategy of geographic redundancy ensures that even if one location experiences a failure, backup data remains secure and accessible from another location.

Engaging with Salesforce's support and professional services can provide additional resources and guidance for disaster recovery and backup strategies. Salesforce offers various support options, including technical assistance, best practices, and advice on optimizing your Salesforce environment for resilience. Leveraging these resources can enhance your recovery efforts and provide insights into the latest tools and techniques for data protection.

Training and awareness programs are also vital components of a successful disaster recovery strategy. Ensuring that all relevant staff members are trained in the procedures and tools related to data backup and recovery helps build a knowledgeable and responsive team. Regular training sessions, combined with practical simulations and drills, reinforce the importance of preparedness and ensure that team members are well-equipped to handle real-life scenarios.

Finally, compliance with regulatory requirements and industry standards is an integral part of disaster recovery and data backup strategies. Depending on your industry and location, there may be specific regulations governing data protection, backup, and recovery practices. Ensuring that your strategies comply with these regulations not only helps avoid legal issues but also builds trust with your stakeholders by demonstrating a commitment to data security and integrity.

In summary, developing and managing effective disaster recovery and data backup strategies involves a multifaceted approach that includes selecting appropriate backup solutions, creating and testing recovery plans, ensuring data integrity, and addressing scalability and geographic distribution. By integrating these elements into a cohesive strategy and fostering a culture of preparedness, you can enhance your Salesforce environment's resilience and safeguard against potential disruptions. Continuous improvement, training, and adherence to regulatory requirements further support the robustness and effectiveness of your data protection efforts.

CHAPTER 31: SALESFORCE CPQ: CONFIGURING QUOTES, PRICING, AND CONTRACTS

Salesforce CPQ (Configure, Price, Quote) is a sophisticated tool designed to enhance the efficiency of the sales process by automating and streamlining quoting, pricing, and contract management. The primary objective of implementing Salesforce CPQ is to ensure that sales teams can quickly generate accurate and consistent quotes while adhering to pricing rules and contract terms. To achieve this, it is essential to configure CPQ features properly, manage pricing rules effectively, and understand the interplay between different components of the CPQ system.

The first step in configuring Salesforce CPQ involves setting up the core components, which include products, pricing, and quote templates. Products are the items or services that your company sells, and in CPQ, these are managed through product records. These records need to be detailed and accurately reflect the various attributes of each product, such as descriptions, units of measure, and categories. It's important to configure product options and bundles to provide sales representatives with a comprehensive view of the available offerings and their respective configurations.

Once products are set up, the next crucial aspect is configuring pricing rules. Pricing rules determine how prices are calculated based on various conditions and criteria. This can include discounts, special pricing for specific customer segments, or volume-based pricing adjustments. To manage pricing effectively, you need to set up discount schedules, price books, and custom pricing logic. Discount schedules allow you to define discount structures based on factors like quantity or customer type, while price books enable you to manage different pricing strategies for various markets or customer groups.

In addition to pricing rules, it is vital to configure quote templates to ensure that quotes are generated in a consistent and professional manner. Quote templates determine the layout and content of the quotes that are presented to customers. These templates can include various sections such as product details, pricing summaries, and terms and conditions. Customizing these templates to reflect your company's branding and ensure clarity in communication helps maintain a high standard of professionalism in your sales documentation.

Configuring Salesforce CPQ also involves managing contract terms and approvals. Contracts represent the formal agreement between your company and the customer, outlining the terms of the sale, including payment terms, delivery schedules, and any other relevant conditions. It is essential to set up contract templates and approval workflows to ensure that all contracts are reviewed and approved before finalization. This process helps mitigate risks and ensures compliance with company policies and legal requirements.

To support efficient sales operations, Salesforce CPQ provides various tools for managing quote and contract lifecycles. These tools include features for tracking quote statuses, managing revisions, and handling amendments. Sales representatives can use these features to monitor the progress of quotes and contracts, make necessary adjustments, and ensure that all necessary steps are completed before finalizing a deal.

In addition to configuration, it is important to understand how to leverage Salesforce CPQ's advanced features to optimize the sales process further. This includes utilizing guided selling, which helps sales representatives navigate through the configuration process by providing prompts and recommendations based on customer inputs. Guided selling ensures that sales reps select the appropriate products and configurations, reducing errors and improving the overall accuracy of quotes.

Another advanced feature to consider is the integration of CPQ with other Salesforce modules and external systems. Integration with CRM systems, ERP systems, and other business applications allows for seamless data flow and enhances the overall efficiency of the sales process. For instance, integrating CPQ with your CRM system ensures that customer information and sales data are synchronized, providing a unified view of customer interactions and sales activities.

To ensure the successful implementation of Salesforce CPQ, it is crucial to engage in thorough testing and validation. This involves simulating various scenarios to ensure that pricing rules, quote templates, and contract management processes are functioning as expected. Testing helps identify and resolve any issues before going live, ensuring a smooth transition and minimizing disruptions to your sales operations.

In conclusion, configuring Salesforce CPQ involves a

comprehensive approach to setting up products, pricing rules, quote templates, and contract management processes. By focusing on these areas and leveraging advanced features and integrations, you can streamline your quoting, pricing, and contract management processes, leading to increased efficiency and accuracy in your sales operations. Proper configuration, testing, and ongoing management are key to maximizing the benefits of Salesforce CPQ and supporting your sales team in achieving their goals.

To fully harness the capabilities of Salesforce CPQ, one must delve into the intricacies of product configuration and pricing management. At the heart of this process is the setup of products and product families, which provides a structured approach to organizing and managing offerings. Each product within Salesforce CPQ can be detailed with attributes such as part numbers, descriptions, and unit prices. This detailed setup not only ensures that sales representatives have access to accurate and comprehensive product information but also facilitates the application of complex pricing rules and configurations.

One critical feature of Salesforce CPQ is its ability to handle product bundles and configurations. Product bundles allow you to group related products together, offering them as a package to customers. This bundling can be set up to reflect real-world sales scenarios, such as a hardware-software combination or a service package. The configuration of these bundles involves defining which products can be included in a bundle, the dependencies between different components, and any upsell or cross-sell options that may be relevant. This setup ensures that sales representatives can offer comprehensive solutions tailored to customer needs while maintaining control over product availability and pricing.

Pricing management is another crucial aspect of Salesforce CPQ, involving the implementation of pricing rules and discounting strategies. Salesforce CPQ offers various mechanisms for managing pricing, including price books, discount schedules, and custom pricing logic. Price books enable the assignment of different prices to products based on customer segments or market conditions. For example, you might have separate price books for wholesale and retail customers, each reflecting different pricing strategies.

Discount schedules provide a framework for applying discounts based on quantity or other criteria. For instance, you can set up tiered discount schedules where the discount percentage increases as the order quantity rises. This feature helps incentivize larger purchases and align pricing strategies with business objectives. Custom pricing logic allows for more complex pricing scenarios, such as volume-based pricing, contract-specific rates, or special promotions.

Effective quote management is central to the Salesforce CPQ experience. Quotes are formal documents provided to customers that detail the products or services being offered, along with their prices and terms. Salesforce CPQ simplifies the creation and management of quotes by automating many of the manual processes involved. This includes generating quotes from predefined templates that can be customized to fit your company's branding and formatting requirements. The system allows you to include various sections in the quote, such as product details, pricing summaries, and terms and conditions.

A key feature of Salesforce CPQ is the ability to manage quote revisions and amendments. As negotiations progress, quotes may need to be updated to reflect changes in pricing, product configurations, or contract terms. Salesforce CPQ supports this by allowing sales representatives to create revisions of existing quotes, track changes, and maintain a history of amendments. This ensures that all updates are documented and that the most current version of the quote is always available.

Contract management is another integral component of the Salesforce CPQ solution. Once a quote is accepted, it typically leads to the creation of a formal contract. Salesforce CPQ facilitates this process by allowing you to generate contracts based on the finalized quote. Contracts can be customized with terms and conditions that align with your business policies and legal requirements. Additionally, the system supports approval workflows to ensure that contracts are reviewed and approved before they are finalized.

To enhance the overall sales process, Salesforce CPQ provides tools for managing and tracking the entire lifecycle of a quote and contract. This includes monitoring the status of quotes, tracking approval processes, and managing contract renewals and amendments. By centralizing this information, Salesforce CPQ ensures that sales teams have a clear view of their activities and can efficiently manage their tasks.

Integrating Salesforce CPQ with other Salesforce modules and external systems can further enhance its functionality. For example, integration with Salesforce CRM provides a unified view of customer interactions and sales activities, allowing for more informed decision-making and better customer insights. Integration with ERP systems can streamline the flow of order and pricing information between systems, reducing errors and improving operational efficiency.

To ensure a successful implementation of Salesforce CPQ, it is essential to invest in proper training and support for your sales team. Understanding how to navigate the CPQ interface, utilize its features, and apply best practices will maximize the benefits of the system. Regular review and optimization of your CPQ setup are also important to address any evolving business needs or changes in sales processes.

In summary, configuring Salesforce CPQ involves a thorough understanding of product setup, pricing rules, quote management, and contract management. By leveraging the system's features and integrating it with other tools, businesses can streamline their sales processes, improve accuracy, and enhance overall efficiency. Proper setup, ongoing management, and training are critical to ensuring that Salesforce CPQ delivers the expected benefits and supports the sales team in achieving their goals.

In optimizing Salesforce CPQ, one must consider the integration of advanced features that further refine the quoting and pricing process. Among these features are guided selling and approval processes, which are instrumental in enhancing the efficiency and accuracy of the sales workflow. Guided selling provides a structured approach for sales representatives, guiding them through a series of questions and prompts to ensure that they select the most appropriate products and configurations for their customers. This tool not only helps in reducing errors but also ensures consistency in the sales process, making it easier for new and experienced sales reps alike to navigate complex configurations.

The setup of guided selling in Salesforce CPQ involves defining rules and criteria that will be used to direct users through the selection process. These rules can be based on various factors, such as product compatibility, customer preferences, or business logic. For example, if a particular product requires certain accessories or services to function correctly, guided selling can automatically recommend these additional items when the product is selected. This feature streamlines the sales process by reducing the time required to configure solutions and minimizing the likelihood of missing critical components.

Approval processes are another essential aspect of Salesforce CPQ, particularly when dealing with complex pricing scenarios or high-value deals. An approval process ensures that quotes and discounts are reviewed and authorized by the appropriate stakeholders before being finalized. This is crucial for maintaining control over pricing strategies and ensuring compliance with company policies. Salesforce CPQ allows you to set up multi-tiered approval workflows that can be customized based on the specific needs of your organization. For instance, you might have different approval levels for different types of discounts or deal sizes, with each level requiring the approval of specific individuals or teams.

Implementing these approval workflows involves configuring approval rules and setting up notification mechanisms to alert stakeholders when their input is required. It is important to design these workflows in a way that balances control with efficiency, avoiding unnecessary delays while still ensuring that all necessary approvals are obtained. The flexibility of Salesforce CPQ in handling complex approval scenarios helps maintain the integrity of the sales process and supports better decision-making.

Another key area to focus on is the management of contracts within Salesforce CPQ. Effective contract management is essential for ensuring that terms are clearly defined and that both parties adhere to the agreed-upon conditions. Salesforce CPQ supports this by offering tools for creating, managing, and tracking contracts throughout their lifecycle. This includes features for generating contract documents from finalized quotes, integrating contract terms into your CRM system, and monitoring contract performance.

Contract templates play a significant role in streamlining this process. By creating standardized templates that include commonly used terms and conditions, you can expedite the creation of new contracts and ensure consistency across all agreements. Salesforce CPQ allows you to customize these templates to reflect your company's specific legal and business requirements, making it easier to manage complex contracts and reduce the risk of errors.

Additionally, Salesforce CPQ provides tools for tracking contract milestones, such as renewal dates or expiration terms. Automated reminders and alerts can be configured to notify relevant stakeholders when key contract dates are approaching, ensuring that timely actions are taken to renew or renegotiate agreements. This proactive approach helps prevent lapses in coverage or service and supports better management of customer relationships.

The integration of Salesforce CPQ with other Salesforce modules and external systems further enhances its effectiveness. For instance, integrating CPQ with Salesforce CRM provides a unified view of customer interactions and sales activities, allowing for better coordination and data sharing across teams. Similarly, integration with ERP systems can streamline the flow of pricing and order information, improving accuracy and efficiency in managing sales and fulfillment processes.

To maximize the benefits of Salesforce CPQ, ongoing optimization and maintenance are crucial. Regularly reviewing and updating your CPQ configurations, pricing rules, and approval workflows ensures that the system continues to meet your evolving business needs. Additionally, providing training and support for your sales team helps ensure that they are proficient in using the CPQ features and can leverage them effectively in their daily tasks.

In conclusion, Salesforce CPQ offers a comprehensive suite of tools for managing the sales process, from product configuration and pricing to quote generation and contract management. By leveraging guided selling, approval workflows, and contract management features, businesses can enhance the efficiency and accuracy of their sales operations. Integration with other systems and ongoing optimization further ensures that Salesforce CPQ supports your organization's goals and adapts to changing requirements. Proper setup, management, and training are essential for realizing the full potential of Salesforce CPQ and driving successful sales outcomes.

CHAPTER 32: LEVERAGING SALESFORCE PARDOT FOR MARKETING AUTOMATION

Salesforce Pardot is a powerful marketing automation platform that seamlessly integrates with Salesforce, providing robust tools to enhance and streamline marketing efforts. In this discussion, we will explore how to effectively implement and manage Pardot to optimize lead generation, nurturing, and campaign management. By leveraging Pardot's capabilities, you can drive marketing success and ensure alignment with sales objectives, thus maximizing the overall efficiency of your marketing and sales processes.

To begin with, the implementation of Pardot requires a clear understanding of its core components and how they integrate with Salesforce. Pardot is designed to manage the entire marketing lifecycle, from lead generation to nurturing and conversion. The platform enables marketing teams to automate repetitive tasks, track engagement, and gain valuable insights into campaign performance. Successful implementation starts with configuring Pardot settings to align with your organization's marketing strategy and goals.

The first step in leveraging Pardot effectively is setting up lead generation tools. Pardot offers various methods for capturing leads, including web forms, landing pages, and lead generation campaigns. Web forms are essential for collecting contact information from website visitors, while landing pages are used to create targeted, stand-alone pages designed to drive conversions. When configuring web forms and landing pages, it is crucial to ensure that they are optimized for user experience and designed to capture relevant lead information. Additionally, Pardot's form handlers allow for the integration of external forms with the Pardot platform, offering flexibility in how leads are collected.

Once lead generation tools are in place, the next focus is on lead nurturing. Pardot excels in automating lead nurturing through its powerful drip marketing campaigns and engagement programs. Drip marketing involves sending a series of automated emails to leads based on their behavior or engagement level. These emails can be personalized and tailored to guide leads through the sales funnel, providing them with relevant content and offers at each stage. Pardot's engagement programs offer a more advanced approach, allowing marketers to create sophisticated workflows that respond to lead actions and interactions in real-time.

Setting up lead nurturing campaigns involves defining the criteria for triggering automated communications and creating content that resonates with your target audience. Pardot's segmentation and dynamic lists play a vital role in this process by enabling marketers to categorize leads based on specific attributes or behaviors. This segmentation allows for highly targeted and relevant messaging, which is key to effective lead nurturing. For example, leads who have shown interest in a particular product or service can be automatically added to a nurturing campaign focused on that product, ensuring that they receive timely and pertinent information.

Campaign management in Pardot involves planning, executing, and analyzing marketing campaigns to achieve desired outcomes. Pardot's campaign management tools enable marketers to create and manage campaigns from start to finish, including setting objectives, defining target audiences, and tracking performance. The platform offers robust analytics and reporting capabilities, providing insights into campaign effectiveness and ROI. By leveraging Pardot's reporting features, marketers can assess key metrics such as email open rates, click-through rates, and conversion rates, allowing for data-driven decision-making and continuous optimization of marketing efforts.

Integration with Salesforce is a critical aspect of Pardot's functionality, as it enables seamless data sharing and collaboration between marketing and sales teams. Pardot's integration with Salesforce ensures that lead and campaign data is synchronized between the two platforms, allowing for a unified view of customer interactions and engagement. This integration supports lead scoring and grading, enabling sales teams to prioritize leads based on their likelihood to convert. Additionally, Salesforce's CRM capabilities provide valuable context and insights into lead activity, enhancing the ability to follow up and close deals effectively.

Implementing Pardot also involves configuring user access and permissions to ensure that team members can effectively utilize the platform while maintaining data security. Pardot offers a range of user roles and permissions, allowing administrators to control access to various features and functionalities. It is essential to establish clear roles and responsibilities for marketing team members, ensuring that they have the necessary access to perform their tasks while protecting sensitive data.

In summary, leveraging Salesforce Pardot for marketing

automation involves a strategic approach to setting up lead generation, nurturing, and campaign management. By configuring Pardot's tools and features effectively, you can automate marketing tasks, enhance lead engagement, and achieve greater alignment with sales objectives. The integration with Salesforce further strengthens the synergy between marketing and sales teams, providing a comprehensive solution for driving marketing success and optimizing overall performance. Through careful implementation and ongoing management, Pardot can become a valuable asset in achieving your organization's marketing and sales goals.

To effectively harness the power of Salesforce Pardot for marketing automation, a nuanced understanding of its advanced features and functionalities is crucial. This exploration continues by delving deeper into Pardot's lead management capabilities, including lead scoring and grading, and its role in creating personalized marketing experiences.

Lead scoring is a pivotal component of Pardot's lead management system. It involves assigning numerical values to leads based on their engagement and interactions with your marketing materials. This process helps prioritize leads according to their likelihood of conversion, ensuring that sales teams focus their efforts on the most promising prospects. Pardot's lead scoring model is highly customizable, allowing you to define scoring rules based on specific criteria such as email opens, clicks, form submissions, and page visits. For instance, if a lead frequently engages with content related to a high-value product, they can be assigned a higher score, indicating a greater potential for conversion.

Lead grading, on the other hand, assesses the quality of a lead based on predefined attributes such as job title, company size, and industry. This grading system helps determine whether a lead fits the ideal customer profile for your organization.

By combining lead scoring and grading, Pardot provides a comprehensive view of lead potential, enabling sales teams to prioritize their outreach efforts effectively. For example, a lead who scores high due to frequent interactions but also has a low grade due to an unsuitable job title might still be valuable if further engagement is warranted.

Another significant feature of Pardot is its ability to create personalized marketing experiences through dynamic content and segmentation. Pardot's dynamic content functionality allows marketers to deliver tailored messages to different segments of their audience. This personalization can be based on various factors such as the recipient's past interactions, demographics, or behavior. For example, dynamic content can be used to display different offers or messages in an email depending on whether the recipient has previously shown interest in a particular product or service. This level of personalization enhances the relevance of your communications and increases the likelihood of engagement.

Segmentation in Pardot involves dividing your audience into specific groups based on criteria such as lead source, behavior, or engagement history. Pardot's segmentation tools include dynamic lists and static lists. Dynamic lists automatically update based on the criteria you set, ensuring that your segments remain current and relevant. Static lists, on the other hand, are manually created and do not change unless updated by the user. Effective segmentation enables targeted marketing campaigns that resonate with specific audience segments, improving the overall efficiency of your marketing efforts.

Pardot also offers robust reporting and analytics capabilities that provide valuable insights into campaign performance and lead behavior. The platform's reporting tools allow marketers to track key metrics such as email open rates, click-through rates, and conversion rates. Additionally, Pardot's campaign reports provide a comprehensive view of how different campaigns are performing in terms of lead generation and engagement. These insights are crucial for evaluating the effectiveness of your marketing strategies and making data-driven decisions to optimize future campaigns.

Integrating Pardot with Salesforce's CRM system further enhances its capabilities by providing a unified view of lead interactions and sales activities. This integration allows for seamless data sharing between marketing and sales teams, enabling better alignment and collaboration. For instance, when a lead converts into a customer, the data is automatically synchronized between Pardot and Salesforce, ensuring that both teams have access to up-to-date information. This integration supports lead nurturing by providing sales teams with context about a lead's engagement history and interactions, facilitating more informed and personalized follow-ups.

Moreover, Pardot's automation rules and engagement programs play a crucial role in streamlining marketing operations. Automation rules allow marketers to create workflows that automatically execute actions based on predefined criteria. For example, you can set up automation rules to assign leads to specific sales reps based on their geographic location or industry. Engagement programs, as mentioned earlier, offer a more sophisticated approach to automation by enabling the creation of complex workflows that respond to lead behavior in real-time. These programs can include multiple steps, such as sending follow-up emails, assigning tasks, or updating lead scores based on specific actions.

In summary, leveraging Salesforce Pardot for marketing automation involves a comprehensive approach to managing leads, personalizing marketing efforts, and analyzing performance. By utilizing Pardot's lead scoring and grading, dynamic content, segmentation, and reporting features, you can create effective and targeted marketing campaigns that drive engagement and support sales objectives. The integration with Salesforce's CRM system further enhances the platform's capabilities, providing a cohesive solution for optimizing marketing and sales processes. With a strategic approach to Pardot's features and functionalities, you can achieve greater efficiency in your marketing operations and drive meaningful results for your organization.

As you delve deeper into leveraging Salesforce Pardot for marketing automation, it's essential to focus on optimizing campaign execution and analyzing results to continuously improve your strategies. Effective use of Pardot involves not only setting up and managing various features but also understanding how to refine and adapt your approach based on performance insights.

One of the key aspects of optimizing Pardot campaigns is mastering the use of engagement studios. Engagement studios are powerful tools for creating complex marketing automation workflows. They allow you to design multi-step campaigns that guide leads through a series of interactions based on their behavior and engagement. This feature is instrumental in nurturing leads, as it helps deliver personalized content at the right time, based on where the lead is in their buyer's journey.

Creating an engagement studio involves mapping out the steps of your workflow, including triggers, actions, and rules. Triggers initiate the workflow when a lead meets specific criteria, such as filling out a form or clicking on a link. Actions are the steps that Pardot performs as a result of the trigger, such as sending an email or updating a lead's score. Rules define the conditions that guide the workflow's progression, allowing you to tailor the automation based on lead behavior and interactions. For example, if a lead opens an email but does not click a link, you might set up an engagement studio to send a follow-up email with additional information or a special offer to re-engage them.

In addition to engagement studies, Pardot offers robust tools for managing and analyzing marketing campaigns. Pardot's campaign management features enable you to track the effectiveness of your marketing efforts by providing insights into key performance indicators (KPIs) such as lead conversion rates, email click-through rates, and campaign ROI. By analyzing these metrics, you can identify which campaigns are driving the most engagement and which areas may need improvement.

One effective way to manage campaigns is through the use of Pardot's campaign reports and dashboards. Campaign reports provide a detailed view of campaign performance, including metrics such as total leads generated, conversion rates, and revenue attributed to each campaign. Dashboards offer a visual representation of this data, making it easier to monitor and analyze performance trends over time. By regularly reviewing these reports and dashboards, you can gain valuable insights into how your campaigns are performing and make data-driven decisions to enhance your marketing strategies.

Another crucial aspect of Pardot is the integration with Salesforce's CRM system, which provides a unified view of lead and customer data. This integration ensures that marketing and sales teams have access to the same information, facilitating better collaboration and alignment. For instance, when a lead is converted into a customer, Pardot automatically updates Salesforce with the relevant details, ensuring that sales teams have up-to-date information for follow-up. This seamless data flow helps maintain consistency across marketing and sales efforts and supports more effective lead nurturing and follow-up.

To further optimize your Pardot usage, consider leveraging

advanced features such as A/B testing and multi-touch attribution. A/B testing allows you to test different versions of your emails, landing pages, or forms to determine which version performs best. This approach helps you refine your marketing materials based on real-world performance data, leading to more effective campaigns. Multi-touch attribution provides insights into the various touchpoints a lead encounters before converting, helping you understand the impact of different marketing channels and touchpoints on the conversion process.

Effective management of Pardot also involves staying current with platform updates and new features. Salesforce regularly releases updates and enhancements to Pardot, which can offer new capabilities and improvements to existing features. Staying informed about these updates and incorporating new functionalities into your marketing strategies can help you stay ahead of the competition and continue to drive success with Pardot.

Additionally, it is important to maintain best practices in data management and compliance. Ensure that your marketing efforts adhere to regulations such as GDPR and CAN-SPAM, and that you are managing lead data responsibly. Pardot offers tools for managing lead preferences and opt-ins, which helps you comply with these regulations and maintain a positive relationship with your leads.

In summary, leveraging Salesforce Pardot for marketing automation requires a comprehensive approach that includes setting up and managing advanced features, optimizing campaign execution, and analyzing performance data. By mastering engagement studios, utilizing campaign management tools, integrating Pardot with Salesforce CRM, and staying informed about platform updates, you can enhance your marketing efforts and drive better results. Implementing best practices for data management and compliance further ensures that your marketing automation strategies are effective and sustainable. With these strategies, you can fully harness the power of Pardot to achieve marketing success and align your efforts with your sales objectives.

CHAPTER 33: PREPARING FOR SALESFORCE CERTIFICATION EXAMS

Successfully preparing for Salesforce certification exams requires a structured approach, given the depth and breadth of knowledge these exams cover. These certifications are designed to validate your expertise in Salesforce administration, development, and specialized areas, providing a significant advantage in the job market. As such, understanding how to effectively prepare for these exams can be crucial to achieving certification and advancing your career.

The first step in preparing for Salesforce certification exams is to familiarize yourself with the exam format and the types of questions that will be asked. Salesforce certification exams typically consist of multiple-choice questions that assess your knowledge of various Salesforce features and best practices. These exams are designed to evaluate not only your theoretical understanding but also your practical skills and ability to apply Salesforce concepts in real-world scenarios. Each exam has a specific number of questions and a time limit, so understanding the structure helps you manage your time effectively during the exam.

To begin your preparation, it's crucial to review the official Salesforce exam guide. This guide provides an overview of the exam topics, the number of questions for each topic, and the weight of each topic in the overall exam. By studying this guide, you can create a focused study plan that targets the most critical areas. For example, if the exam guide indicates that a significant portion of the exam covers data management and security, you should allocate ample study time to these topics.

Once you have a clear understanding of the exam format and topics, the next step is to gather study materials and resources. Salesforce offers a variety of resources to aid in your preparation, including online courses, study guides, and practice exams. Salesforce's Trailhead platform is an excellent place to start, offering a range of modules and trails tailored to each certification exam. These interactive modules cover essential topics and provide hands-on experience with Salesforce features, helping reinforce your learning through practical exercises.

In addition to Trailhead, consider investing in study guides and practice exams from reputable sources. These materials are specifically designed to mimic the actual exam format and help you familiarize yourself with the types of questions you will encounter. Practice exams are particularly useful for identifying areas where you may need additional review and for gauging your readiness for the actual exam. Regularly taking practice exams can also help reduce test anxiety by making you more comfortable with the exam process.

Another effective study strategy is to participate in study groups or forums. Engaging with others who are preparing for the same certification can provide valuable insights and support. Study groups often discuss challenging topics, share resources, and provide motivation. Online forums and communities, such as Salesforce's own forums and LinkedIn groups, are also excellent places to seek advice and connect with other professionals who have already achieved certification.

As you prepare for the exam, it's important to regularly assess your readiness. Self-assessment tools, such as practice tests and quizzes, can help you evaluate your understanding of key concepts and identify areas that require further study. Salesforce offers official practice exams that simulate the actual test environment, providing a realistic assessment of your knowledge and readiness. Reviewing these practice exams and analyzing your performance will help you focus your study efforts on the areas where you need the most improvement.

In addition to reviewing study materials and taking practice exams, it's essential to approach the exam with a strategic mindset. Develop a study schedule that allows you to cover all exam topics systematically. Break down your study sessions into manageable chunks, and set specific goals for each session. Avoid cramming the night before the exam; instead, focus on reviewing key concepts and reinforcing your understanding.

During the exam, time management is crucial. Familiarize yourself with the exam interface before the test day to ensure you are comfortable with navigating the questions and tools provided. Read each question carefully and consider all answer choices before making a decision. If you encounter a challenging question, it's often best to move on and return to it later, ensuring that you have enough time to answer all questions.

Preparing for Salesforce certification exams involves a combination of understanding the exam format, utilizing available study resources, and strategically managing your study time. By familiarizing yourself with the exam structure, leveraging Salesforce's resources, participating in study groups, and regularly assessing your readiness, you can approach the certification exam with confidence. Effective preparation not only enhances your knowledge and skills but also increases your chances of achieving certification and advancing your career in Salesforce administration.

Preparing for Salesforce certification exams involves a systematic approach to ensure you cover all relevant topics and are well-prepared for the test. After familiarizing yourself with the exam format and gathering study resources, the next step is to deepen your understanding of key concepts and effectively manage your preparation process.

One of the most critical aspects of preparation is to ensure that you have a thorough understanding of the core concepts and functionalities of Salesforce relevant to the certification you are pursuing. This involves not only reading through study guides and documentation but also applying what you've learned through hands-on practice. Engaging with Salesforce's features in a real or sandbox environment allows you to explore the functionalities and gain practical experience, which is often reflected in the exam questions. Practical experience with the Salesforce platform helps solidify theoretical knowledge and provides context for how various features are used in actual scenarios.

In addition to hands-on practice, it is beneficial to review Salesforce's official documentation and release notes. Salesforce frequently updates its platform, and understanding these updates can be crucial, as they may impact the exam content. Salesforce's release notes provide detailed information about new features, enhancements, and changes to existing functionalities. Staying up-to-date with these changes ensures that your knowledge reflects the most current practices and features available on the platform.

Another valuable strategy for exam preparation is to create a comprehensive study plan. This plan should outline what topics you need to cover, how much time you will allocate to each topic, and when you will review key concepts. A well-structured study plan helps ensure that you systematically cover all necessary material and do not overlook important areas. It also allows you to track your progress and make adjustments as needed. Setting specific goals for each study session and regularly reviewing these goals helps maintain focus and ensures that you are making steady progress toward your exam preparation.

As part of your study plan, it's also important to incorporate different types of study materials and methods. While reading textbooks and official guides is essential, supplementing your study with various resources, such as video tutorials, webinars, and online forums, can enhance your understanding. Video tutorials and webinars often provide visual demonstrations and real-world examples that can make complex topics more accessible. Engaging with online forums and communities allows you to discuss challenging topics with peers, seek clarification on confusing concepts, and gain insights from those who have already passed the exam.

Effective study also involves regularly testing your knowledge through practice exams and quizzes. Practice exams are a critical tool for assessing your readiness and identifying areas where you need further review. They simulate the actual exam environment and help you become familiar with the types of questions you will encounter. After completing practice exams, review your answers carefully, especially those you got wrong. Understanding why an answer is correct or incorrect helps reinforce your knowledge and improve your problem-solving skills.

When preparing for Salesforce certification exams, it's also essential to develop test-taking strategies. Familiarize yourself with the format and structure of the exam to avoid surprises on test day. Practice managing your time effectively during the exam to ensure you can answer all questions within the allotted time. If you encounter a difficult question, don't get stuck on it—move on and return to it later if time permits. This approach helps ensure that you maximize your chances of answering all questions accurately.

On the day of the exam, ensure you are well-rested and prepared. Get a good night's sleep before the exam and arrive at the testing center or log in to the online exam platform with plenty of time to spare. Bring any required identification or materials, and ensure your testing environment is free from distractions if you are taking the exam online. Managing stress and maintaining a calm and focused mindset during the exam can significantly impact your performance.

After completing the exam, take the time to review your performance and reflect on your study process. Regardless of the outcome, analyzing your performance helps identify areas for improvement and provides valuable insights for future preparation efforts. If you pass, celebrate your achievement and use the certification to advance your career. If you don't pass, review the exam feedback, adjust your study plan, and retake the exam with renewed focus.

Effective preparation for Salesforce certification exams involves a combination of understanding exam formats, utilizing diverse study resources, practicing hands-on skills, and developing test-taking strategies. By following a structured study plan, staying current with Salesforce updates, and engaging with various learning methods, you can enhance your knowledge and increase your confidence, ultimately leading to successful certification and professional growth.

After completing your preparation and taking the exam, the final step is to evaluate and reflect on your performance to ensure continuous improvement and readiness for future challenges. This process begins with analyzing your exam results, which can provide insightful feedback on your strengths and areas for further development.

Once you receive your exam results, carefully review the performance report provided. This report often includes details on which sections you performed well in and which areas need improvement. For instance, if the results indicate that you struggled with specific topics or question types, this feedback can guide your subsequent study efforts. It's essential to take note of these areas so that you can focus your review on the topics where you need the most improvement. Revisiting study materials, re-engaging with practice exams, and seeking additional resources on these topics will strengthen your knowledge and prepare you better for future exams.

Reflection on your preparation strategy is also crucial. Assess how well your study plan worked and whether there were any areas where you could have improved. Consider whether you allocated enough time to each topic and if your study methods were effective. This reflection allows you to adjust your approach for future certification exams or professional development efforts. If you find that certain study techniques were particularly beneficial, you might want to incorporate them into your ongoing learning routine.

Additionally, engaging with Salesforce communities and professional networks can offer support and valuable insights. Many online forums, user groups, and professional networks are filled with individuals who have recently taken or are preparing for the same certification exams. Participating in these communities can provide you with practical tips, study resources, and encouragement. Sharing experiences with peers who have gone through similar challenges can also help you gain new perspectives and strategies for overcoming obstacles.

Continuous learning and staying current with Salesforce updates is a key component of ongoing professional development. Salesforce regularly updates its platform, and staying informed about new features, best practices, and industry trends is vital for maintaining your certification and expertise. Subscribing to Salesforce newsletters, attending webinars, and participating in relevant training sessions will help you keep your knowledge up-to-date and ensure that you remain proficient in using Salesforce.

Maintaining your Salesforce certification also involves fulfilling any continuing education requirements, if applicable. Some certifications may require periodic renewals or additional coursework to stay current. Keeping track of these requirements and ensuring you meet them will help you retain your certification status and continue to demonstrate your expertise in Salesforce.

Lastly, remember that obtaining certification is not just about passing an exam; it is about demonstrating your ability to effectively use Salesforce to solve real-world business challenges. Applying what you've learned through your certification in your professional role will reinforce your skills and contribute to your overall success. Look for opportunities to leverage your certification to take on new projects, drive improvements within your organization, or even mentor others who are pursuing their certifications.

In summary, preparing for Salesforce certification exams involves a comprehensive approach that includes understanding the exam format, utilizing diverse study resources, practicing hands-on skills, and developing effective test-taking strategies. After the exam, reviewing your performance, reflecting on your preparation methods, and engaging with professional communities are essential steps for continuous improvement. Staying current with Salesforce updates and fulfilling any continuing education requirements will help maintain your certification and expertise. By integrating these practices into your professional development routine, you can ensure ongoing success and growth in your Salesforce career.

CHAPTER 34: FUTURE TRENDS AND INNOVATIONS IN SALESFORCE

As we advance towards the future of Salesforce, it becomes increasingly important to understand and anticipate the trends and innovations that will shape the landscape of Salesforce administration. This forward-looking perspective allows us to remain agile, adapt to emerging technologies, and leverage new features to optimize our Salesforce environments.

One of the most notable trends in Salesforce is the growing emphasis on artificial intelligence and machine learning. Salesforce has been integrating AI capabilities into its platform through Salesforce Einstein. Einstein leverages machine learning algorithms to provide advanced analytics, predictive insights, and automation features. For example, Einstein's predictive lead scoring helps prioritize leads based on their likelihood to convert, thereby enhancing sales efficiency. Similarly, Einstein Bots offer automated customer service solutions, improving response times and customer satisfaction. As AI and machine learning continue to evolve, Salesforce will likely introduce even more sophisticated tools that enable deeper insights and more automated processes.

Another significant trend is the expansion of Salesforce's focus on customer experience through enhanced personalization. With features like Dynamic Forms and Dynamic Actions, Salesforce is pushing the boundaries of personalized user experiences. Dynamic Forms allow administrators to tailor the layout and visibility of fields based on user interactions and record data, creating a more intuitive and relevant user interface. Dynamic Actions enable the customization of action buttons based on context, improving user efficiency. As personalization technology advances, Salesforce will continue to develop tools that enable more granular customization and improved engagement with end users.

The integration of Salesforce with other technologies and platforms is also a key area of development. With the rise of cloud computing, businesses are increasingly utilizing a variety of cloud-based solutions. Salesforce's ability to integrate seamlessly with other platforms, such as Amazon Web Services (AWS) and Microsoft Azure, enhances its versatility and functionality. Integration tools and APIs are becoming more robust, allowing for smoother data flow and interoperability between Salesforce and external systems. This trend towards greater integration will likely continue, providing more opportunities for businesses to create unified and cohesive technology ecosystems.

The adoption of low-code and no-code development platforms is transforming the way custom applications and automations are created within Salesforce. Salesforce's Lightning Platform provides a low-code environment that enables users to build applications and workflows without extensive programming knowledge. This democratization of development allows more users to contribute to the creation and customization of Salesforce solutions, accelerating innovation and reducing development time. As the demand for rapid application development grows, Salesforce will continue to enhance its low-code and no-code offerings to empower users and streamline processes.

In addition, the focus on data privacy and security is becoming increasingly critical as organizations handle more sensitive information. Salesforce has been at the forefront of implementing security features and compliance measures to safeguard data. Innovations in this area include advanced encryption options, enhanced user authentication methods, and more granular control over data access. Staying ahead of regulatory requirements and ensuring robust data protection will remain a priority for Salesforce as privacy concerns and regulations evolve.

The rise of mobile technology and remote work has also influenced the development of Salesforce features. With a growing number of users accessing Salesforce from mobile devices, there is a continuous push to enhance mobile functionality and ensure a seamless user experience across different devices. Salesforce Mobile SDKs and Lightning Experience are designed to provide a consistent and efficient mobile interface. Future innovations are likely to further improve mobile capabilities, making Salesforce more accessible and user-friendly for remote and on-the-go users.

As we look to the future, it's also important to consider the evolving best practices in Salesforce administration. The shift towards a more agile and iterative approach to implementation and customization is becoming increasingly prevalent. Agile methodologies emphasize flexibility, collaboration, and iterative development, allowing teams to adapt quickly to changing requirements and feedback. Embracing these best practices can help organizations stay aligned with their business goals and respond effectively to new opportunities and challenges.

In summary, staying informed about future trends and

innovations in Salesforce is essential for maximizing the potential of the platform. Embracing advancements in artificial intelligence, personalization, integration, low-code development, and data security will help ensure that your Salesforce environment remains cutting-edge and effective. By adopting agile best practices and leveraging emerging technologies, you can continually improve your Salesforce administration and drive business success. As Salesforce continues to evolve, keeping an eye on these trends will enable you to stay ahead of the curve and make the most of the opportunities that lie ahead.

The rapid evolution of Salesforce is characterized by its ability to adapt to new technologies and shifting market demands. One area where this adaptation is particularly evident is in the expansion of Salesforce's cloud offerings and the integration of advanced technologies. As we look toward the future, understanding these innovations and their implications is crucial for optimizing Salesforce environments.

Salesforce is increasingly focusing on enhancing its capabilities through the integration of blockchain technology. This technology, known for its decentralized and secure nature, offers significant potential for improving data integrity and transparency. Salesforce's Blockchain Cloud aims to provide enterprises with a platform to build and manage blockchain networks. This integration enables businesses to track and verify transactions more securely and transparently, which is especially valuable in industries like finance, supply chain management, and healthcare. By leveraging blockchain technology, Salesforce users can expect to see more secure and efficient ways to manage and validate data.

Another notable trend is the enhancement of Salesforce's analytics and reporting capabilities through advanced data science and artificial intelligence. The Salesforce Einstein Analytics suite is continually evolving to offer deeper insights and more sophisticated data analysis tools. Future developments in this area are likely to include more advanced predictive analytics, real-time data processing, and AI-driven insights that help organizations make more informed decisions. As data becomes more integral to business strategy, leveraging these advanced analytics tools will be essential for gaining a competitive edge and driving business growth.

The rise of the Internet of Things (IoT) is also influencing Salesforce's development strategy. IoT refers to the network of interconnected devices that collect and exchange data. Salesforce's IoT Cloud allows businesses to connect IoT devices to their Salesforce environment, enabling them to capture and act on real-time data from various sources. This capability facilitates more proactive customer service, predictive maintenance, and personalized experiences based on real-time information. As IoT technology continues to advance, Salesforce is likely to integrate even more sophisticated features that enhance connectivity and data utilization.

The growing importance of user experience (UX) and user interface (UI) design is another key trend. Salesforce is placing a strong emphasis on creating intuitive and user-friendly interfaces to improve adoption and productivity. The Lightning Experience, with its modern and customizable interface, exemplifies this focus. Future enhancements are expected to further streamline navigation, enhance personalization, and incorporate more user-centric design principles. By prioritizing UX/UI improvements, Salesforce aims to make its platform more accessible and efficient for users across various roles and industries.

The concept of "no-code" and "low-code" development is revolutionizing how businesses create and deploy applications within Salesforce. With tools like Salesforce Lightning App Builder and Process Builder, users can now build custom applications and automate processes without needing extensive programming knowledge. This trend towards no-code and low-code solutions is empowering more users to participate in app development and process automation, accelerating innovation and reducing reliance on specialized developers. As these tools become more advanced, we can expect even greater ease of use and functionality, enabling faster and more flexible development of Salesforce solutions.

As data privacy and security concerns continue to grow, Salesforce is enhancing its focus on compliance and data protection. Innovations in this area include more robust encryption methods, improved data governance features, and enhanced auditing capabilities. Salesforce's commitment to meeting global compliance standards, such as GDPR and CCPA, reflects the increasing importance of data security in the digital age. Future developments are likely to include even more sophisticated security measures and compliance tools to ensure that user data is protected and that organizations can meet regulatory requirements effectively.

The integration of Salesforce with emerging technologies such as augmented reality (AR) and virtual reality (VR) is also on the horizon. These technologies offer new ways to engage with customers and visualize data. For example, AR and VR can be used for immersive training experiences, virtual product demonstrations, and enhanced customer interactions. As these technologies become more mainstream, Salesforce is likely to incorporate them into its platform to provide innovative solutions that enhance user engagement and interaction.

In summary, the future of Salesforce is characterized by the integration of cutting-edge technologies and a strong focus on enhancing user experience and data security. As Salesforce continues to evolve, staying informed about these trends and innovations will be essential for maximizing the platform's potential. Embracing advancements in blockchain,

AI, IoT, UX/UI design, no-code development, and emerging technologies will help organizations stay ahead of the curve and leverage new capabilities to drive success. By proactively adapting to these changes and continuously improving Salesforce environments, businesses can achieve greater efficiency, innovation, and competitive advantage in the ever-evolving digital landscape.

As Salesforce continues to evolve, staying ahead of technological advancements and understanding their implications is crucial for leveraging the platform effectively. Among the emerging trends, the integration of artificial intelligence (AI) into Salesforce's ecosystem is perhaps the most transformative. Salesforce Einstein, the AI-powered component of the platform, is poised to enhance decision-making, automate complex tasks, and deliver personalized customer experiences. As AI capabilities become more sophisticated, Salesforce will likely incorporate deeper learning algorithms and more advanced predictive analytics to refine business processes and customer interactions.

Einstein's AI-driven features, such as predictive lead scoring and opportunity insights, are designed to help sales teams prioritize their efforts and focus on high-value prospects. By analyzing historical data and identifying patterns, Einstein can forecast which leads are more likely to convert, thereby improving sales efficiency and effectiveness. Future advancements may include even more granular insights and recommendations, driven by continuous learning from new data inputs and interactions.

Another significant trend is the growing emphasis on integrating Salesforce with other enterprise systems and platforms. As organizations adopt a more holistic approach to managing their IT landscapes, seamless integration between Salesforce and third-party applications becomes increasingly important. Future innovations are likely to include enhanced connectors and integration tools that simplify the process of linking Salesforce with ERP systems, marketing automation platforms, and other business-critical applications. This will enable a more cohesive flow of information across systems, enhancing data accuracy and operational efficiency.

The shift towards a more personalized customer experience is also driving innovation within Salesforce. As customers expect more tailored interactions and services, Salesforce is focusing on expanding its capabilities to deliver hyper-personalized experiences. This includes leveraging customer data to create targeted marketing campaigns, personalized product recommendations, and customized service offerings. Advanced machine learning models and more refined data segmentation techniques will likely play a key role in achieving these personalization goals, making it essential for businesses to harness these capabilities to meet evolving customer expectations.

In parallel with these advancements, Salesforce is enhancing its focus on mobile solutions. With the increasing reliance on mobile devices for business operations, Salesforce is committed to providing a robust mobile experience that mirrors the functionality of its desktop applications. Future developments may include improvements to mobile app performance, additional offline capabilities, and more intuitive interfaces designed specifically for mobile users. This will ensure that Salesforce remains accessible and effective for users on the go, supporting productivity and engagement across various devices.

The evolving landscape of data privacy and security is also influencing Salesforce's development trajectory. With growing concerns about data breaches and regulatory compliance, Salesforce is likely to introduce more comprehensive security features and compliance tools. This could involve advanced encryption protocols, more granular access controls, and enhanced auditing and monitoring capabilities. As regulations become stricter and data protection becomes more critical, Salesforce's focus on security will be paramount in maintaining user trust and safeguarding sensitive information.

Additionally, the rise of low-code and no-code development platforms is reshaping how organizations build and customize their Salesforce applications. These platforms empower users with minimal technical expertise to create and deploy applications, streamline workflows, and automate processes. Salesforce's investment in low-code and no-code tools, such as Lightning App Builder and Flow, is expected to grow, making it easier for users to tailor the platform to their specific needs without relying heavily on traditional coding. This democratization of app development will likely accelerate innovation and enhance agility within organizations.

Looking ahead, the integration of augmented reality (AR) and virtual reality (VR) into Salesforce is another area to watch. While still emerging, AR and VR technologies offer new possibilities for immersive customer experiences and innovative use cases. For example, AR could be used for virtual product demonstrations or enhanced field service experiences, while VR might support virtual training sessions or interactive customer engagements. As these technologies mature, Salesforce's ability to incorporate AR and VR into its platform could provide unique advantages for businesses looking to leverage cutting-edge tools.

In summary, the future of Salesforce is characterized by a continuous influx of innovative technologies and an increasing emphasis on personalization, integration, and security. The integration of AI, enhancements in mobile and personalization capabilities, advancements in data privacy, and the rise of low-code/no-code development platforms are all shaping the trajectory of Salesforce's evolution.

Staying informed about these trends and understanding their implications will be crucial for effectively leveraging Salesforce and driving organizational success. By embracing these advancements and adapting to the ever-changing technological landscape, businesses can optimize their Salesforce environments and remain competitive in an increasingly dynamic market.

www.ingramcontent.com/pod-product-compliance
Lightning Source LLC
Chambersburg PA
CBHW052141220526
45471CB00004B/1469